BITTERSWEET

BitterSweet

The Memoir of a
Chinese Indonesian Family
in the Twentieth Century

Stuart Pearson

MEMOIR

NUS PRESS
SINGAPORE

OHIO UNIVERSITY PRESS
RESEARCH IN INTERNATIONAL STUDIES
SOUTHEAST ASIA SERIES NO. 117

OHIO UNIVERSITY PRESS
ATHENS

First published by:

NUS Press
National University of Singapore
AS3-01-02, 3 Arts Link
Singapore 117569

Fax: (65) 6774-0652
E-mail: nusbooks@nus.edu.sg
Website: http://www.nus.edu.sg/npu

ISBN 978-9971-69-425-8 (Paper)

Published for distribution in the United States by:

Ohio University Press
Ohio University Research in International Studies
Southeast Asia Series
Athens, OH 45701, USA

Executive editor: Gillian Berchowitz
Area consultant: William H. Frederick

Website: http://www.ohioswallow.com

ISBN-10 0-89680-264-7
ISBN-13 978-0-89680-264-3

© 2008 Stuart Pearson
E-mail: stuart@bigpond.com

National Library Board Singapore Cataloguing in Publication Data

Pearson, Stuart, 1952-
    BitterSweet : the memoir of a Chinese Indonesian family in the twentieth
century / Stuart Pearson. – Singapore : NUS Press, c2008.
    p. cm.
    Includes bibliographical references and index.
    ISBN-13 : 978-9971-69-425-8 (pbk.)

    1. Sudibjo, An, 1912- 2. Sudibjo, An, 1912- – Family. 3. Chinese – Indonesia
– Biography. 4. Chinese – Indonesia – Social life and customs – 20th century.
5. Chinese – Indonesia – History – 20th century. I. Title.

DS632.3.C5
305.89510598 – dc22   OCN225854023

Cover: Sugarcane in East Java, 1910 (KITLV #2440)

Printed in Singapore

To the two people who made this book possible,
An and Eddie Sudibjo

Contents

CONTENTS

List of Figures

List of Illustrations

Foreword

It gives me much pleasure to recommend this unusual book to anyone interested in the modern history of the ethnic Chinese in Southeast Asia and specifically in Indonesia.

Most books about Chinese Indonesians address societal issues in the broad rather than the refracted experiences of individual lives. Social scientists and historians tend, almost inevitably, to make generalizations about Chinese Indonesians as a minority group. These can easily reinforce the popular negative stereotypes which so often distort the lived experience of individual people. Personal memoirs help to provide an antidote to the poison of these stereotypes.

The few books which do focus on individual lives of Chinese Indonesians are usually autobiographies (or biographies) of men who have played a prominent role in politics or business. Very little has been written by or about individual ethnic Chinese women. The memoirs of Koo Hui-Lan and Queeny Chang are the best-known of those available in English.[1]

This volume is a welcome addition to the field. It is a memoir of a Chinese Indonesian family in the twentieth century. Described as a "family history", it is based on extensive interviews which Stuart Pearson has edited and recast into first-person narratives.

The principal "voice" is that of his mother-in-law, An Utari Sudibjo, who was born in the east Javanese town of Kediri in 1912 under the name Tan Sian Nio. When Pearson began his project, An was more than

---

[1] Koo, Hui-lan [Madame Wellington Koo]. 1943. An autobiography as told to Mary Van Rensselaer Thayer, New York: Dial Press [later version published as Koo, Madame Wellington (with Isabella Taves) 1975. *No feast lasts forever*, New York: Quadrangle/New York Times Book Co.]. Chang, Queeny. 1981. *Memories of a Nonya*, Singapore: Eastern Universities Press. Blussé, Leonard. 2002. *Retour Amoy: Anny Tan, Een vrouwenleven in Indonesië, Nederland en China*, Amsterdam: Balans.

90 years old and her husband Eddie Sudibjo was in his eighties. One of the interesting aspects of the book is the unusually long span of An's memories. Her narrative is punctuated by great events that influenced the course of her life: the vicissitudes of the sugar industry in Kediri in the 1920s; the economic depression of the 1930s; the Japanese invasion and occupation of Indonesia in 1942; the Indonesian struggle for independence after the Japanese surrender in 1945; the dislocation caused by the campaign against Dutch economic interests in 1957; the inflation and political instability of Sukarno's Guided Democracy from 1959 to 1965; and the subsequent frightening transition to Suharto's New Order. An's account of her life reflects upon these fast-changing contexts.

She was born and grew to adulthood in what was then the Netherlands Indies. Despite graduating from the Dutch Chinese elementary school (*Hollandsche-Chineesche School*, or HCS) in Kediri with results that ranked her second in the entire colony, she was unable to follow her older brother into a prestigious Dutch secondary school (*Hogereburgerschool*, or HBS) because of her father's bankruptcy. At the age of twelve, An was sent instead to the Dutch Chinese Teachers' College (*Hollandsche Chineesche Kweekschool*) in Batavia, the colonial capital. After five years of study there she qualified as a primary school teacher with the additional distinction, shared with only one other student in her cohort of about thirty, of qualifying to teach in the European elementary schools (*Europeesche Lagere School*, or ELS) as well as the HCS. In the following three years, while teaching at the HCS in Jember in East Java, she successfully studied by correspondence to become a high school teacher of mathematics and physics. She was active in the teachers' union (*Nederlands Indisch Onderwijzers Genootschap*, or NIOG), rising to be national Secretary in 1940.

In 1939 she became deputy principal of the HCS in Salatiga and soon afterwards, while still in her twenties, was promoted to be principal of the school when the Dutch principal was called up for military service. This was remarkable progress for a young woman in a male-dominated colonial society.

The Japanese occupation of Indonesia interrupted An's stellar career. Soon after the Dutch surrender in March 1942, all Dutch-medium schools were compelled to close. An locked up her school and made her way to Tanggul (near Jember), where her father was by now supervising six rice mills for a cousin. Accompanying her on this journey was her future husband Eddie (born Kang Hoo Bie), who had been a boarder at her primary school in Jember and was now a student at a high school in Solo which had also been forced to close. She soon found herself responsible for feeding a detachment of Japanese soldiers who were billeted in Tanggul. In 1944 she married Eddie, who was nine years her junior. Their son John (one of the "voices" in the book) was born in Jember in October 1945, shortly after the Indonesian declaration of independence. In mid-1947 they escaped from the insecurity of East Java and settled in Jakarta, where their second child Ingrid (later to be Pearson's wife and another "voice") was born.

An resumed her career in Jakarta teaching mathematics and physics at a combined junior and senior high school, where she was soon promoted to principal when the Dutch head resigned to leave Indonesia. As Ingrid's birth approached, she had to stop classroom teaching and was deployed to a special task force translating school text books from Dutch into Indonesian. An was responsible for the translation of the mathematics and physics textbooks, which she then used when in August 1949 she returned to active teaching of mathematics and physics to trainee teachers at a new senior teachers' college (*Sekolah Guru Atas*). Within a few years she was principal of the college, where she stayed until 1967. Meanwhile her husband Eddie had found employment with the Dutch airline KLM and did management training which led to a career in civil aviation.

Nevertheless, this memoir is more than the story of their careers. We learn much about An's Chinese families and their relationships with indigenous Indonesians. Unlike Koo Hui-Lan and Queeny Chang, who were born into two of the wealthiest and most prestigious Chinese families in the Indies, An had to work for a living. Although she was not from their social stratosphere, she is overly modest in claiming that she is "just an ordinary individual". Her maternal grandmother was a member of the Djie family in Kediri, one of Java's great peranakan dynasties and in which there were numerous Chinese officers. Indeed, she mentions that her uncle (probably great-uncle) Djie Thay Hien, who was *Majoor der Chineezen* in Kediri, had a car with a chauffeur as early as 1916. Her own father was able to borrow the car during Chinese New Year holidays so they could visit relatives to pay their respects. Djie Thay Hien's son and a brother were both appointed as a *Kapitein der Chineezen* in Kediri. Another brother was the opium revenue farmer in Madiun. Three Djie cousins — also probably first cousins of An's mother — featured in a 1935 Who's Who of the Chinese of Java.[2]

---

[2] Rush, James R. 1990. *Opium to Java: Revenue Farming and Chinese Enterprise in Colonial Indonesia, 1860–1910*, Ithaca and London: Cornell University Press, p. 55.

An's father's family was not in that top bracket but the Dutch education that she and her siblings received put them in the upper stratum of twentieth-century peranakan Chinese society. She and her older brother Tan Swan Bing — who was already important enough to be included in the same Who's Who[3] — themselves achieved high status but through educational achievement rather than ascription.

The Chinese community in Kediri was much smaller and more provincial than those of Semarang and Medan where Koo Hui-Lan and Queeny Chang were born and raised. An's family was also closer to the local indigenous Indonesians than their families. At the time of An's birth, her parents were living in Ngronggot, a small rural village close to Kediri.

Her father enmeshed the village into the wider cash economy: he developed local quarries and employed local people to build roads into the village; purchased the copra output of the district and sold it in Kediri; built a large house which became the family home and a general store, run by his widowed younger sister, where the Javanese villagers were able to spend the money they received for their copra to buy previously unobtainable goods; and built sixteen more shops from which he derived a rental income. He even bought a gamelan orchestra and paid for a teacher to train local villagers to play, so that every market day there would be performances of the Javanese shadow puppet theatre (*wayang kulit*) accompanied by the gamelan.[4] For the first twenty years of her life, although she spent many of them away at school in Kediri and Batavia, this Javanese village was An's home base. She remembers it with nostalgia and describes it vividly.

She is less nostalgic about Kasminah, the 15-year-old Javanese girl little older than herself, who was "given" by An's mother to be her father's concubine. Here is a real-life version of the *nyai* (concubine) portrayed in Pramoedya's *This Earth of Mankind*, albeit without the heroic aspects. Their three children were adopted as full members of the family. Kasminah lived in An's maternal grandmother's house in Kediri until Kasminah's death in 1971. During the revolutionary struggle, An's parents fled Tanggul for the

Tan, Hong Boen 1935. *Orang-Orang Tionghoa Jang Terkemoeka di Java* [Prominent Chinese in Java], Solo: The Biographical Publishing Centre, pp. 85–6.
[3] Ibid., p. 141.
[4] Pausacker, Helen. 2005. "*Peranakan* Chinese and *Wayang* in Java", in Tim Lindsey and Helen Pausacker (eds.), *Chinese Indonesians: Remembering, Distorting, Forgetting*, Singapore and Clayton: Institute of Southeast Asian Studies and Monash Asia Institute, pp. 185–208.

relative security of Kediri and for many years lived under the same roof as Kasminah.

In Ngronggot, An was influenced by a Javanese mystic who put a "protective spell" over the family house, including its contents and family members. When she was sick with malaria, *Pak Kiai* Koermen meditated for her and her health improved immediately. She believes that, together with an excellent diet in her childhood, the psychic and spiritual healing of this mystic was responsible for her good health over her long life.

Much later, in the 1960s, An and her husband found another Javanese spiritual guide, Raden Mas Soedjono (or Mas Djon), following him on . pilgrimages to Pelabuhan Ratu on the south coast of Java, where they would meditate overnight. When she and Eddie adopted Indonesian names, it was Mas Djon who selected the names for them. During the crisis period of 1965–66, they would go to Mas Djon every night and meditate, sometimes until one or two o'clock in the morning. Once again An felt "cocooned in a protective force". She and Eddie believe that, without the help of Mas Djon, they would have died during the vicious aftermath of the attempted coup. It is worth noting here that in their attachment to Javanese mysticism, the Subdibjos were by no means unique. Other ethnic Chinese have been active in various Javanese mystical sects and also the Theosophical Society.

The Sudibjos lived in the fashionable Menteng district of Jakarta for twenty years in a house at Jalan Jogja 7 which was large enough to hold several families. For several years Jan Nielsen, a Dutch teacher, and his wife Gerda were fellow tenants. Long after the Nielsens' emigration to Australia in 1951 they adopted the two Sudibjo children when they went to Australia to study.

When Dutch schools were closed by presidential decree in December 1957, An obtained government approval to establish her own private school Harapan Kita at Jalan Jogja 7. At first the school had only three students, including her son John, but it grew to about eighty students by 1967. The school was barely profitable on an accounting basis but paid off as an investment in elite social networking. An augmented her SGA salary by running a catering business. She also invested her energies in managing a Jakarta restaurant during the 1962 Asian Games.

For most of their time at Jalan Jogja 7, the house was shared with Indonesian army officers. In the last ten years, their relationship with these officers was tense. In 1967, when An was on holiday in Australia, one of these officers took advantage of her absence to take over the house and evict the school. This was the spur to An's emigration to Australia, where she has lived for the past forty years.

In Australia, An resumed her side career in catering on the basis of her experience in Tanggul and Jakarta by buying the Toby Coffee Lounge in central Sydney. When forced to vacate the premises two years later, she bought another Sydney restaurant and renamed it Warung Indonesia. At the same time Eddie bought a fish shop business in what An called an "unsavoury" location. The two businesses continued in competition for three years until the building in which Eddie carried on his fish business was destroyed by fire.

One of the interesting features of the book is that An, Eddie and their children all found a home in Australia. It was, of course, not uncommon for Chinese Indonesians to leave Indonesia to find a better life elsewhere. In the 1950s and 1960s most emigrated to China or the Netherlands. For a Dutch-educated peranakan like An, China would have been an unusual destination. Her sister Roostien qualified for Netherlands citizenship because her husband was one of the few ethnic Chinese who had been naturalized as Dutch citizens (*gelijkgesteld*) during the colonial period. In 1962 An herself was offered a teaching job and a house in Holland by a Dutchman, her former headmaster, who also offered to sponsor her for Dutch citizenship. She did not consider the offer seriously, because Eddie did not want to live in such a cold climate. Later on, in the mid-1980s, when Warung Indonesia was in financial difficulty, she went to the Netherlands and tried to claim a Dutch pension. The claim was then rejected because in 1976 she had already become an Australian citizen.

In the early 1960s, the restrictive immigration policy (better known as the White Australia Policy) was still in operation in Australia. At that time it would not have been possible for An and Eddie to emigrate but it was possible for Asian students like their children to study in Australia. To ensure a longer right to residence, it was agreed that the Nielsens should adopt them. By 1967, the White Australia Policy was beginning to crumble but it was still difficult for Asians to settle in Australia. An came to Australia on a three-month visitor's visa, which she could apply to extend three months at a time up to a total of twelve months. Remarkably, they bought the coffee lounge under the cloud of that uncertain immigration status.

When the year was about to expire, An returned to Jakarta and obtained another similar visitor's visa. It was obviously impracticable to continue running the coffee lounge on such a basis. Fortunately a Dutch customer introduced them to an Australian friend, Senator Tony Mulvihill, who was at the time chairman of the Commonwealth Immigration Advisory Council. Senator Mulvihill pressed their case to the Minister for Immigration, who in early 1970 granted them two-year temporary residence visas. Their visas were repeatedly extended until 1976, by which time the White Australia Policy had been officially abandoned. They were then granted permanent residence and allowed to proceed directly to be naturalized as Australian citizens.

Unlike so much of the genre, this memoir is no hagiography. It is in fact a remarkably unvarnished portrait of An. She does not spare herself, nor does her family spare her. A great deal of dirty family washing is displayed for all to see: her controlling and manipulative qualities, her disputes over money with family and friends, and her arguments with her husband. This is a portrait with warts and all but in the final analysis we, along with her family, end up admiring her extraordinary life and her resilience. She is not "just an ordinary individual". We can be grateful for her Dutch colonial education and her ability to reflect so objectively on her own experience and the events which have influenced her life.[5] We should also be grateful to her son-in-law who has made it possible for us to share her story.

Charles A. Coppel
University of Melbourne
August 2007

---

[5] Govaars, Ming. 2005. *Dutch Colonial Education: The Chinese Experience in Indonesia, 1900–1942*, Singapore: Chinese Heritage Centre.

Preface

.

This is the story of the Tan family and their journey over five generations and 170 years from China to Indonesia and eventually to Australia. It is told through the memory of the oldest surviving descendent, Tan Sian Nio, who is now 95 years old and has been known as An Sudibjo for the past sixty years.

When An was approaching her 90th birthday, her children decided to celebrate this milestone with a big birthday party. This called for some kind of testimonial. Her children knew a good deal about their mother's life through oral and anecdotal history but nothing had been recorded. As the son-in-law, I was drawn into researching the salient points of her life and that of her husband Eddie. Through a brief conversation I discovered that these two apparently ordinary people had lived extraordinary lives spanning Dutch colonial rule, the Great Depression, World War II and the Japanese Occupation, Revolution and two decades of political instability before they moved in the late 1960s to join their children and live in Australia.

The short document prepared in haste for the birthday party was, as I later discovered, full of inaccuracies, but it suggested that an even richer story was there to be told if I was willing to pursue it. Having time on my hands, I approached other relatives and friends and also sought the professional opinion of a retired academic, Dr Rudy de Iongh, who is a specialist in Indonesian history. I took his advice to use an interview process structured according to the main political events of Indonesia's twentieth-century history.

The detailed interviews with An and Eddie became a fascinating process lasting more than two years. For each session I would ask a series of prepared questions about a certain phase of their lives. These interviews were recorded on Dictaphone and then painstakingly transcribed. The text was then given back to An and Eddie, which allowed them to elaborate, clarify and sometimes contradict the emerging story.

All material was eventually edited into a plain English style likely to be the most appealing to the general reader. The narrative is in the first person and I have been careful to keep the text as close as possible to what the interviewees said. English is not, however, An or Eddie's first language. An prefers to converse in a mix of Dutch and Indonesian, which gave rise to all sorts of linguistic challenges as I tried to interpret her original statements. For example, her frequent use of the word *dinges* (Dutch for "thing"), was mostly edited out as being too awkward. Where editorial comment has been necessary, this has been provided in the form of footnotes, which are entirely my responsibility.

Before the reader ventures forth into the extraordinary lives of An and Eddie Sudibjo, a note of caution is in order. This memoir is not presented as fact, but as an attempt to explore fact. No history, let alone personal history, is ever entirely factual. It is influenced by the opinions and perceptions of those who lived it, as well as those that record it. Just like individuals, families too have their myths but even those myths can be understood differently by each member of the family. The accounts of relatives, friends and even family members are not always consistent and these inconsistencies remain in the text for readers to interpret.

In her early life An was a teacher, well read in Dutch and Indonesian history and she continued to read widely into old age. She therefore relates her own story to a more formal history, without being in any way beholden to it. Again, the reader must at times decide how to relate An's own memory and experience to the received version. I myself am not a trained historian, so I have tried to leave the text as clean of comment and interpretation as possible.

I have been informed that historical accounts of ordinary Indonesians are rare, and for ordinary Chinese Indonesians rarer still. As far as I am aware, this memoir is one of the first personal histories of a non-elite Chinese Indonesian and perhaps the first to be written in English.

A recurring theme in An's interviews was the issue of nationality and how uncertain An was with her various allegiances. Nationality is about belonging. Like many other Chinese Indonesians, An had little sense of belonging to any nation. She never signified any tangible connection with her ancestral homeland of China. Yet despite being raised in the then Netherlands Indies, she did not feel welcomed or wanted in her place of birth either. The feeling of alienation deepened during the Revolution and after the independence of modern Indonesia. When growing insecurity and anti-Chinese discrimination finally drove them to seek Dutch citizenship in the late 1960s, it was too late. However, that feeling of insecurity began to dissipate after they joined their children to live in Australia. They fell in love with the place and eventually succeeded in becoming Australian citizens. In An's own words: "In my entire life, it was the first place where I felt safe and comfortable." Now, almost forty years after they first came to Australia, they have become so thoroughly Australian that they no longer acknowledge their Indonesian past or their Asian heritage. For them it is simply enough for the family to be known as Australians. An's story and that of her Tan ancestors is also an account of the wider Chinese Diaspora.

Stuart Pearson
Sydney, 2007

Acknowledgements

No attempt to record the history of any individual can be achieved without the valued input of many other resources and people. This life history is no exception. The author wishes to express his sincere appreciation to retired Senior Lecturer Rudy de Iongh (School of Asian Affairs, Sydney University) for the many, many hours of diligent and insightful research he provided to this family history. Without his outstanding contribution, this exercise would have resulted in a history of significantly diminished quality.

In addition, I would also like to express my appreciation to all the unsung and in some cases unknown authors who have provided a wealth of background material on the World Wide Web and in libraries that was used freely as background research. Without access to these resources I know this biography would have resulted in a document of much poorer quality. Wherever and whenever possible the contribution of these people has been acknowledged. I would like to specifically acknowledge my appreciation of the Royal (Netherlands) Institute of Linguistics and Anthropology (KITLV — *Koninklijk Instituut voor Taal-, Land- en Volkenkunde*), which kindly gave me permission to use a number of photographs from its vast archives for this biography. I wish to also thank Scott Merrillees who was introduced to me by Professor Charles Coppel just before the manuscript was completed. Scott kindly provided me with a number of rare images of the Teachers' College in Jakarta where An went to study. I am indebted to Scott for this unexpected assistance.

Then there is the crucial input of friends and relatives of the Sudibjo family. I received assistance from a number of people scattered around the globe who willingly gave me their own interpretations and recollections on the life and times of An Sudibjo. Responses from individuals in Singapore, Australia, Indonesia and Holland played a significant role in adding depth and meaning to my study. I pay special appreciation to An's two children, who both allowed themselves to be interviewed extensively. Thank you all.

After I had completed my preliminary draft and was attempting to secure a publisher, I was assisted by Professor Howard Dick (University of Melbourne and Editor of the ASAA Southeast Asia Publications Series) who helped me reshape the text into the form of a memoir that would be more suitable for publication. He introduced me to NUS Press and took on the responsibility of editing the manuscript on behalf of this respected organization. I am also grateful that Professor Charles Coppel agreed to write such a detailed Foreword to this publication. His support for this memoir is much appreciated. I wish to thank Ian Heywood, Cartographer for providing the excellent maps used in the memoir.

Several times during the editing process my wife, Ingrid, took on the painstaking task of proofreading and correcting the manuscript for typographical and grammatical errors. This is a thankless undertaking which she did enthusiastically and accurately. The quality of the text is mainly down to her commitment and thoroughness.

My greatest appreciation is reserved for the two individuals who have contributed the most to the success of this venture — An and Eddie Sudibjo. Without their cooperation, this exercise would have failed from the start. They both willingly submitted themselves to endless hours of tape-recorded interviews that took almost two years to complete. Even when the questions became personal, or seemed to challenge their perceived wisdom of events, they never stopped the interviewing process. It was as much of an act of devotion for them as it was for me.

I shall be eternally grateful that they allowed their lives to be recorded and themselves to be opened up to inevitable scrutiny. To my parents-in-law in general and to my mother-in-law specifically, I thank you from the bottom of my heart for this singular opportunity of sharing your lives with the world and simply say: I love you both very, very much.

I would welcome any suggestions, comments or corrections concerning the content of this book to the following email: stuart@bigpond.com

A Note on
Spelling and Grammar

Words from nine languages are used in this book; English, Dutch, Bahasa Melayu/Indonesia, Japanese, Arabic, old Javanese, French, Indian and even Latin. While English is the prime language of communication — after all it is a book written by an English speaker for an English-speaking audience — words from these other languages are interspersed throughout the text, especially to describe locations, names, and a peculiarity of a particular culture.

The challenge is to establish what form of spelling is to be adopted when using words from these nine languages. The Dutch and Indonesian languages have undergone several official revisions over the past half century and the process is still incomplete. Further, the English language itself is so dynamic that no official publications can keep up with the rapidly evolving and changing language. Wherever possible, I have adopted the most current spelling available, but there are some notable exceptions to this rule which need to be pointed out.

First, I have not changed the spelling of personal names to conform to contemporary orthography unless the person concerned has done so him or herself. For example, I have spelt the names of the first two Presidents of Indonesia as Sukarno and Suharto, even though at the time they were born their names were spelled as Soekarno and Soeharto, because both used the revised forms internationally, especially in official documents.

Secondly, I have a preference to use Indonesian place names wherever possible: thus Kalimantan rather than Borneo, Jakarta rather than Batavia, but where indigenous names have become accepted outside Indonesia I have used the spelling of place names that would be familiar to the English-speaking reader. For instance, I have used Sumatra rather than Sumatera which is Indonesian usage.

Thirdly, I have used the old Dutch spelling for institutions for which no contemporary spelling is available.

A number of locations have changed their names or their spelling over the centuries. For example, Jayakarta became Batavia, then Djakarta and finally Jakarta; Makassar was the original name of the large port city in Sulawesi, but was changed to Ujung Pandang in the 1970s and then changed back to Makassar a few years ago; and Solo was previously known as Surakarta. Wherever possible I have used the current terminology and spelling except where quotations are drawn directly from older sources.

Throughout the text the generic term "Indonesia" and "Indonesian" is used for the Javanese. This is not meant to be a slight on the Javanese people — who are a distinct ethnic group and still prefer to be known as Javanese rather than Indonesian — but a device to simplify complex issues of ethnicity within a "patchwork" nation of 200 million people, 15,000 islands, hundreds of languages and hundreds of ethnic categories.

Finally, it is often the convention in the text to write foreign words in italics. When I followed that protocol in my original draft, I discovered that there were so many words in italics that they became a distraction. I have opted to write all foreign pronouns, titles, and short words in normal font and use italics where all other foreign words appear for the first time only in the body of the text. Thereafter, all foreign words are in normal font.

PART A

The Voice of
An Utari Sudibjo
(Tan Sian Nio)

1

Introduction

I was born with the Chinese name of Tan Sian Nio in the regional city of Kediri, East Java on 11 July 1912. My family name is Tan after my father and Sian Nio means "angel girl". I also had a Dutch first name, which was Anna.[1] When I married in 1944, I took on my husband's family name of Kang and became *Ibu* (Mrs) Kang Hoo Bie Tan. Later still, when Chinese Indonesians were forced to adopt Indonesian names in the mid-1960s, my name became Ibu An Utari Sudibjo and that is how I am known to this day.

These name changes are not unusual for Chinese living in Indonesia throughout the turbulent twentieth century. Hopefully the following history of my life will help explain how one person could have so many different names.

According to me, history is only about the life and times of exceptional people. I was never a political leader, nor a military commander. I have never received a Nobel Prize and I did not found any great social movement. In every respect, I am just an ordinary individual. So I do not really understand

---

[1] When An's older brother was the first to go to the Dutch primary school in Kediri, her parents discovered that the Dutch teachers, who had recently arrived from Holland, were unfamiliar with Chinese-sounding names. The parents decided to give their children European first names that could be used alongside their Chinese names to make matters easier, particularly with the Dutch teachers. An's older brother was also known as Klaas, and her older sister became Roostien, because her first name in Chinese was "flower". Using the same linguistic connections, An became also known as Anna, which was the closest Dutch-sounding approximation to the translation of her first name in Chinese, "angel". However, by the time An's youngest brother went to the same school in Kediri (nine years after the oldest child) teachers had become more comfortable with Chinese names and the family ceased this practice.

why anyone would be interested in the story of my life. However, I have been informed that even common folk may have something to say about the extraordinary times they have lived through and without doubt I have witnessed some exceptional events in my life.

I have lived through Dutch colonial rule; the Japanese occupation; the National revolution; Communist insurgency; the institution of a New Order Government; and finally emigration to Australia, where I have lived for the past forty years.

Even though I consider my personal history unremarkable, I hope it may help others understand how extraordinary events affected the lives of the ordinary.

2

The Background to My Birth

In my opinion, the first forty years of the twentieth century constituted the high-water mark of Dutch colonial rule in the Netherlands East Indies or what I will refer to from here on as Indonesia. By the early 1900s Dutch control of the vast archipelago of over 15,000 islands was virtually complete: from the provinces of Aceh in the west to Papua in the east the Royal Netherlands Indies Army (*Koninklijk Nederlandsche Indisch Leger,* KNIL) and the Dutch Civil Administration (Binnenlandsche Bestuur, BB) enforced what became known as *Pax Neerlandica* (Dutch Peace).

Although Pax Neerlandica created a feeling of safety and reassurance in Dutch rule from Sabang to Merauke,[1] it also brought with it the seeds of its own destruction. No sooner had the wars and rebellions finished, than the first signs of a nationalist awakening began to emerge.

Young educated Indonesians eagerly used the newly created, unified geographic and political entity of Indonesia to pursue a greater say in the politics and economy of the colony. The first nationalist movements arose during the early years of the twentieth century and were inspired by the Japanese defeat of the mighty Russian navy in 1905. For aspiring Indonesian nationalists, it dispelled the myth of European invincibility and convinced them that their long-term goal of an independent Indonesia was achievable.

---

[1] After the transfer of sovereignty in 1949, these two towns located at either extreme of the Indonesian archipelago became a famous phrase often repeated by Indonesian leaders to define the limits of the new nation.

Dutch control was strong but benign — at least around the East Javanese region of Kediri, where I grew up. I have since learned that this was not the case everywhere in Indonesia at the time but during my youth I did not have any recollection of any violence towards or from the Dutch. In fact our household enjoyed a very good relationship with the Dutch. My parents were always visiting Dutch people and doing business with them. I had Dutch friends my own age and we frequently played in each other's houses.

I can say that the Dutch tended to treat the races as three distinct people. Thinking about it now, maybe the Dutch policy was deliberately based on a hierarchical separation of the races. The three distinct groups of Dutch, Chinese and indigenous Indonesians maintained their own cultures, while interacting with each other socially, economically and politically. In commerce, for example, the Europeans controlled the lucrative large-scale export-import trade; Chinese maintained the intermediate trade while most of the food production, unskilled labour and small-scale trade remained in the hands of native Indonesians.

Another area where people were treated differently was in the education system. At Primary School level, Europeans went to their own schools, called Europeesche Lagere School, ELS; the Chinese to the Hollandsche-Chineesche School, HCS; and only the best and brightest indigenous Indonesians went to the *Hollandsche-Inlandsche School*, HIS. From these three types of primary school only the smartest could continue on to the very few secondary schools (Hogereburgerschool, HBS) and eventually tertiary education, either in the Netherlands or, from the 1920s, in Indonesia.

Such was the Dutch educational policy in Indonesia. Indigenous Indonesians received only basic education, if they received any education at all, and only the brightest went on to get the same level of education as the Chinese and the Dutch. In the HIS, HCS and ELS schools all teaching was in Dutch, as it was for all secondary and tertiary schooling. If you could not speak Dutch in Indonesia, your educational opportunities were virtually non-existent, no matter how intelligent you were.

The involvement of Chinese in the Indonesian archipelago dates back centuries, but did not lead to large-scale migration until encouraged by the Dutch in the early 1800s. After Indonesia's independence from the Dutch in the mid-twentieth century had ended the steady influx of Chinese migrants, the total population of people of Chinese descent living in Indonesia had exceeded two million out of an estimated total population of sixty million. The Chinese filled a niche in the social order sandwiched between the mass of native Indonesians at the bottom of the hierarchy and the small number of Dutch as colonial masters at the top.

Our family was involved in trade and, apart from hiring indigenous labour and leasing land from them, all the important matters, such as finance, buying and selling material, and supplying produce to factories were conducted with the Dutch or other Chinese.

My Father's Background

My father's name was Tan Ting Bie (born circa 1880 in Kertosono, died 1966 in Kediri). Tan is my family name and Ting Bie is the Chinese equivalent of a first or personal name. In Chinese, Ting Bie literally means "plenty rice", but is more correctly translated as "prosperity". Rice was, and still is, the staple food crop throughout Asia and the Chinese used it as a metaphor for abundance — the more rice you have, the more prosperous you are. My father was the second generation of *peranakan* Chinese born in Indonesia[2] and the second born of four children, having an older and a younger sister and one younger brother.[3]

My grandfather on my father's side was Tan Tik Ie (born circa 1860, died in the mid-1920s). He was born and lived most of his life in and around Kediri. My grandfather's first wife had died in the late 1880s and by the time I can remember meeting him around 1916 (when I was four or five), he had already remarried. He died when I was in Batavia (which from now on I shall refer to as Jakarta) while I was attending Teachers' College during the late 1920s, but unfortunately I could not get leave to attend his funeral. Even though my grandfather and his second wife lived near where we lived, they did not exercise anywhere nearly the same influence on me as my own parents, or even my maternal grandmother. They were quiet, while my parents and my· maternal grandmother were much more dynamic, determined people.

I never met my great grandfather, Tan Kim Hok. He was dead a long time before I came into this world, but I was told by my father that he was born near the coastal north-eastern Chinese province of

---

[2] Peranakan Chinese are those born in Indonesia and includes Chinese of mixed parentage; *totok* Chinese were born in China. According to An, it was better to be peranakan than totok because it meant you were culturally oriented towards Indonesia, not China.

[3] See Family Tree (Appendix A).

Shandong, alongside the Yellow Sea in the late 1820s, or perhaps the early 1830s. He started his professional life in China as a textile merchant dealing in cloth made from cotton and especially Chinese silk. In his youth he travelled to many locations throughout Asia, including Taiwan and Indonesia, to expand his textile business and to gather raw material. Tan Kim Hok came to Indonesia as a trader when he was a young man, possibly in the early 1850s, and established himself in the East Javanese city of Kediri, conveniently located on the *Kali* (river) Brantas, which was navigable by barge down to the busy port of Surabaya. In the mid-1850s, he married a locally born Chinese girl from Kediri whose surname, I believe, was Liem.

When my great grandfather arrived in Indonesia, he spoke only the Chinese Jiaodong dialect of his native province, making it impossible for him to converse with Indonesians (who mainly spoke Javanese or Bahasa Melayu, which later became Bahasa Indonesia), Europeans (mainly from Holland, who spoke Dutch) and also fellow Chinese (who, predominantly coming from China's southeast, spoke Cantonese or Hokkien).

After he was married, my great grandfather continued to travel back and forth between Indonesia and his homeland in Northern China but, according to my father, something happened back in China during the late 1850s that caused my great grandfather to settle permanently in Kediri.[4] When his circuit of international textile trade was broken, he turned to trading locally in a then new product that was quickly becoming popular, kerosene.[5]

The family lived modestly in a rented house on the main road of Kediri, Jalan Alun-Alun, which was owned by a local Chinese family who would later become related to the Tan family by marriage. According to my father, great grandfather Tan died in Kediri around 1890.

My grandmother arranged for father to be tutored at home for literacy and numeracy until she died, when I think he was around 9 years old. After her death, my father went to work for his late mother's brother-in-

---

[4] During this period in China, there were periodic bouts of civil unrest, such as the Taiping Rebellion of 1850–64 and this may have caused great grandfather Tan to cease connections with his homeland.

[5] According to Tan Swan Bing (An's older brother and only surviving sibling at the time of writing this memoir), great grandfather Tan made a modest living as a wholesaler of kerosene, which he sold from a shop at the front of the family home in Kediri. This trade was continued by his son, Tan Tik Ie.

Kediri, East Java in the early twentieth century. (KITLV #26313)

law, Tjioe Djie Kwie, who was a successful commodity trader in Kediri. As a teenager, he started off by assisting his uncle in any way he could and along the way saved a little bit of pocket money to help out his family. In return, my father's basic literacy and numeracy were advanced under his uncle's tutelage to the level needed of a businessman. He became proficient in reading and writing a number of languages including Arabic, traditional Javanese script and Melayu. He spoke all levels of Javanese including the highest, which is spoken at the *kraton* (palace). In his adulthood these linguistic skills would give him an advantage when dealing with high-ranking Javanese officials. He could also speak passable Dutch and Hokkien.

Over the next ten years his uncle also taught him all the necessary attributes of being a successful trader. From an early age my father bought and sold many commodities such as rice, soy-beans, and corn on behalf of his uncle. Towards the end of his informal apprenticeship, when he was now in his late teens, he was paid ƒ15 (Dutch *guilders*) a month plus board at his uncle's house in Kediri. I vaguely remember someone telling me that he did not get along with his stepmother.

Tjioe Djie Kwie (and the Tjioe side of the family) was much wealthier than the Tan side of the family. It seems that Uncle Tjioe took my father

9

"under his wing" to give him a better opportunity in life after the unexpected death of my father's mother.

By the early 1900s, my father was making a small name for himself in the district as a trader and his business was beginning to prosper. But Uncle Tjioe did not limit my father's education to just financial matters. He was a sophisticated, cultured man who introduced my father to many activities that my father's own family could not afford.

For example, Uncle Tjioe owned his own *gamelan* (a Javanese orchestra playing traditional native music) and employed a full time *kapelmeester* (bandmaster) who taught my father how to play. Years later, when my father was a successful and wealthy trader in his own right, he established his own gamelan orchestra and spent many enjoyable hours seated on floor mats singing and playing various instruments alongside other musicians in the orchestra, also teaching local villagers how to play.

My Mother's Background

My mother Njoo Hing Tjie (born 1884, died 1964) was the third generation of peranakan Chinese born in Indonesia. She was born and raised in the port city of Makassar (recently known as Ujung Pandang) in South Sulawesi. But apart from that small scrap of information, I do not know when the first member of the Njoo family arrived in Indonesia or what he did. However, my mother told me that by the time she was born in Makassar her family had become very wealthy and influential.

Her father, Njoo Djie Kiem (born in the late 1850s) supplied food and equipment to the Dutch army garrisoned at Fort Rotterdam in Makassar and had extensive business interests throughout the eastern region of the Indonesian archipelago (Sulawesi, eastern Java, and possibly the islands of Nusa Tenggara).[6]

He may have been a Christian because he was one of the earliest graduates of the colony's first Dutch High School established in Jakarta, being educated there possibly in the late 1860s or early 1870s.[7] He married

---

[6] For several centuries the Dutch used Makassar as the civil and military centre for their control of the eastern half of Indonesia. Large numbers of troops and a sizeable number of naval vessels were stationed there to transport soldiers to any trouble spot in the eastern archipelago.

[7] Koning Willem III (King William III) School was established in 1859 in Jakarta, where being a person of influence, Dutch-speaking and a Christian were prerequisites of entry.

Djie Djioe Nio of Kediri in the 1880s and had two daughters, one by adoption (Njoo Hong Tjie) and my mother by birth.

According to my mother, her father's business interests often took him away from Makassar for long periods of time and this possibly explains why my mother was adopted and placed under the protection of the Sultan of the local Kingdom of Gowa, who was also a school friend of her father. During these long absences, he left his power of attorney with his brother in Makassar. Unfortunately, his brother either embezzled or badly mishandled funds to the extent that my grandfather became bankrupt in the late 1880s.

Apparently much of the documentation (ledgers, accounts and bills) was destroyed at the time, so without any written proof my grandfather was not able to recover monies owed to him. Some people did feel honour-bound to repay their debts, but it was insufficient to save the business. Within a few years my grandfather died a broken man at the relatively young age of thirty-something, leaving my grandmother a destitute widow in her early thirties. My mother was only six years old at the time.

In 1893 or thereabouts, after the death of my grandfather, my *Oma* (grandmother) Njoo returned to her birthplace of Kediri, taking her two daughters with her (my mother then aged about nine and the older sister).[8] She was now poor but Oma Njoo made enough income through dressmaking to maintain appearances and even employ a servant. As was the custom of the time for a Chinese widow with children, she never remarried.

Decades later, my grandmother's brother and his children came to visit us in Kediri but my grandmother refused to see him. To this day, I do not know his version of events. By the time of my childhood in the late 1910s the two sides of the Njoo family had irreconcilably gone their own separate ways.

When my mother reached maturity, my father's uncle Tjioe Djie Kwie and his wife brokered a marriage between the Njoo and Tan families, to whom they were both related. My parents did not know each other before the marriage and the first time they met was on their wedding day.[9] Both the Njoo and Tan families were equally poor in wealth and status, but I

---

[8] All grandparents were addressed by the Dutch form of either *oma* (female) or *opa* (male).

[9] According to Chinese custom, young girls after the age of 12 rarely, if ever, ventured out into public alone. They stayed in the home assisting their parents and learning how to become a good wife, being instructed in such matters as cooking, cleaning, sewing and running a proper household. On the rare occasions they left the house, they went with the family or a chaperone.

think the reason why the two families agreed to the arrangement was that my father, who was still working for Uncle Tjioe Djie Kwie, appeared to be the best available person to raise both families out of their lowly position. In other words, he seemed like a good catch.

My Family's Beginnings

My mother and father were married in December 1902 in Kediri at the ages of 18 and 22 respectively. As they were not well off, it was not a big wedding and perhaps only about 50 people attended.[10] After the marriage my father continued working for Uncle Djie Kwie and received an increase in wages to ƒ25 per month. In about 1910 my parents relocated to Ngronggot,

A typical kampung in East Java in the 1920s. According to An, Ngronggot was very similar. (KITLV # 25625)

---

[10] Traditionally, weddings in Indonesia were viewed as an outward demonstration of one's wealth — the more guests you have, the wealthier you must be. Some wedding ceremonies involve thousands of guests and take several days to complete but even the average wedding has hundreds of people attending. To invite only a few dozen people is a clear sign of your financial hardship.

several kilometres off the road between Kediri (18 kilometres away in one direction) and Kertosono (about 15 kilometres away in another direction).

At this time, Ngronggot was a small underdeveloped rural *kampung* (village) with possibly less than a thousand inhabitants who were exclusively *asli* (native) Indonesians. No Chinese or other foreigner had ever lived in the village before my parents arrived.

Uncle Djie Kwie advised him to go there and possibly lent him some money to establish himself.[11] My father started out by building new roads in the area for the Dutch colonial government. Up to that time there were only tracks through the countryside.[12]

My father began by developing local quarries to produce the road-base, then paid local labour to lay the road-base to create new and wider roads to the village of Ngronggot and beyond. In return, the Dutch paid him a set amount per kilometre of roadway constructed.[13] As soon as the government contract to improve the roads into and around Ngronggot was fulfilled, my father quickly reverted back to his chosen profession of trading.

His first private venture involved buying the entire district's surplus copra from the locals and transporting it along his new roads to the large market town of Kediri, where it was sold for a profit, most likely to Uncle Djie Kwie. By about 1912 my father felt secure enough financially to buy two blocks of land right in the centre of the kampung. On one he built the largest house in the village, a house we would call our family home for the next twenty years or so. On the other block, opposite the village *pasar* (market), my father erected Ngronggot's first general store (*toko kelontong*), where the local people could buy goods such as pots and pans, textiles, kerosene lamps, torches and batteries hitherto only available in Kediri, a day's walk away.

It was never my father's intention to operate the store himself. In fact the purpose was to provide an income for his recently widowed younger sister, Kira, whom I only knew as *Tante* (Aunt) Kira. Tante Kira

---

[11] The Dutch colonial government had restricted Chinese to living in the major towns and cities of Indonesia, but this limitation was officially lifted in 1910, inducing a large number of Chinese to move into small country towns and take up residence. It is likely that An's father moved to Ngronggot after these restrictions were removed.

[12] Ngronggot was linked to the main Kediri-Kertosono road by a meandering track through the open countryside and rice fields that took an hour or so to walk. Its narrowness severely hampered the movement of goods.

[13] An's parents were possibly sent to Ngronggot to satisfy a Dutch contract secured by Uncle Djie Kwie to provide a new road connecting Ngronggot to the Kediri-Kertosono rail line.

arrived and soon had the store running smoothly. The venture proved to be very popular with the locals, who were now receiving regular cash payments from my father for their copra and wanted to spend it on personal, farm and household items, such as tobacco, clothes, cooking equipment, and farming tools that were previously unaffordable. From this time Tante Kira started paying my father rent. Within a year or two Tante Kira, who as a childless widow was always eligible to marry again, felt financially comfortable enough to look for another husband.[14] Shortly after, she agreed to marry Kwee Soen Sian, a local-born Chinese from Kediri, as her second husband and together they continued to run the store in Ngronggot.

By the mid-1910s, my father was buying in seed and teaching the local people how to better farm and grow a number of different cash crops such as rice, soy-bean, and corn. Of course, any money the locals accumulated was usually spent at the general store operated by Aunt Kira and her husband.

Interior of a typical Chinese shop in East Java in the 1910s. (KITLV # 4212)

---

[14] According to Chinese tradition, widows without children were actively encouraged to remarry while widows with children were discouraged from re-marrying.

My father watched the small village develop and with more produce being grown, traded, and transported, saw a need for an enlarged and modernised market. He convinced the village elders to sell him more land in the centre of town on which he expanded the existing *pasar* (market) by building nine new shops. He also constructed seven more shops outside the pasar on the main street near our house. Within months they were fully leased to merchants, craftsman, retailers, public notaries and other business people who were attracted to the growing town. To avoid any possible criticism that he was favouring the Chinese, my father made sure that the tenants were mainly indigenous and the local people genuinely appreciated him for it.

With sixteen new commercial premises producing regular income, together with the existing rental income from Auntie's store and high returns from his ventures in trading seasonal crops, my father had quickly become the largest landholder and the wealthiest citizen in Ngronggot.

We even had our own gamelan orchestra at our disposal. Before my father's arrival in Ngronggot, the village did not possess such a luxury, which in Java is regarded as a sign of a community's sophistication and wealth. Realizing this, one of the earliest initiatives my father implemented after he got established was to create a fifteen-piece gamelan orchestra.

First he purchased all the instruments — percussion instruments of wood and brass — and then paid for a music teacher to come from Kediri to train the local villagers in playing them. After the orchestra was established and a band leader or kapelmeester appointed, they played at weddings and other celebrations in the local area with my father always paying the musicians a small fee.

Every forty days, coinciding with a regular market day my father had "open house" at our home.[15] All the villagers could come and partake of finger food while they listened to their gamelan orchestra along with a *dalang* (story-teller), whom my dad had hired to entertain the locals

---

[15] The Javanese week, which was still being used extensively in the early twentieth century in rural Java, is of only five days duration and the frequency of market days was determined by the size of the township. A village such as Ngronggot had one market day a week (i.e. one every five days); small towns had two market days every week and places like Kediri had a pasar every day of the (Javanese) week. Forty is an auspicious number in Javanese society and is believed to originate from religious practice. For example, naming ceremonies for a baby occur forty days after birth; mourning traditionally proceeds for forty days after death. Therefore An's father organized "open house" in the kampung of Ngronggot to take place every eighth market day, or once every forty days.

with tales of love and war in the *wayang* (shadow puppet play) tradition that drew on stories from the great Hindu epics of *Ramayana* and the *Mahabharata*. The local people loved these evenings for they regarded such events as putting their little town "on the map" and were grateful to my father for making it happen.

Once the orchestra even played at the *Regentswoning* (Regent's house) in Kediri, which the villagers regarded as a great achievement.[16] From my perspective, in just over a decade of astute business practice, my father had personally turned a sleepy backwater of a kampung into a thriving and vibrant community and the villagers admired him for it. By the time I was a little girl in the early 1920s, everyone in Ngronggot addressed him as *Ndoro*, which in the local Javanese language means "gentleman of noble birth".

Looking back, life for me as a young girl in the village of Ngronggot was peaceful, enjoyable and idyllic. I had no concerns about my safety, nor for the safety of any of my family and I was totally quarantined from the anti-Dutch and anti-Chinese sentiment that was growing ominously elsewhere. I basked in the reflected admiration the villagers held for my father and I adored him totally.

---

[16] Regent is the Dutch equivalent of district head, now *bupati*.

3

Growing Up (1912–24)

Life in Ngronggot

Out of my mother's thirteen pregnancies, I am the third of only four children who survived beyond infancy.[1] There were six other babies that my mother miscarried and three more who died in their first year of life. My mother fell pregnant regularly between 1906 and 1922 and even though we lived throughout this time in the countryside at Ngronggot, all births occurred in the nearby main town of Kediri, where midwives and sometimes a doctor were available.[2]

I was born with a small birthmark on my upper right buttock. It is in the shape of the two letters "I" and "T", which happen to be the name of my paternal grandmother who died when my father was a young boy. Dad told me this was a certain sign that I was the reincarnation of his mother. According to my father, he was his mother's favourite child and her re-embodiment in me, my father believed, meant that she had returned to be close to him and continue her love for him. In return, my father

---

[1] The other three surviving children, are:
- Tan Swan Bing (meaning "bright teacher") ("Klaas"), born 1906
- Tan Tien Nio, ("flower girl"), ("Roostien"), born 1910
- Tan Siauw Djie, ("small child"), born 1916.
Also see Family Tree (Appendix A)

[2] In early twentieth-century Indonesia, most births occurred without sophisticated medical supervision and often without even a midwife present, but as An's mother suffered from a chronic heart condition that became more serious with age and successive pregnancies, all her deliveries were performed at Kediri, the nearest location where a midwife and doctor could assist. In 1922 she experienced a near-fatal heart attack with the delivery of her last child, who was stillborn. To complicate matters further, she was diagnosed with diabetes in her later childbearing years.

loved me and treated me with special kindness as a sign of respect and love for his mother. As my father's favourite, I was allowed to do whatever I liked as long as I was happy.

The very first memory I have is at the age of three or four and involves being affected by the disease Malaria Tropica. There were no medicines such as quinine available for me then, so it took me over a year to recover fully. I was given a special diet which included oat porridge, extra eggs, imported Ovaltine and Scott's Emulsion (containing fish oil), plus fresh milk every day from a cow which my parents purchased and kept on our property especially for me. My parents started giving this food to my brothers and sisters to make them strong as well but, whereas they only received it once a day, I was given it twice a day. I believe all this special food I had when I was a little girl helped me to become strong and healthy to this day.

Pak Kiai Koermen

In Ngronggot, my family had daily business dealings with the indigenous Indonesians, one of whom was a local leader who supplied thousands of coconuts for our family's copra business. His name was Pak Kiai Koermen. (*Pak* means father; *Kiai* is Javanese for religious teacher; and Koermen was his Javanese family name). These honorific titles indicated that he was not only an important local leader but also well off for he could afford what was then a rare and expensive journey to Mecca to confirm his faith in Islam. In fact it was reported that he had performed the Haj to Mecca at least three times![3] He was about ten years older than my father and his children had all left home.

However, Pak Kiai Koermen was more than just a wealthy and influential leader in the community — he was an impressive mystic as well. He had a reputation for being able to "see" into the future, "cure" illnesses, "protect" crops, execute powerful "spells" and "fulfil" wishes.[4]

When I was growing up, I was told that Pak Kiai Koermen possessed more power than the *dukun* (faith healers), who were plentiful throughout Indonesia at the time and could perform magic spells or tell fortunes.

---

[3] Even though the majority of indigenous Indonesians were Muslim, the pilgrimage to Mecca (one of the five major tasks of the religion) was beyond the financial resources of all but a wealthy few.

[4] The closest Western description that could be applied to Pak Kiai Koermen is that he was a very powerful Javanese mystic.

During the coconut season, my mother paid him to deliver more than a thousand coconuts every month to our property for processing into copra. The contents were scraped out and left to dry in the open air, which also exposed the drying copra to theft. Pak Kiai Koermen put a spell on my family's property to protect it against anyone attempting to steal the drying copra. He said that if people ventured onto the property with any criminal intentions, they would become so confused they would be unable to find their way out!

Once, several strangers from outside the kampung did in fact come to steal the copra at night but were found wandering confusedly about our property the next morning, when they were quickly dealt with by the local villagers. A local police presence did not yet exist in this part of Java, so they were let off with a stern warning, a small beating, and a promise from them that they would never return. Word quickly spread far and wide that my parent's property was "protected".

Later, another stranger climbed up one of our coconut trees to steal coconuts. He became so disoriented and frightened by what he said later were spirits attacking him that he stayed up in the tree all night and half the next day, to the delight of a growing crowd of villagers who had assembled throughout the morning to hear his hysterical jabbering. Eventually, Pak Kiai Koermen finally arrived and "released" the man from the "spell". Thereafter, absolutely no-one tried to steal from us again.

At this point even my parents were so impressed with Pak Kiai Koermen's prowess that he became more than a mere business acquaintance — he became a close personal friend. To cement the friendship, Pak Kiai Koermen put a "protective spell" over my family's house, including its contents and family members.

He created a *raksasa* or giant spirit-person to guard the home against intruders — my father told me his name was Tjodrono. The first time I actually saw him was a few months later when I was alone in the house one evening and became frightened by some unusual noises coming from outside. He was almost two metres high and possibly weighed about a hundred kilograms, which to the rest of us Chinese and Indonesians made him a giant. He appeared to be ethnic Javanese, except that his deep brown skin and face was covered in thick black body hair (Javanese are comparatively hairless). Like a native, he wore a *sarong* (skirt) and was bare-chested and barefooted. He had a thick mane of black shoulder-length hair and the most piercing eyes I have ever seen. Lastly, Tjodrono wore a *keris* (dagger) about 30–35cm long in a sheath tied to a belt that held up

19

his sarong. If his appearance was not frightening enough, then somehow you knew that Tjodrono would use the knife to deadly effect. From the instant I saw Tjodrono I stopped being scared. Instinctively I knew he was there to protect the house and the people who lived in it, including me. I calmed down straight away and went off to bed, reassured in the knowledge that I was now perfectly safe.

One day my cousin Tjiekdee Tjie Hwie came to stay at our house. She was about my age and the daughter of my mother's sister. She did not believe in Tjodrono and scoffed at the whole idea of spirits. That evening the whole house was woken up by her screams of distress and cries for help. She had gone to the servant's toilet by mistake, which was out-of-bounds to us and been confronted by Tjodrono. She was terrified and from that point on became a believer.

From time to time over the next several years I would see Tjodrono occasionally standing at the end of corridors, or moving silently through rooms in the house. Each time he made an appearance I felt comforted, protected and in safe hands. Once or twice in my adult life Tjodrono has appeared to me in dreams to warn me about dishonest people. After I moved to Australia he advised me to dismiss a worker in my restaurant in Sydney, but in the dream he refused to tell me why. When I spoke to this person the next day about the dream, she suddenly confessed she had been stealing money from my restaurant for months, but at the time no one else knew about her criminal activity — only Tjodrono.

Pak Kiai Koermen regularly meditated in a very small room in his house that was specially set aside for him. The room was only two metres square, had an earthen floor and was completely bare save for a central bamboo pole against which he would rest his back while he meditated and prayed for up to twenty-four hours at a time. During these sessions he would abstain from all food and drink. No one was allowed into the room except for me. I was only four or five years old at the time and still suffering from malaria. Pak Kiai Koermen took it upon himself to help make me better. I went to his house many times and was very naughty for while he was trying to pray for me, I kept on asking questions such as "What are you doing there?"; "Can I come in?"; "Let me join you". He "adopted" me, meditated for me and immediately my health improved significantly. Pak Kiai Koermen renamed me *Waras*, which means "healed" in Javanese. I felt safe and comfortable in his presence.

For many years after that, I visited him to pay my respects whenever I returned home from school. He was a very good man and so was his wife. Knowing that school holidays were approaching, they always set aside the very best fruit for me to eat in anticipation of my end of school visits. Years later, when I was away in Jakarta attending Teachers' College and after our family had moved away from Ngronggot, my parents informed me that Pak Kiai Koermen had passed away.

For many years after his death I felt a spiritual emptiness in my life that was not filled until I found another spiritual leader to replace him, Mas Djon (see Chapter 9). As well as the special food I was given when I was young, I believe the psychic and spiritual healing of Pak Kiai Koermen was the other main factor in the good health I still enjoy to this day.

Our Home

My parents' house in Ngronggot seemed to be constantly full of people and was a very exciting place in which to grow up. I remember that the house accommodated all the family of six, plus servants and the occasional guests. When my father entered the sugar industry in 1918 (more on that later) we also housed up to ten employees working for my father at the local fields or mills. Counting family, servants and sugar employees during the peak sugar cane harvesting season, a total of two dozen people or more could be comfortably accommodated at our home. The servants (always native Indonesians) and workers (always Chinese) lived in separate quarters adjacent to the main house.

The Chinese workers acted as my father's supervisors during harvesting. They ate with us in the main dining room, but the Indonesian servants always ate on their own. The Chinese workers stayed with us between four and six months a year during the harvest season, then returned to their wives and families. My father treated all his Chinese employees — including a few who were relatives — very well indeed. He always paid them more than other employers in the district and often reported back to their parents or family. Therefore many of them were happy to return year after year.

Our family home in Ngronggot was the largest house in the village by far and was located opposite the pasar near the central square on the back road to the railway junction of Kertosono. We employed five household servants in all, being a cook, a housekeeper, and three general servants. When I was an infant, I also had an *amah* (personal nurse) but I do not remember her well. By the time I was of school age — about six — my

21

surviving grandmother (on my mother's side) said I was old enough to do without such an indulgence and my amah was dismissed.

In our household, the indigenous Indonesians were definitely at the bottom of the social ladder. We knew that we were better than they, but we also knew that we were inferior to the Dutch. There was one occasion when we prepared frantically for the overnight visit of important Dutch guests. This necessitated moving our servants out of their compound to make way for the servants of the Dutch. However, something prevented the Dutch from arriving and we merely told our servants to return the house to normal and, oh by the way, they could move back into their rooms. We never mistreated our servants, but we never really held them in high regard either. I guess relationships between the Dutch, Chinese and indigenous Indonesians in our household were a reflection of the attitudes between the races in the general community. If Dutch people came to our house we behaved deferentially to them and we expected the same to us from indigenous Indonesians.

In this three-tiered Indonesian society, the Chinese were "sandwiched" between the small number of Dutch (0.2 per cent of the population) who ruled, and the millions of indigenous Indonesians (97 per cent of the population) who served. We always performed a delicate balancing act of trying not to offend either side. My father would sometimes repeat the Dutch phrase common at the time to summarize how all three ethnic groups were meant to co-exist — *rust en orde* (tranquillity and order) — and it seemed to express his wishes too. However, this description of the social order is also a gross over-simplification. The fabric of society was much more complex and complicated than that.

There were Indonesians from rich sultans down to even poor village elders who wielded significant economic, political or social power. Yet some Dutch had no influence or standing at all and virtually lived as peasants. Lastly, while a few Chinese enjoyed enormous privileges, many others toiled like everyone else just to make a living. But in reality, while the social structure was always blurred, there was an underlying principle at work. In general the Dutch were the economic and political masters, the Chinese were deputed to manage the economy and the indigenous Indonesians mainly provided the workforce.

As a defence against the many on one hand and the powerful on the other, the Chinese community developed an informal network to support each other — economically, socially and politically — to ensure that their own kind maximized any successes. Originally based on blood ties alone, the network of support later expanded to include any ethnic Chinese living in Indonesia.

Even though we were ethnically Chinese, we regarded Indonesia as our home. My forebears had come to live in Indonesia more than a century earlier and, depending on which side of the family you looked at, I was either the third or fourth generation peranakan Chinese living in Indonesia. Indonesia was my country and my future, but it was an Indonesia under Dutch rule. My parents wanted us to go to Dutch schools and speak Dutch fluently because they believed Dutch-educated people had better opportunities in their careers and work. In short, my parents were trying to turn us into Dutch people. Both parents insisted on a very good education for us children — that is a Dutch-based education of course — but it is a quote from my father that he repeated so often that I remember it well. Dad would frequently say, "It is more important to give children a good education than to leave them an inheritance of money". His words became a mantra for us children. Later, when we in turn had children of our own, we likewise insisted they be educated to the highest levels possible.

Religious Beliefs of My Family

The religion of my family at home was mainly Buddhism. My father would often take the family to visit the local Chinese *klenteng* (temple) and lead us in observing Buddhist practices. The family was also influenced by Confucianism in the form of revering and worshipping our ancestors. At home while I was growing up there was an altar or shrine in our house. It was on a special table and housed the ashes of my ancestors (such as my grandparents and great-grandparents) in a number of silver urns. On the 1st and 15th day of each Chinese month, prayers were offered to the ancestors accompanied by food, such as fresh fruit, cakes, sweets, rice and the favourite dishes of the departed.

There was never a statue of Buddha in our house. It was only later when we children were going to Dutch schools that Christian beliefs started to exercise an influence on our household.

Our servants were Muslim, but I had no understanding of this religion, other than that they prayed to Allah at certain times of the day. When I was growing up, Islam in Indonesia was not as strictly observed or its followers as devout as now. For example, it was not then the habit of Muslim women to wear headscarfs, at least not in Java. I do remember that at the end of the Islamic holy month of *Ramadan*, the servants in

A typical Chinese Buddhist Temple (Klenteng) in East Java in the early twentieth century. The Klenteng in Kediri was surrounded by rice fields. (KITLV # 3480)

our household always returned to their traditional villages for a week or two during *Lebaran* (Muslim New Year), leaving us to fend for ourselves. Even though Lebaran was a religious holiday, the majority of the people did not place much religious significance on it. Instead, most people viewed it as a holiday, like many in the West currently regard Easter and Christmas.

As children, the Dutch education system exposed us to Christianity in the form of Religious Education. My brothers converted to Catholicism first when they were at school and much later, when she was an adult, my sister Roostien also became a Catholic. Even though some members of the family were Christians, others Buddhist with Confucian overtones, and the servants Muslim, there was no conflict in our household over religion.

No-one was religiously fundamental or zealous and everyone, including the servants, tolerated each other's beliefs to the point where we even enjoyed participating in each other's religious practices. For example, all the family still worshipped our ancestors after some of we children had become Christians and sometimes we would join our servants in celebrating Islamic rituals such as Muslim New Year's Day. At the time Indonesia was made up of many religions, but nobody was so fanatic that they would fight and kill one another over their religious beliefs.

My own children were baptised into the Roman Catholic Church in their early years, but I was not baptised into the Roman Catholic Church until June 1995, when I was 82 years old.

A Memorable Day

I saw my first motor vehicle of any kind when I was a little girl of about four in 1916. My parents had taken the whole family to Kediri to celebrate the elevation of my Uncle Djie Thay Hien[5] to the distinguished honorary position of *Majoor der Chinezen* (Major for the Chinese) of the Kediri district by the Dutch authorities.[6] He had been *Kapitein der Chinezen* since 1899 but the rank of Majoor was the highest status possible under the Dutch. It was a hugely significant occasion and our family must have been impressed by the ceremony and importance, but at my tender age I can only remember the car!

I had never seen anything like this machine before — a vehicle that moved without animal power. It oozed luxury, having leather seats, wooden trim and deeply polished black paintwork that shone in the sun. It was huge, noisy, and came complete with a chauffeur, who was resplendent in his own uniform of coat, cap and gloves.

My uncle's residence was opposite my father's house in Kediri, so I crossed the road to join the many native Indonesians who had excitedly crowded around the limousine and caused a commotion observing this contraption. Depending on their point of view, they muttered amongst themselves that the vehicle was either the grandest thing they had ever seen, or the work of the devil. For my part, I thought the car was absolutely fantastic.

I cannot remember whether I travelled in the vehicle on that particular day, but I do remember subsequent years when my father would borrow the car (and driver) from my uncle and the family would travel the countryside on holidays during Chinese New Year in order to pay our respects to relatives. We would drive down the roads with the wind in my hair and watch Indonesians rush to the sides of the roads to greet us. I felt special and important during these journeys and even today I still enjoy being taken for a car trip.

---

[5] Related to Oma Njoo, whose maiden name was Djie Djioe Nio.
[6] Regeeringsalmanaak voor Nederlandsch-Indië.

Motor vehicles of any kind were still uncommon in Eastern Java for decades after this event. For years, only the rich or the Government could afford them. In the two decades or so that our family resided in Ngronggot, we never owned a car. We personally used *dokar* (horse-drawn carts) and employed *cikar* (horse-drawn wagons) for the transport of raw sugar to the mills. It was only when our family moved to Tanggul in the late 1920s and my father became the Supervisor of several rice mills that we obtained our first car and driver. Even during the Second World War the majority of Japanese troops mainly used bicycles for personal transport, because there were not enough motor vehicles in Indonesia to confiscate. During the 1920s I did see motor lorries in Jakarta when attending Teachers' College, but I did not see my first motor lorry in the countryside until the early 1930s and they were still a rare sight years later.

Majoor Djie Thay Hien was a distant relative on my mother's side of the family, being a cousin of my maternal grandmother, Oma Njoo. I am not sure if or how he influenced our lives specifically, but I do know that as Indonesians of Chinese descent in the Kediri area we were certainly part of his responsibility and being related he probably had a greater say over our lives than I was aware of as an infant. He was a very rich man and known throughout the district as a *groothandelaar* (wholesaler) of tobacco, which he exported to Hamburg, Germany. He owned a number of tobacco plantations throughout east and middle Java and in Kediri itself he operated a drying house to "cure" the tobacco prior to being exported.

Djie Thay Hien was an old man when he was elevated to the position of Majoor and I believe he died around 1924. His son, Djie Ting Loen took over the family business and was immediately elevated to *Luitenant der Chinezen* by the Dutch.[7] Over the next decade or so he was promoted to Kapitein and then finally Majoor der Chinezen, but the invasion of the Japanese in 1942 put an end to this colonial system and from then on no special privileges of rank were again conferred on the Chinese in Indonesia.

There were other relatives who exercised significant influence over my family in a more direct and memorable way. For example, Tjioe Djie Kwie was Grandmother Tan's (my paternal grandmother) brother-in-law and helped my father get established. Then there were the brothers Lie Djing Han and Lie Djing Tjay (related to Great Grandmother Tan), who

---

[7] Regeeringsalmanaak voor Nederlandsch-Indië.

assisted my father into the sugar industry. And lastly, Tjioe Sien An (my father's cousin), who came to my father's rescue after the sugar collapse by employing him as a Superintendent of his rice mills in the Tanggul area.

Holidays

My father leased a small piece of land high up on the slopes of the extinct volcano Gunung (Mount) Wilis, which soared over two kilometres above the plains about 45 kilometres to the west of Kediri. There he erected a holiday bungalow which was large enough to accommodate our family of six and four of our servants. It had a large kitchen, a big dining room and four bedrooms. Each long school holiday my parents would take the family (and servants) to our lodge, where we would stay for three or four weeks enjoying the cooler climate and high country rainforest around us.

The daytime temperatures were a mild 20 degrees Celsius and at night it sometimes got cold enough for the family to have to wear jumpers. Other families borrowed the bungalow from time to time and I do not think they were ever charged for it.

Dad was happy to have people use the holiday home as he did not want it empty for most of the year. He said that a vacant bungalow only encouraged squatters and vandals. I can remember spending our long holidays at Gunung Wilis for many years until about the mid-1920s, when the family's financial circumstances changed dramatically and this property had to be sold.

Life in Kediri

Kediri was a big, bustling regional town of over 30,000 people and intensely proud of being the seat of an ancient Javanese kingdom that produced Indonesia's greatest prophet-king, Joyoboyo during the twelfth century. The city had several primary schools — one each for the Dutch, Chinese and indigenous Indonesians — and a Junior High School or MULO (*Meer Uitgebreid Lager Onderwijs*) for the education of the children. There were also many Dutch expatriates living in Kediri at the time. For example, all the teachers at the Dutch Primary School for Chinese (HCS) were Dutch. The Chinese got on well with the Dutch, and vice versa. I played with the children of my father's Dutch Government friend who was a *Controleur* (District Officer). My father had developed a personal relationship with the *Controleur* and his assistant during the time when he first moved to Ngronggot and sold road base to the Dutch Government.

My childhood in East Java was blessed. I enjoyed a safe and secure upbringing. I never experienced prejudice of any kind until I was in my early teens in the mid-1920s and went to a high school in Jakarta. Surprisingly, the only prejudice there came from the Dutch teachers. Maybe it was because I was in the capital city and therefore at the very heart of the colony, but my Dutch teachers did treat me differently. They would sometimes point out to the rest of the class (of Dutch, Chinese and Indonesians) that I was not as important as my fellow Dutch students. They would also put down the Indonesians students too as being inferior to both the Chinese and especially the Dutch, thereby reinforcing the "approved" social order.

None of us spoke Chinese at home. Having lived for several generations in Indonesia, the family knew nothing of China or its language(s). We had come to view ourselves as citizens of colonial Indonesia and beholden to its masters, the Dutch. Only those people we regarded as still "hopelessly" attached to China would speak any of its languages. The family spoke mainly Bahasa Melayu to each other at home and we children — being Dutch-educated — spoke Dutch to people outside the home environment. Dad spoke enough Dutch to get by in his dealings with the Dutch authorities, but Mum did not speak the language at all. All the family learnt to speak Javanese to converse with our servants, who did not speak either Dutch or Bahasa Melayu.

My Father

My father was definitely the greatest influence on my life. From my earliest days I can remember him as a good, good friend. He played with us, combed my hair, and gave me medicine when I was sick.

My father seemed more sophisticated, more cultured and more educated than any other adult family member (including my mother) and I can remember he had a presence about him that I would call charismatic. Notwithstanding his busy life involving commercial and social matters, my father always found time to be with us children.

He passed on to us many of his thoughts and beliefs in the form of sayings which I carry as part of my belief system to this very day. For example, my father had a passionate dislike of wasting food. This may have come from his own experiences for it was not unusual for Indonesians at the time to undergo periods of malnutrition and even starvation. He would often remind us that, "food is a gift of the gods and should never be wasted as it would anger them". These sentiments I repeated to my own children years later.

He would sit with us and sometimes read us stories and ask us about our day, but most importantly he would look after us when we were sick. We children did not know it at the time but our mother was not well. She had a weak heart plus diabetes and her condition was further complicated by her perpetual state of pregnancy between 1906 and 1922. Dad decided to lighten mother's work load as much as possible and this included personally nursing us back to health when we were seriously ill.

With so many children and so many already dying of disease in their infancy, my father must have nursed us back to health many times, but the two occasions I can specifically remember are in about 1916, when I was just four and stricken with malaria, and again in 1918 when my older brother Swan Bing, then aged 12, almost died from typhoid fever. Of course our mother would have been quarantined against the risk of infection while pregnant, but what I remember is father taking time off from work to give us so much individual attention. Because of this all four children felt a very special and close bond with father.

He rented a house for us to stay in Kediri and put my maternal Grandmother Njoo in it so that she could look after us while we attended primary school. The house, which was large enough to accommodate a growing number of children and servants, was located opposite the old Tan family home and store on Jalan Alun-Alun. Oma Njoo operated her own business selling ice, syrup, and salted eggs. All the children went to live with Oma Njoo when they, in turn, came of school age.

From my earliest recollections I can remember that my father looked after my paternal Grandfather and supplied him with all the necessities as well as many of the luxuries needed for a comfortable life. He relocated Opa Tan and his second wife to Ngronggot when he could afford to do so in order to look after him in his latter years. He provided him with a house and servants, plus monthly living expenses, care and subsequently paid for his funeral.

My father eventually built or bought six houses in the vicinity of where my grandfather lived in Ngronggot so that he could live off the rental income. When I was about twelve I can remember going around collecting the rent from the tenants while I was on holidays. I can remember that my Grandfather was, in his earlier years before I was born, described as a Groothandelaar, a wholesaler of products and in this case specifically kerosene, but I saw no evidence that he was *groot* (great) in any way. To me, he was really just a modest shopkeeper selling small amounts of kerosene to the natives.

School Days in Kediri

At the age of five I had fully recovered from malaria and it was time for me to go to school. I was thus sent to live with my Oma in Kediri. At the time, there were no schools suitable for us in Ngronggot.[8] I sometimes had to journey home by train and disembark at the nearest station at Papar. From there, I travelled by ferry over the Brantas river, then by dokar past rice fields to Ngronggot about four kilometres away. Most of my early schooling years were spent with Oma Njoo, in Kediri.[9]

One of my discoveries at Kediri was how modern this large town felt compared to our rural kampung. Even though I was only five at the time, I can still recall being amazed by such civil improvements as flush toilets, tram cars, and electrical street lighting. We even had electricity at Oma Njoo's home in Kediri, while it was never available in Ngronggot during the time we lived there. During my first days in the house I remember playing with the switches repeatedly in total amazement at being able to illuminate a room so easily.

As my parents had already taught me the basics of reading, writing and arithmetic at home, I was sent to a higher class in the Primary School after only half a year in kindergarten. The kindergarten was run privately, by parents of the children I think, and was co-located in the same building as the Primary School, which was a Government-run HCS.

Oma Njoo was very strict. She checked all my homework before I went to bed and, if she thought I had not completed it, she threatened to make me stay up until it was. But my Oma could not read Dutch and therefore did not know whether I was studying or reading novels instead.

---

[8] An believes her father, along with many other influential Chinese businessmen in the Kediri region, were instrumental in successfully lobbying the Colonial Government to establish a new HCS in Kediri in the late 1910s. Up to then the nearest HCS was over 100 kilometres away in Surabaya.

[9] When An went to school in Kediri her parents sent a *genduk* (child maid) to accompany her. Her name was Saartje and she was only 5–8 years older than An. Saar stayed in the family's employment for the next thirty years.

All she saw was that I had a book in my hands and that seemed to satisfy her. I read books about children in Europe, mainly Holland. Often I hid from her to avoid doing chores around the house by climbing onto the roof with my latest book.

The books I read when I was young were all in the Dutch language and I could not get enough of them. I read girls and boys books without hesitation and would read from morning to night if I could get away with it. Some of the books I enjoyed so much that I can still remember their titles eighty years later were *Dik Trom, Lies en Hock, 1001 Nachten, Hans & Grietje,* the Dutch versions of Huckleberry Finn, Mark Twain, The Last of the Mohicans, and Tom Sawyer.

Serialized comic books had just become available and I remember reading the instalments of *Kuifje en Kapitein Haddock* (the famous Belgium animated character Tin Tin), but I especially liked the science-fiction novels of the Frenchman Jules Verne (translated into Dutch of course) such as *Around the World in 80 Days*, *20,000 Leagues under the Sea* and *Journey to the Centre of the Earth.* The books I loved most involved adventure and science fiction, although I did read a few romantic novels as well.

A Hollandsche-Chineesche School (HCS) in Java in the early 1920s very similar to the school in Kediri most of the Tan children attended and where An later taught in Jember and Salatiga. (KITLV # 34587)

When we had holidays that were longer than a week, Oma would close the house in Kediri and all the children would return home. In Ngronggot I was allowed to run and jump and play and back at home with my parents I was very happy. It was intended that all my brothers and sisters, who stayed with Oma, would go on to High School.

There was a Chinese-language school in Kediri called *Tionghoa Hwee Kwan* that I could have attended, but instead my parents chose the Government School because they wanted me to speak Dutch. The Chinese School mainly taught craft subjects such as sewing, embroidery and lace-making, plus Chinese languages and history. It did not teach mathematics, languages, geography or history. My parents were determined that all their children would grow up with the best prospects for advancement as possible, which meant a Dutch-speaking education at a Dutch-run school.

The HCS started at 7:30 am and finished at 1:00 pm, six days a week. After lunch and a rest, most students went on to pursue other activities in the afternoon from 4:00 to 6:00 pm at the previously mentioned private Chinese School (Tionghoa Hwee Kwan). There the girls learned skills like sewing — I can remember making a handkerchief — and the boys learned manual skills such as woodworking. After 6:00 pm everybody went home, had dinner and then we completed our homework. I was a bright student and usually finished my homework in less than an hour, whereas my siblings often took two hours or more to finish theirs. As I loved reading, and still do, I would read novels after finishing my homework to fill in the time.

Secondary School

At the time there was a choice of two types of high school in Indonesia. The elite Public High Schools (Hogereburgerschool, or HBS), of which there were less than a dozen for the whole of Indonesia and therefore extremely difficult to enter, and the recently introduced Junior High Schools (Meer Uitgebreid Lager Onderwijs, or MULO). There were possibly twice as many MULO schools across Indonesia, but they only offered four years of secondary education, which was equivalent to only three out of the five years at HBS. Children had to attend the HBS if their parents wanted them to receive a university education in Holland.

These high schools were not organized along strictly racial lines. Being the top level of secondary education in Indonesia, the Chinese, Dutch and Indonesians alike could go there, but only if they could afford it and had

32

met the necessary tough qualification standards. In the 1930s school fees were beyond the reach of all but the wealthiest. For indigenous Indonesians, this meant that only the children of sultans, regents, and high-ranking government officials went to the HBS. As proportionately more Chinese and Dutch were wealthier than indigenous Indonesians, there were more Dutch and Chinese present at these schools.

When my older brother graduated from Primary School in Kediri, he went to the oldest and most prestigious HBS in Indonesia at Bandung. This was a great achievement for him and the family but it did put the family under considerable financial pressure. By the time I had graduated from the same primary school in mid-1924 and was ready to follow him to the same HBS in Bandung, my family's financial situation had radically changed.

The Sugar Industry

About 1918, when I was at Kediri in Primary School, my father entered the sugar industry as a supplier of raw cane to recently constructed sugar mills in the Kediri district. Anyone could grow sugar cane, but all *suikerfabrieken* (sugar mills) were licensed by the Dutch. For many years the Dutch had encouraged the building of private sugar mills across East Java and from the early 1900s some wealthy relatives of ours — the Lie family — progressively obtained licences and built a total of six modern rice mills in the district at Baron, Djuwono, Kudjon Manis, Papar, Poerwoasri and Waroedjeng. In the vicinity were also two large Dutch-owned mills at Minggiran and Mritjan, making sugar the most important crop in the district.[10]

Because my father had close relations with the Lie family, they asked him to become a supplier of raw cane to the mills. This meant that he had to organize and pay for the planting, tending and harvesting of large tracts of cane with the indigenous landowners in the district. Basically, he acted as a middleman between the mill owners and the landowners.

The financial rewards seemed considerable, but so also were the risks. This undertaking required all of my father's own money, plus a

---

[10] Refer to maps at Appendix B in which the modern spelling is used — Baron (same), Juwono (for Djuwono), Kujon Manis (for Kudjon Manis), Papar (same), Purwodadi (for Poewoasri) and Warujayeng (for Waroedjeng). The two Government-operated mills are at Minggiran (same) and Mrican (for Mritjan).

Aerial view of the sugar mill at Mritjan near Kediri in 1925.
(KITLV # 18226)

Administrative office of Mritjan sugar mill near Kediri. An's father would
have stood in these rooms conducting business. (KITLV # 30694)

substantial loan from his Uncle Tjioe in Kediri again. Dad spent some time in Kediri learning all about this new crop before he entered the industry and came back determined to make a new fortune. Having paid a lot of money to lease land from the local villagers, he then supplied them with young cane cuttings and taught them how to plant, raise and harvest the sugarcane. The mills agreed in advance to pay my father a set price per tonne. If he could cut, collect, and transport the sugarcane to the closest mills for less than what the millers paid him, he would make a handsome profit.

In those days, sugar growing in the Kediri district of East Java was not like you see in a modern developed western country today, such as in Australia. There were no large plantations consisting of hundreds of hectares spread out in the countryside far removed from local townships. Instead there were many small fields, such as family plots of 0.5–10 hectares each, scattered in and around the local villages.

The workers were always close enough to a village to buy their lunches (*makan siang*) if they wished from a nearby roadside stall (*warung*). At harvest time, his ten or so employees (all Chinese) would supervise about a hundred locals, broken up into work gangs of equal size to move from plot to plot, cutting down the ripened cane. The cane was then transported on cikar — large flat wagons pulled by oxen — to the nearby mill where Dad had contracts to supply agreed quantities of raw sugarcane at a previously negotiated price.

The sugar mills were built close to villages and railway lines but not close to each other. It would have taken a week or so to walk around all eight sugar mills in the Kediri district. The mills themselves were large factories, each employing a hundred or more locals crushing the raw cane in huge steam-driven machines and then refining the juice through stages of heat evaporation into white sugar.

When I was on holidays I would visit some of these mills, but I was only allowed on the premises before work commenced in the morning. The smells and tastes were pleasant and sweet. As a treat, I was often given a stick or two of unprocessed sugarcane to eat.

Apart from the government-owned railway (*Staatsspoorwegen*) there were no narrow-gauge railways or motorized transport in our district at the time. Ox-carts were used to transport the raw sugar cane from the fields to the mills and, in the case of the suikerfabrieken at Waroedjeng, Baron and Djuwono, the refined sugar from these mills to the railhead at Kertosono. Only later, when I was about 10 years old, did I see

Machinery inside Minggiran sugar mill in 1920. (KITLV # 7785)

motorized transport carrying refined sugar to Kertosono. Even then, my father and other suppliers still used ox-carts to convey the raw sugarcane to the mills to begin the process of refining. A cikar can carry up to two tonnes of produce or material but it travels slowly due to the lumbering pace of the oxen.

The Djuwono mill was very important because it had a large warehouse and was located closest to the rail junction at Kertosono on the main rail line that ran between Surabaya and the capital of Jakarta. The mills at Baron and Waroedjeng were not located on a railway line and sent their sugar to Djuwono, where it was stored before transport by rail to the coastal port of Surabaya for export.

All the other mills, including the Dutch-owned mills, were located at towns or sidings along railway lines or main roads and could ship their sugar directly to the ports for export.

Although my father started off in a relatively small way, he grew to become one of the main suppliers to the local mills in just a few short years. He was involved in the scientific development of new sugar cane crops and trialled a new variety — I believe was known as *EK-111* — that

Transport of sugar cane by *cikar* to *suikerfabrieken* in the Kediri district in 1926. (KITLV # 7743)

Photo showing *cikars* laden with sugar cane assembled outside a *suikerfabrieken* in East Java, similar to how Tan Ting Bie's cikars would have been around the mills in the Kediri district in the 1920s. (KITLV # 2708)

was successful in giving a higher yield of sugar.[11] This new strain of sugar cane was developed at a recently-built government-run *proefstation* (research station) in nearby Kudjon Manis run by a Dutch scientist named van der Veen. I was told that after *EK-111* was successfully trialled, it was exported to Cuba, enabling that country to rapidly become a major competitor in the international sugar market.[12] There were a number of new varieties planted by growers across Java at the time, including the very successful variety known as *POJ-2878*, but it was not one of the new strains my father planted.

The Lie brothers who owned the sugar mills were even richer than Tjioe Djie Kwie, the uncle who had originally helped my father get established in Ngronggot. As with most Chinese businessmen in the area, they helped each other out by lending money and making investments in each other's enterprises. My father supplied raw sugar cane to as many of the eight mills as he could and the brothers sold refined sugar to overseas markets.

That was, and still is, the way with the Chinese. Related families pooled their capital and labour so that all would prosper. It was safer to trust family members than the authorities or banks.

All these uncles and cousins lived in the Kediri area, sending their children to the local ELS. When I was young and of the same age as their children, our family had a close relationship with these relatives on Oma Njoo's side. At Chinese New Year we had to visit the oldest relative, who lived in a huge house in Kudjon Manis (near the above-mentioned research station and sugar mill) to pay our respects. However, most of the Lie family relocated to Surabaya when their children started attending secondary school at the expensive Dutch-language HBS there. I believe this was in the early 1920s. The Lie family felt that their children would benefit by mixing more with Dutch-speaking pupils, including the sons and daughters of the colony's Dutch masters. Only during sugar harvesting time did Lie Djing Han and Lie Djing Tjay return to the district, staying in residences attached to their mills.

---

[11] There may be number missing from this code. Experimental strains of sugar cane were usually denoted by an alpha-numeric system containing letters followed by four numbers.

[12] Sugar variety *EK-111* may well have been exported to Cuba, but Cuba was already a major global supplier of sugar by the first decade of the twentieth century.

After Oma Njoo died in the mid-1920s, we did not see them as much as we had previously and our two families lost touch.[13] They never returned to Kediri and I suspect that many members of their family went to Holland to live. However, I was informed much later that some members of the Lie family remained in Surabaya for decades and invested heavily in tobacco in East Java.

My Father's Concubine

Kasminah was my father's "second wife". It was the custom at the time for wealthy Chinese to take a second or even a third wife. This was a sign of their status and virility.

Though these relationships were not officially recognized under Dutch law, many Chinese, Indonesian and even Dutch men had long-term relationships with women whom we would now call mistresses or concubines.

Kasminah was a local asli Indonesian girl who had started working as a cook's assistant to my Oma Njoo in Kediri as a 14-year-old in 1921. She was young, attractive and healthy, while my mother was approaching forty with a worsening heart condition. My mother's last childbirth had produced a stillborn baby and almost killed her and the pregnancy before that had ended in a miscarriage. It had been five years since the last child born had lived past infancy, but despite the risk to her health my father wanted to continue an intimate relationship.[14]

In 1922, my mother arranged to "give" Kasminah, then aged 15, to my father to gratify his sexual needs. He was 42.[15] She was elevated from a lowly servant girl to the more privileged position of mistress and now had servants herself.

After Oma's death, my father allowed Kasminah to operate Oma Njoo's business, thereby giving her an independent source of income. My father also provided her with some money, clothing, and jewellery,

---

[13] It would appear that Oma Njoo may have been the lynchpin to inter-family relationships between the Njoo, Djie, and Lie families because after her death the three families drifted apart.

[14] At the time there were no effective birth-control methods commonly available. For An's mother, more sex meant more children and therefore the distinct possibility of death.

[15] According to Kasminah's daughter, Tan Liem Nio, Tan Ting Bie had already slept with other young girls from the town.

which reinforced her status and she was envied by many other indigenous people. Nevertheless, my mother would not allow her to live under the same roof as herself. Kasminah continued to live at my Oma's house in Kediri, but now she had her own bedroom. When my father visited Kediri on business — which was as often as two or three times a week — he would sometimes sleep overnight with Kasminah. She also looked after my youngest brother during his schooling in Kediri and stayed in this house in Kediri until her death in 1971.

The relationship produced three children, of whom all were adopted by my parents as full members of the Tan family.[16] About 1939, when Tjien (whom everyone called by her Dutch name, Erna) was ill with typhus, her younger sister Kien was sent to live with me in Jember. She was about eight at the time and enjoyed herself so much that she begged to stay permanently with me, even after Erna's health improved. Everybody consented and Kien continued to live with me until her untimely death from influenza at the age of nearly eleven in 1942. Kien was a gorgeous child with a lovely disposition and her death saddened me greatly. It was said that Kien was the reincarnation of Oma Njoo and that is why everyone in the family got on so well with her. The one thing my mother insisted on was that all three children call herself "mother" — the children were only allowed to refer to Kasminah by her first name. As they grew older, each child eventually knew who their real mother was, but while my mother was still alive no child was ever allowed publicly to acknowledge Kasminah as their mother.

My relationship with Kasminah was not a good one either. I could not get along with her. For a start she was only about five years older than me, which forced me to the uncomfortable realization that my father was sleeping with an adolescent girl who was similar in age to his daughter. Secondly, I had this belief at the time that she was greedy. I thought that Kasminah demanded every piece of my mother's jewellery from my father and that he complied. It upset me to think that Kasminah could have appropriated my mother's entire jewellery collection and left my mother with nothing.[17]

---

[16] Tjien (b. 1923), Kien (b. circa 1931) and Liem (b. circa 1943).

[17] According to An's brother, Tan Swan Bing, personal possessions including family jewellery were sold to pay off debts caused by the failure of Tan Ting Bie's sugar interests. Further, Tan Liem Nio states that Kasminah independently accumulated her own collection of jewellery, which was handed to Tan Liem Nio after Kasminah's death.

Deep down, however, I was offended how this practice made females less equal to males. Men could have more than one wife, but women were forbidden to have more than one husband.

This custom made me feel insecure and for years I avoided marriage because I was afraid any future husband of mine would do the same as my father and get himself a second wife, even if I objected. Logically, I should have blamed my father for this practice, or perhaps my mother for allowing it, but instead I focused my resentment on Kasminah because in my mind she was the person at fault.

4

A Local Sugar Crisis and
Its Aftermath
(1924–30)

The Lie family's financial arrangements were messy. One brother held the all-important mill licences in his name while the other owned the buildings and their contents. The running of the mills was left to one of the brother's two sons, Lie Djing Han and Lie Djing Tjay. However, when their father and uncle both died in the early 1920s, the uncle's family fought over the estate and disputed the inheritance, claiming that they were the rightful owners of the mills. As lack of documentation could not determine which brother had obtained the valuable licences and which brother had provided the finance to build and equip the mills, expensive legal challenges were mounted by both families.

The dispute within the Lie family coincided with a drop in the world sugar market. The boom which followed upon World War I came to a sudden end during 1920. By the early 1920s there was global overproduction of sugar, resulting in a drastic fall in prices.

The first I heard about these big events was in mid-1924 when I was not able to start my secondary school education at the expensive Dutch-speaking HBS School in Bandung. My father told me that he could not get rid of his sugar cane and our family was ruined. It cost Dad 1 guilder and 20 cents per tonne to plant, grow and harvest the season's sugarcane of 1924, but he received only 30 cents per tonne when he came to sell it.

Being only twelve at the time, I did not fully understand the situation.[1] All I knew was that my father was wiped out financially. He said he was *afgelopen* (finished). We still employed a number of house servants, including Saar (who by now we called by the endearing diminutive term of Saartje), but all the cane workers and Chinese supervisors were dismissed. I remember this time with much sadness.

My father's loss became very personal when, instead of following my older brother to the Hogereburgerschool in Bandung, I was sent to a much cheaper school in Jakarta. Up to that point I had believed that I was destined to go to the HBS, graduate and depart for Holland, where I could study to become a doctor of medicine. This was a dream so bold and so outrageous that I had not shared it with anyone. But before I could start the journey, the dream was taken away. I was crushed and to this day I regret the missed opportunity.

The bankruptcy was perhaps the single most important event in my life. It totally changed my life's direction and affected everything that has happened to me since. Even though I had gained the second highest mark out of all the candidates across Indonesia, the HBS board and tuition fees at a minimum of *f*20 per month were now beyond the reach of my parents. So instead of going to the HBS in Bandung, it was arranged that I attend a new Teachers' College in Jakarta, where my tuition and boarding fees were heavily subsidized by the colonial government. My father had to pay only *f*5 a month for tuition and boarding combined.

I arrived there in the second half of 1924. It was a five-year course and I graduated in June 1929 with a diploma which allowed me to teach in both the Chinese and Dutch primary schools.

---

[1] An's youthful recollections about the sugar crisis are rather confused and have required some heavy editing. She claims that the Lie family mills closed down as a result of the legal dispute between family members, but this is contradicted by figures from the annual *Koloniale Verslag* (Colonial Report) which shows that mill production remained at much the same levels throughout the mid-1920s. It would seem that she has conflated her father's ruin in 1924 with the later Java-wide collapse of the sugar industry that occurred in the Great Depression of the 1930s. It was in this later period that the Lie family mills did indeed go out of production and in most cases never reopened. Allowing that cane contracts would be signed about two years before a harvest, the most likely explanation of An's father's financial crisis is either that he signed fixed-price contracts in the early 1920s which, in a falling market, the mills did not honour, or that he had speculated on a market recovery which did not eventuate in time. By 1925 the market was indeed recovering but by then it was too late. The exact period of the Lie family's internecine legal dispute is also not verified.

Because it was a two-day train journey back to Kediri with an overnight stay in Yogyakarta, I returned home only during the long school vacations. Sometimes I stayed weekends with relatives in Jakarta, but that was not often.

My siblings were also affected. My older brother by six years, Tan Swan Bing, had completed three out of his five years of education at the HBS in Bandung as a boarder with relatives when the local sugar crisis struck down the family's finances in 1924. He did not return for the start of his fourth year, instead attending the next two years at a much cheaper HBS in Surabaya, where he stayed with relatives to avoid the extra cost of boarding fees as well.

My older sister (Roostien), who had been attending this same HBS in Surabaya, was relocated to the MULO in Kediri, which did not offer the same educational opportunities, though that did not bother Roostien who, at the age of 14, was already more interested in marriage than in pursuing a professional career like me. Roostien did not like education and soon she dropped out of school altogether to prepare herself for marriage. In 1927 at the age of 17, Roostien was finally married by arrangement to Liem Sing Giap, who was about ten years older and a senior bureaucrat with *PTT* (*Post, Telegraaf & Telefoon*, the Dutch Post and Telegraph service).

The Secondary School I went to was the Hollandsche-Chineesche Kweekschool (Dutch-Chinese Teachers' College) that produced teachers for the HCS primary school system. I graduated as a primary school teacher at the age of 17 years. If teachers graduated with sufficiently high marks they could study a further three years in a specialized area, such as Mathematics, Physics, Geography or a Language, and gain a higher diploma so that they could teach in high school.

My Oma Njoo died in 1925 within a year of my father's failed venture into the sugar industry. Even though she was in her early sixties, the family attributed her death to the stress and heartbreak associated with the bankruptcy of her son-in-law (my father). I overheard adult relatives whispering among themselves that, "It's bad Karma, you know! As a young girl, she witnessed her mother suffer from poor financial decisions. Then she had to watch the same thing happen to her own daughter. She just could not take it, you know."

Life in Teachers' College

The Teachers' College in Jakarta was located on *Leonielaan* (Leonie Lane), which ran off the main road to Bogor near the turnoff to Bekasi in the suburb of Meester Cornelis (now Jatinegara) and it was laid out as below.

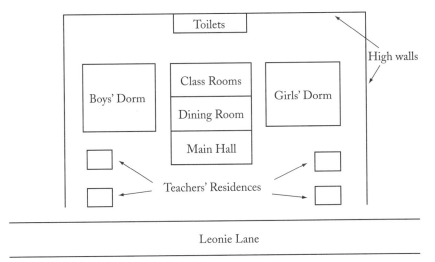

Teachers' College, Meester Cornelis, Batavia (Jatinegara), Jakarta (circa 1925–30).

The Teachers' College in Jakarta was a boarding school designed for about 150 students but it opened with only half that number.[2] By the time I arrived in the mid-1920s, the number of students had climbed to about 120 with equal proportion of males and females. While students were segregated into male and female boarding houses, every other activity by the school was combined, including teaching, eating and assemblies.

The purpose-built college was part of one of the last great legacies of the colonial government, whereby during the 1920s and 1930s they attempted rapidly to expand education across Indonesia and needed more teachers (and hence more teachers' colleges) to achieve this. I think there were then only five teachers' colleges across the whole country. Two were in Jakarta (one for the Dutch and the one I attended, for the Chinese); a third and fourth in Central Java, one for indigenous Indonesians and

---

[2] According to Ming Govaars, *Dutch Colonial Education: The Chinese Experience in Indonesia, 1900–1942* (p. 128), the school was opened in 1918.

Front of Teachers College from Leonie Lane (early 1920s).

another run by the Protestant Christian Church; and a fifth in Semarang operated by the Catholic Church and open to members of any ethnic group if they could afford it.

The Teachers' College which I attended was under the headmastership of *Meneer* (Mister) Doornik, who was from Holland, as were four of the other five teachers on staff. In years one to three, I was in the class of Mr Streuding who would take us for general instruction together with basic English, Dutch and Malay languages. Mr Doornik, as well as being the Director of the college, taught us physics and mathematics. Mr Hoekendijk conducted classes in general teaching methodology (pedagogy) while in later years Mr Nijhof took us for higher English and special teaching classes. Finally, Mr van Dinter, who was of mixed Indonesian and Dutch parentage, taught us music and singing.

We arose each weekday at 6:00 am, performed our morning ablutions and by 7:00 am were dressed for breakfast, which was held in the common dining room for all students. All students and teachers wore a white uniform, which was standard for public servants in the Dutch colonial administration. The girls and boys ate a separate tables with some of the teachers seated at their own table in the middle of the dinning room, so dividing the boys from the girls. At 7:45 am school started and we continued classes with a mid-morning break through to 1:00 pm, when we all had lunch in the dining room again until 2:00 pm.

A senior class of students being taught physics at the college (early 1920s).

In the afternoon, students were allowed to pursue their own activities such as sport, craft, or study, or even organized activities outside the college. After 5:00 pm, we all had "free time" until dinner. Some students occasionally went on leave to the city to buy items they needed but the majority stayed in the college reading, studying or socializing on the wide verandas that enclosed the boarding houses. I spent my time mainly reading and, in my later years at college, studying for the extra diploma that I wanted to pass. At 7:00 pm we had dinner in the main dining hall and after 8:00 pm went back to our own rooms to study, this being conducted under the supervision of a different teacher rostered on each night. At 9:30 pm we prepared ourselves for sleep by having "quiet time" and then at 10:00 pm the lights were extinguished.

Our dormitories consisted of rooms facing out onto a veranda that went around the building. Each room had four beds where we slept and stored our belongings, but we actually studied on the veranda because it was less stuffy and slightly cooler than inside.

The supervising teacher would walk around the outside of the building to see that we were all studying and help us with any questions. There were also one or two teachers on duty in the dining hall every time we ate. During the school year the routine repeated itself every day of the week. On the weekends, however, we were free to pursue

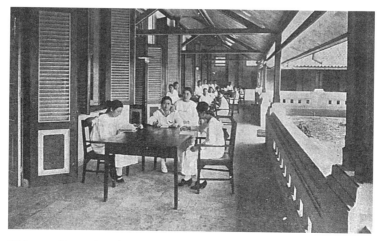

Girls casually passing the time on the veranda outside their bedrooms (early 1920s).

whatever we liked as there were no organized activities such as study or sport.

Every year about two dozen students graduated as teachers from our school in Jakarta which, when added to all the other students graduating from the other teachers' colleges, came to less than a hundred across Indonesia. With half that number of teachers leaving the profession annually through the normal attrition of resignations and retirements, there were still insufficient number of teachers to fill the new classrooms and schools being built under the colonial government's expansion program. In fact, under-investment in the supply of new teachers — only one new teachers' college had been built in Indonesia during the previous twenty years — meant that the government's stated aim of educating the people was highly unrealistic. For all the government's rhetoric on education, the results were dismal. The simple devastating truth is that by the high point in colonial rule in 1930, 80 per cent of all children were *not* being educated and a similar proportion of adults were illiterate.

The chronic shortage of educators meant that classroom sizes increased to levels that would be unacceptable by the teaching standards of today. For example, the first class I taught had forty-eight pupils and throughout my public teaching career never dropped below forty. This perennial shortage of teachers is why the government opened the one new teachers' college I attended and offered scholarships to all qualified trainee teachers.

Nevertheless, to be eligible, I and every other trainee teacher had to obtain an average grade of 75 per cent or higher from our respective primary schools.

During my five years at Teachers' College (June 1924–June 1929) I was a diligent student. I never got into trouble and did not even take unauthorized leave. I knew that I had to work hard because my parents were financially suffering. I was a member of a student's youth organization called the *Chung Shiok* that students in the Dutch Chinese Teachers' Colleges across Indonesia joined. It was purely voluntary and I enrolled because it seemed that everyone else had already done so and I did not want to feel left out. I think it was more like a social club and certainly not a political organization. Apart from attending parties and trips arranged by the organization, I do not think I gained any other benefits out of being a member. There was another organization at the time called the *Chung Hwa Hui*. This was a progress organization formed to promote the activities of all the ethnic Chinese in Indonesia. I think it might have been pro-Dutch and conservative, but I do not know much about this organization as I was never a member.

Whilst at college, I was obliged to learn a musical instrument. I chose the violin, which I played in the school orchestra and sang in the school choir, but I knew I did not have enough musical talent to pursue it as a career. When I started teaching I did not continue these musical pursuits.

During my final year, I also sat for an extension to my diploma, one that allowed me to teach in the primary schools for the Europeans (ELS) who were mainly Dutch. Studying for the more onerous ELS teaching certificate as well as the normal HCS teaching diploma certainly did not leave me much time for extra-curricular activities during my last few years at college. The reason I sat for the extra certificate was purely financial. The Diploma for the HCS schools was worth a wage of *f*110 a month, but the ELS Certificate entitled me to *f*180 per month. This further qualification was more difficult to obtain. Out of the dozen or so final year students at our college in Jakarta, only two of us had sufficient grade to warrant being allowed to sit for this extra exam that my classmate (Jo) and I both passed with flying colours.

Towards the end of my time at the college Meneer Doornik, the Director, decided that the bare school grounds could do with some beautification and organized a tree-planting program. On the day of the ceremony I was selected to dig several holes together with other senior

49

boys and girls. With great fanfare the Director and other staff planted many small trees which everyone hoped would provide much needed shade in years to come.

When I graduated from Teachers' College at the age of 17, there was such a severe shortage of teachers in Indonesia that many graduates were successful in obtaining teaching positions in locations of their choice. Otherwise, the usual rules applied and they were sent where the government needed them. I was fortunate to be posted to Jember, which was the location I had requested, being the closest school to my family's new home in Tanggul.[3] During my years at Teachers' College my family had moved from Ngronggot to Tanggul (a distance of about 300 kilometres further east in Java and about 30 kilometres away from the regional centre of Jember).

Earliest photo of An (right) (circa 1928) when she was about 16 years old with sister Roostien (far left), Roostien's son Adolf (2nd from left) and the mother of the two girls (Njoo Hing Tjie).

---

[3] According to other family members, as soon as An was settled into Jember her parents sent Saartje to become An's main servant. From this point on Saartje was employed by An, not her parents. While An was at Teachers' College, Saartje had married and was now a young mother herself.

My first teaching position in July 1929 at Jember was a HCS primary school comprising seven other teachers (5 for primary and 2 for infants). Because no other teacher at Jember had obtained an ELS Teaching Certificate, I started with the highest teaching qualifications, even though I was the newest and youngest teacher. Thus, I automatically became the primary school teacher to the 6th Class in the morning and the 7th Class (the highest) in the afternoon.

While teaching primary school at Jember, I decided to improve myself further. I wanted to elevate myself from a primary school teacher to a secondary school teacher. But first I needed to upgrade my qualifications. Therefore, I enrolled in the only transition course possible at the time, a correspondence degree from the Dutch Government in Holland. For the next three years I endured the hardship of no tutors, no help and protracted delays in correspondence to complete the course. As the course was administered directly from Holland and based exclusively on the Dutch educational model, the final exam was conducted at the Dutch Education Offices in Jakarta.

Towards the end of my third year of teaching at Jember, I obtained leave to journey to Jakarta and sit for these exams. I was very nervous. I simply did not know whether my efforts — completed without any help over the preceding three years in a rural backwater — would be sufficient to gain me a pass. I arrived at Jakarta by train on the appointed day and made my way anxiously to the Head Office building of the Department of Education. There were several dozen other candidates assembled, some of whom spoke Dutch so fluently that I felt sure they would pass the exam more easily than me. Nevertheless, I swore to myself that I would do my best.

Six months later in 1933, I received a letter from the Dutch Government in Holland informing me that I had passed the exams and been awarded a Degree (*Akte*) allowing me to teach Mathematics and Physics in High School. My wage rose again to *f*250 a month, an income that was considered very high for a woman during the Great Depression.

Older Brother Does Well

Tan Swan Bing finished his HBS in June 1926 when he was about nineteen and was very lucky indeed to receive a scholarship from the Dutch Government to continue his education at a university in Holland. At the time a degree from a Dutch university was considered superior to any academic qualifications obtained from Indonesian colleges. My brother and the whole family were overjoyed.

Tan Swan Bing left immediately to commence a 5-year degree course in Commerce at the *Handelshogeschool* (School of Commerce), now part of the Erasmus University of Rotterdam, where all his expenses, including an allowance for food and accommodation, were paid for by the scholarship on the expectation that he would work for the Dutch Colonial Government for a period of six years after he gained his degree. Because his academic performance was excellent, the Dutch Government kept renewing his annual scholarship each year.

However, in June 1929, my brother was hospitalized with a broken leg and hip from a serious traffic accident and it took him almost six months to recuperate, during which time he could not attend the university. Then the Great Depression of October 1929 struck — which the Dutch call *De Malaise* — and the Government withdrew all scholarships. Nevertheless, my brother decided to stay in Holland and to pay his own way through university. Coincidentally, he received some compensation money for the earlier motor vehicle accident, which, combined with some part time work at the university, enabled him to continue studying.

I also discretely sent him some money whenever I could and he managed to complete his studies without having to disclose to our parents just how tight finances were for him over the last year or so of his course. In the end, he graduated in June 1932 with a *doctorandus* degree in Commerce, entitling him to use the abbreviation of "Drs" in front of his name. My brother returned to Indonesia in early 1933.

My Relationship with My Younger Brother

My younger brother, Tan Siauw Djie, was four years younger than me. He was a sickly child suffering from Malaria Tropica as well as chronic asthma, which continued to afflict him the rest of his life. I never felt very close to Siauw Djie, unlike my loving relationships with Roostien and Swan Bing. Siauw Djie was very intelligent and gifted musically, playing the violin so well that he could have been a professional musician. He was educated at the Teachers' College in Muntilan, near Magelang in Central Java, run by the Catholic Church. Upon completion, he was posted to a Catholic high school in Semarang as a teacher of Mathematics.

5

Relocation and Early Career (1930–42)

Tanggul

After my father's bankruptcy in 1924, which resulted in many of my father's properties being sold off to pay creditors, the network of Chinese family connections built up and maintained by the women did not abandon him. After several years of extreme financial hardship, a cousin (Tjioe Sien An) came to my father's rescue and employed him as a Superintendent at three

Women planting rice in east Java. (KITLV # 17089)

of this cousin's six rice mills located almost 300 kilometres to the east of Ngronggot in the Tanggul area.

Tjioe Sien An's mother and my father's mother were sisters.[1] As the new Superintendent, my father initially controlled only the rice mills which were located within a short 5-kilometre radius of Tanggul. There were two rice mills near Tanggul itself: Tanggul Kulon (west) and Karanglo, about 2 kilometres east of Tanggul. There was a small rice mill further east in nearby Bangsalsari, but my father closed it because it was too small and too close to the Karanglo mill. The three other rice mills, also owned by Tjioe Sien An but located further away from Tanggul — Rambipuji (20 kilometres away), Balung, (30 kilometres), and Bondowoso (50 kilometres) — were still to be operated by either Tjioe Sien An or his sister. In other words, Tjioe Sien An gave my father a chance to prove himself, without jeopardizing his entire operations.

My father wrote regularly to inform me of what was happening and in early 1928, during my third year at college, he informed me the family had moved to Tanggul. The next time I had leave from college I went directly to the new house in Tanggul and never visited Ngronggot again. There was a gap of about three years between my father's bankruptcy in Kediri and the family's move to Tanggul.

In the interim, the family managed to live somewhat less comfortably (due to the enormous debt) from the other businesses (copra, property, and store) which had been established years earlier and had continued to be operated profitably by my mother. Thus we still managed to afford servants throughout this period, even though our involvement with sugar had sent my father bankrupt. Of course I was not in a position to help my parents financially while still at Teachers' College, but from the second half of 1929 when I graduated and started earning a wage, I sent my parents as much money as I could, perhaps as much as a third of my wage through an account I opened at the local Post Office.[2]

---

[1] An's grandmother was the eldest of three sisters, of whom Tjioe Sien An's mother was the youngest.

[2] According to Tan Swan Bing, the financial support of parents was the real cause of friction between he and An. For much of the late 1920s, Tan Swan Bing was not in a position to assist the parents because he was then a university student, newly married without permanent employment. According to Chinese tradition, the eldest son has an obligation to look after parents if he can. This issue re-surfaced in the 1950s and An was still accusing her brother in the 1980s of having shirked his duties over the previous fifty years. Tan Swan Bing's wife, Huguette, had finally had

Post, Telephone and Telegraph office in Tanggul in 1930.
(KITLV # 30367)

The area around Tanggul and Jember in the far eastern part of Java was renowned for the production of rice and sugar. Apart from the rice mills privately owned by my father's relative, the Dutch operated the biggest sugar mill in Indonesia at Jatiroto, about 15 kilometres from Tanggul. My father was given a substantial salary, furnished accommodation and a chauffeur-driven car. As soon as my father became settled, the rest of the family joined him in Tanggul. The Supervisor's position was a heaven-sent opportunity to rescue my father's self esteem and resuscitate the family's fortune and my father threw himself into the task with characteristic determination and aptitude. Within months he had mastered the complexity of managing a modern rice mill and was seeking out ways to expand sales and lower costs. Over the next decade he became so accomplished at his task that Tjioe Sien An eventually gave him responsibility for all six of his rice mills in the area.

My Oma Njoo in Kediri had died before the family moved to Tanggul, so the only close relative who did not relocate was my Opa Tan. He stayed behind in Ngronggot, as he was then in his late sixties and too old and frail to travel. My Opa continued to live in the small house on

---

enough and sent a nasty letter to An saying that she never wanted to see her or any member of her family again. After Huguette's death in 1995, brother and sister remained estranged until the two siblings reconciled during the writing of this book.

a large property that my father had purchased for him years previously, but he no longer enjoyed the rental income he had received earlier as my father had been forced to sell all the houses he owned in 1924 or 1925 to pay off his debts. However, the pasar, which was opposite my Opa's property, was too small for the traders to accommodate all their goods and vehicles (animal-drawn drays and carts) on market day. So once a week when the market was operating, traders rented space on my Opa's land to store their animals, vehicles and extra stock. This provided Opa with a steady income. The property also had enough fruit-bearing trees to provide seasonal fresh food.

Other relatives of ours living in Kediri came regularly to check on Opa. He died in early 1929, a year or so after my parents moved to Tanggul and while I was in my last year of Teachers' College in Jakarta. My recollection is that my father returned much of his remaining property to the village elders of Ngronggot. Our big house was turned into a school and after my Opa died his house was turned into a polyclinic (medical centre).[3]

The Great Depression

The Great Depression first affected me when my brother-in-law, Liem Sing Giap, lost his Government job with the Post and Telegraph service in the early 1930s. Shortly after, other friends and acquaintances lost their jobs too or suffered drastic cuts in salary. Even so, I was not asked to take a pay cut and throughout the Great Depression in Indonesia the rate of unemployment seemed no more than normal and beggars no more prevalent.

When I was posted to the HCS in Jember in 1929, Mrs Lange (the Principal's wife) was heavily involved in both the Girl Guides and Boy Scouts organizations and she encouraged me to join them too. Subsequently, I became a Leader. While I had not mastered swimming myself, I went on to teach and coach others to swim. Some of my protégés went on to win championships for their schools. During this time I had obtained my Dutch teaching degree and was promoted to the position of Deputy

---

[3] According to An, this was an act of philanthropy, yet because of his dire financial straits it seems more likely Tan Ting Bie had to sell them to repay his enormous debts. According to her older brother, Tan Swan Bing, the parents had up to twelve properties in Ngronggot and several more in Kediri. With the exception of Grandmother's home in Kediri and Grandfather's home in Ngronggot, he says they were all sold to pay off accumulated debt. Tan Swan Bing remembers that even the family gamelan orchestra and jewellery had to be sold to meet outstanding commitments.

Principal at Jember in about 1937. Of course, I received a substantial pay increase as well to about ƒ300 a month.

From when I first arrived in Jember I lived in a small house by myself with servants of course, including my head servant Saartje. However, after I had been there some years and obtained my Dutch teaching degree, I was approached by officials from the Chinese progress organization, Chung Hwa Hui. I think this was in 1935. They explained that there were many Chinese families in the region who wanted their children to attend my HCS in Jember, but there was not a suitable or affordable boarding house for the boys and girls to stay at. They offered to accommodate me in a larger home with more servants and give me a small stipend if I would supervise a house full of young boarders. I readily agreed. It would not only increase my wealth, but it would grow the pupil numbers at the HCS and perhaps even lead to an expansion of the school with an accompanying promotion for me.

In no time at all they had rented a large home with many rooms, appointed two assistant housekeepers to help me and filled it with about twenty boys and girls aged from 8 to 15. My headmaster, Meneer Lange, was very pleased indeed. In one move I had added an extra twenty students to the school population of about 250, causing him to request an extra teacher and a higher salary for himself. As his deputy principal, I also received a higher salary.

One of the unintended benefits of running this boarding house was that I would meet and later marry one of my boarders, Kang Hoo Bie or Eddie Sudibjo, but more on that later.

My Siblings

Meanwhile my brother, Swan Bing, continued his education in Holland and had risen to become the Chairman of the Chung Hwa Hui, the same Chinese society I became familiar with in Jember. In this instance Chung Hwa Hui represented all Chinese-Indonesian citizens studying in Holland.[4] In this capacity he invited Mr Tai, the Chinese Ambassador to

---

[4] During his time in Holland, Swan Bing often met another Indonesian, Mohammad Hatta who was studying in the same University in 1922 to 1932 and became a leader of indigenous Indonesians studying in Holland. Dr Hatta went on to become Indonesia's first Vice President under Sukarno.

Wedding of Huguette (bride) to Tan Swan Bing (obscured in background left of Huguette) in Holland in 1932

The Hague, to address the society. When the Ambassador arrived with his daughter, Huguette, Swan Bing immediately fell in love with this vivacious Chinese-French 18-year-old woman.[5] Swan Bing married Huguette and completed his Economics degree from the Handelshogeschool (School of Commerce) in Rotterdam in the same year (1932). He then returned to Indonesia with his new bride when he was about 26 and I was about 20 in early 1933.

Upon his return he worked as a correspondent for the leading Chinese-language newspaper, *Siang Po*, in Jakarta for about two years until he was recruited by the *Matahari* (Sun) newspaper in Semarang to be its economic editor. However, shortly after he had started work, the paper closed down due to the Great Depression. For the next year, with a wife and new family

---

[5] Huguette (Tai Ai Hoa) was born in Paris in 1914 to the former Chinese Ambassador to France and his French wife. At the end of his term as Ambassador (which may have been cut short by political turmoil in China during the 1920s), Huguette's father was allowed to stay in Europe and became a French citizen along with all the members of the family, including Huguette.

he struggled financially to make ends meet. I sent him money from Jember to support him while he got himself a new job.[6]

In 1936, he secured a modest position of bookkeeper at a large trading house based in Semarang, called, *Kian Gwan*[7] (meaning "source of prosperity for everyone"). Under the watchful eye of Oei Tjung Hauw, the son of the company's founder, my brother worked and lived in Semarang for several decades climbing the corporate ladder of Kian Gwan to eventually become *Algemeen Adviseur* (General Counsel) to the whole business. Oei Tjung Hauw sent him to Holland in 1958 along with the remaining Dutch citizens expelled from Indonesia to represent the interests of both the company and himself personally.[8] In 1969, at the age of 63, my brother finally retired. He remained in the Netherlands until his death in 2005.

My younger brother, Siauw Djie, lived with Swan Bing in the pavilion of his home in Semarang during his posting at the local High School. During his stay he was introduced to Khouw Mi Lien, the younger sister of Khouw Bian Tie who was a "bosom friend" of Swan Bing from their university days in Rotterdam.

Salatiga

In 1939, I was transferred from Jember to a similar-sized school at Salatiga, a hill town about 50 kilometres south of Semarang, Java as the Deputy Principal. Actually, I had requested the transfer to move away from my then boyfriend at the time, Oei Hok Tjwan. Mr Hoekendijk, the District Head for the Department of Education in East Java, was a good friend

---

[6] According to An, Huguette regarded this act of kindness as an "insult". Being French and the daughter of an ex-Ambassador, An says it was a great shock for Huguette to end up in a third-world country (Indonesia) without money and then have to rely on financial assistance from relatives. Over time, both Huguette and Tan Swan Bing distanced themselves from the Indonesian side of the family.

[7] Kian Gwan Trading Company was just one of several thriving businesses established by Semarang's most famous citizen, Oei Tiong Ham (1866–1924). At his death, his fortune was valued at a staggering ƒ200 million (over $2 billion in today's currency). His son, Oei Tjung Hauw continued the then unusual, but financially rewarding practice, of appointing highly-qualified outsiders to manage the company and this is how Tan Swan Bing came to secure a management position in the mid-1930s (<www.semarang.nl/mensen/OeiTiongHam>).

[8] Kian Gwan continued to flourish through the war and revolution but, anticipating the political and economic crisis of the 1950s, management systematically transferred almost all of its capital to overseas branches. What was left of the Indonesian office was finally nationalized in 1961 (reference above).

of mine who arranged the transfer after I had spoken to him. Salatiga is situated in the highlands of Java and enjoys a cooler climate.

Years earlier as a young girl, I had spent many enjoyable holidays at the family bungalow high up on the slopes of Gunung Wilis, but I only stayed for several weeks at a time. Now I was staying in Salatiga for as long as I wished. Further, the land around our holiday home on Guning Wilis was virgin rainforest, but in Salatiga it was cultivated and sustained crops suited to its elevated position, such as lychees, apples, peaches, pears, and other exotic stone fruit that I had not tasted before. I took my trusted servant, Saartje, with me to run the household in Salatiga.

I taught in the HCS in Salatiga in the mornings and then travelled by bus about an hour away to teach Mathematics at the HBS in Semarang in the afternoons. I was at Salatiga for only a few months when my Dutch headmaster, Mr Penn, was suddenly called away to serve in the Colonial Army. By this time (circa 1940), Holland had fallen to the Germans in World War II. Even though there was no threat to us from Germany, we became increasingly alarmed about the threat from its Axis ally in the Pacific, the Japanese.

While I was not involved directly in the Dutch military build-up, I still benefited from it. When my Dutch headmaster at Salatiga was called-up for military service, I was immediately promoted to the position of Acting Principal, which was soon after converted to the permanent position of Principal and paid the very considerable sum of ƒ350 a month. All before I was 30![9]

When I transferred to Salatiga I continued my involvement with Girl Guides and to a lesser extent Boy Scouts. After my Principal's call up into the Dutch Army Reserve, I found myself actually running these activities. A few times a year the ex-Principal's wife and I took up to a dozen young girls at a time a short distance away camping into the mountains beside nearby Danau (Lake) Rawapening.

Everyone had to collect firewood daily from the surrounding forest and learn the skill of lighting a fire using no more than three matches. Every day two girls were rostered to walk a short kilometre or two to the town of Banyubiru to obtain food and provisions. Some girls were from wealthy families and objected to this imposition. In their young minds, it was a

---

[9] An believes she was one of the youngest Principals in Indonesia. What made her achievement doubly satisfying was that she was a young single woman of Chinese descent.

task that should be performed by servants only and therefore "beneath them". But they quickly learnt that if no-one performed this duty, no-one ate and there is nothing like empty stomachs to bring haughty girls back to reality.

During school holidays, my nieces and nephews would often come and spend their time with me, firstly in Jember and then subsequently in Salatiga. One of my nephews, Liem Sian Hong (son of Roostien) chose to live with me in Salatiga while he was completing his final year at the HBS in Semarang, even though his uncle and my brother, Tan Swan Bing, actually lived in Semarang at the time and could have easily accommodated him.

In the 1930s I was leading a more Euro-centric or Dutch lifestyle, while other Chinese began proudly promoting their Chinese origins. There was a rising tide of Chinese patriotism in Indonesia that coincided with the ascendency of the Nationalist Government in China, but I kept myself clear of such matters and the potential of conflict with the Indonesian population.

Teachers' Union

There were three teachers' unions in the colony during the 1930s and depending on your qualifications (to teach in European, Chinese or Indonesian schools) it was compulsory for every teacher to join one of them. The teachers' association for European schools, Nederlands Indisch Onderwijzers Genootschap (NIOG – Netherlands Indies Teachers' Society), was the largest and most powerful with several thousand members, followed by the Chinese Teachers' Union (Chineezen Onderwijzers Bond) and, lastly, by the Indonesian Teachers' Union (Serikat Guru Indonesia) with perhaps no more than a few hundred members across Indonesia.

There was no financial remuneration in becoming a union official but there were many indirect benefits. First there was free accommodation at the union-owned and operated European Club in Jakarta, a four-star luxury hotel with silver service and servants galore. Then there were free air flights and transportation for delegates to travel to Jakarta to attend meetings and the annual conference. For a union representative outside Jakarta, these were significant advantages. Most importantly, being an official of the Teachers' Union carried with it a great deal of status and prestige. Union officials were regarded with admiration by fellow teachers, as equals by senior bureaucrats and as very important people by the general populace.

In the early 1930s, while in Jember, I decided to run as a candidate for the vacant position of District Delegate. To my surprise I was elected unopposed. Being young and single, I had plenty of time on my hands and I was drawn to the ranks of union officialdom by the lure of free accommodation and travel.

I kept the position of District Delegate for the rest of the time I was at Jember. When I transferred to Salatiga in 1939, the Union expanded my role to that of regional representative for all of Central Java. This included responsibility for all the European-qualified teachers from Semarang in the North to Yogyakarta in the south and from Solo in the East to Ceribon in the West, several hundred teachers in total. This was one of the prime positions in the Union (second only to that of the Regional Representative for West Java, which contained the capital, Jakarta) and propelled me rapidly onto the National Executive.

In 1940, the Union promoted me again by appointing me Secretary for the whole of NIOG. I would fly to Jakarta every month to attend National Executive meetings. However, a year later I declined the Union's offer to run for National President of NIOG because it would have meant transferring to Jakarta full time if I was successful. I had just been promoted to Principal of the school in Salatiga on a very high salary and this position came with a very comfortable home and servants. If I became National President I would have had to take a lower-paid job in Jakarta (only teachers with much longer seniority than I became Principals in the capital), as well as pay more for my own accommodation and servants in the city for these items were always more expensive in the capital.[10]

I have mentioned before that, ever since I was a young girl and saw my first car in Kediri, I have loved all forms of modern transportation. First it was the car, then travel by train when I journeyed back and forth to school in Jakarta, and finally in the 1930s it expanded to include air travel. Traditional methods of travel — such as walking or by horse — never thrilled me. Actually, it was my father who was the first to travel by plane to attend conferences and business talks when he was Supervisor

---

[10] In 1947, when An resumed teaching for the Dutch Colonial Government, she was so busy as a mother and teacher and re-establishing her family in new accommodation in Jakarta that she never thought about becoming a union official again, despite many requests to do so from her teaching colleagues.

at the rice mills in Tanggul in the early 1930s. Once, I saw him off at the aerodrome in nearby Jember and instantly fell in love with the whole romance and mystique of flying by air.

Air travel in Indonesia was still in its infancy, having been introduced to the archipelago in the late 1920s while a regular air link with Holland was only established in October 1931. Possibly no more than a few thousand people had travelled by air in Indonesia up to this date. In those days in Indonesia the aeroplanes were exclusively Dutch from the Fokker company and relatively small by today's standards, accommodating less than a dozen passengers. My father told me that the service on board was personal and of the highest class and I knew I wanted to enjoy this experience as soon as I could.

My wish came true when I became an official of the Teachers' Union and began travelling by air, first from Jember and then Salatiga, to the national capital of Jakarta. Of course all these trips were paid for by the Union. Before the Japanese invaded Indonesia I had already enjoyed more than ten plane journeys for the Union and one holiday trip on a plane that I paid for myself. It was a luxury that I could afford and it impressed everyone I told.

The Suitors

Many young men wanted to marry me during the 1930s. I was young, fairly attractive and had a well-paid job. I was a good prospect, but I refused most advances. However, I was romantically involved with three people.

The first person was Ong Hok Tie, who had graduated from the same Teachers' College in Jakarta one year ahead of me. He was posted to a school in Balikpapan, Kalimantan, but before he left he promised to save enough money over the next few years to marry me. When I graduated a year later with better qualifications, Ong Hok Tie started correspondence study to raise his qualifications also, but he found this task too difficult. We wrote to each other over the next several years and he came to Java twice to visit me. We were not formally engaged, so when a few years turned into many, I did not mind as I was still in no hurry to get married.

When my father commented on the lengthy courtship, I told him I was afraid that any future husband would take a second wife like he did. My father was not impressed by this criticism of him.

Eventually, the casual relationship with Ong Hok Tie stretched out to eleven years, mainly due to my unwillingness to marry. During this on-again, off-again relationship with Ong Hok Tie, I met and became attracted to a dentist in Jember called Oei Hok Tjwan, but I found out that Oei Hok Tjwan's mother disapproved of the relationship. I was out shopping for a dress one day in Jember and while I was trying on some outfits in the changing room I happened to overhear a conversation by two ladies that had entered the shop after me. I immediately recognized one of the voices as the mother of my boyfriend and heard her say that she was not impressed by me as a potential daughter-in-law. She said I was too ambitious and went on to say that I would be too competitive and too independent. She concluded that what she really wanted for her son was a wife who would have her son's best interests at heart, devote herself to promoting her son's future and stay quietly at home producing babies.

I realized then that being a professional woman would always create conflict between us and that because his mother was so dominant her opinions would strongly influence her son. As much as I liked Oei Hok Tjwan and was growing in love with him, I knew our relationship had no future if it involved this woman as my mother-in-law. In my opinion, it was better to quietly move away and let separation end the relationship rather than contemplate a life of domestic servitude. Hence, I requested a transfer to a school in another district and was successful in moving to Salatiga.

The third person I became involved with turned out to be the man I have been married to for over sixty years — Kang Hoo Bie (Eddie) — but the relationship did not start out romantically. You see, it started when I was his teacher! Kang Hoo Bie is nine years younger than me and I first met him in 1930 when he was a 9-year-old student in my class at Jember HCS. Eddie lived with his parents in the village of Wonosari, about 45 kilometres away, and got up at 5:00 am every day to travel by train to school. During the subsequent school years, Eddie attended many excursions and trips to the mountains and places of interest that were supervised by me and other teachers. So we knew each other quite well.

One day when he was about 13, Eddie had a near-fatal accident on a train when he slipped on the train steps while the train was moving and was luckily rescued by a workman before falling underneath the train wheels. When his father heard about it, he decided that travelling was unsafe and wanted him to board in Jember. As the family had no relatives in Jember, he asked Eddie if there was a teacher that he would like to board with. When my name was mentioned, his father approached me to request that Eddie board with me for payment. I had sufficient room in

Earliest known photo of Eddie (circa 1937) taken during holidays in Pujon, East Java. From L-R: Lieke (Kasminah's daughter), Roostien, Ida, Eddie, Sian Hong (Adolf) on pony. Willem Liem, Eddie's close friend, is on the far right. In 1965 Willem was executed by the Army for being a member of the Communist party (PKI).

my boarding house in Jember and I welcomed the opportunity of earning some extra income.

Eddie stayed with me for four years while he attended the HSC for three years and MULO for one year in Jember. When I was transferred to the HCS in Salatiga, at the start of the school year in August 1939, Eddie moved to a Roman Catholic boarding school in Solo for the following two and a half years until the occupying Japanese closed all non-Indonesian schools in March 1942. Between 1939 and 1942, Eddie spent several school holidays with me in Salatiga. Because he started schooling late (aged 9) and repeated one more year's schooling during his education, he was 21 by the time all Dutch and Chinese schools were closed down by the Japanese. Eddie was no longer a boy and my opinion of him had dramatically altered as well. By 1942, we had become close friends.

Calm Before the Storm

I had heard of the Japanese military expansion into China from 1931 onwards, but at the time it meant nothing to me. I simply ignored it, as did the people I mixed with. I now know that Germany was becoming increasingly aggressive too during the 1930s, but we were not informed about such things at the time. Right through the 1930s, life in Indonesia seemed to be an endless cycle of calm, subject to the manifest superiority of European (Dutch) civilization.

Even after the Dutch were defeated in Europe in mid-1940, I did not see any rise of anti-Dutch feeling in Indonesia. There was no wide spread unrest or large-scale demonstrations in the streets. This may seem strange, but even though our colonial masters were defeated back in Europe, their continued presence in Indonesia maintained the "status quo". For the moment, at least, everything appeared normal.

I have always viewed the period from 1930 until the Japanese invasion in 1942 as the best time in my life. I was young, healthy, single, and wealthy. Professionally, I had reached the exalted status of Principal and was a senior union official as well, all in my early thirties. People everywhere respected me.

As 1940 turned into 1941, I reflected on just how much I had achieved in such a short time. I was very pleased with myself and wished that life would go on like this forever.

6

World War II and Japanese Occupation (1942–45)

On 7 December 1941 I was living in Salatiga as Principal of the local primary school when the Japanese attacked the American naval base at Pearl Harbour, Hawaii. The next day the newspapers and radio were broadcasting the terrible news about the destruction of the American fleet and reporting that the USA, Britain, Australia and the Netherlands had all declared war on Japan. The Dutch declaration of War automatically meant that the Netherlands Indies, a Dutch colony, was also at war with Japan. Overnight the world had changed.

The Japanese launched a series of lightning strikes across Southeast Asia, invading Malaya, Singapore and the Philippines, then striking at Sumatra and Kalimantan. In February 1942, I was informed through a mutual friend that my former boyfriend Ong Hok Tie had been executed by the invading Japanese in Balikpapan, the regional capital Kalimantan, where he had been teaching.[1] I was very sad at this terrible news but

---

[1] The Sakaguchi Brigade of the Imperial Japanese Army executed Dutch, Chinese and (some) Indonesian citizens in Balikpapan, Kalimantan during February 1942 in retaliation for the destruction of the much-needed oil fields by the retreating Dutch defenders. Immediately after the Japanese captured the town about eighty soldiers, nurses, and civil servants including teachers were publicly executed by the Sakaguchi Brigade on the beachfront in front of the local population. Although it cannot be confirmed, it is believed that Ong Hok Tie was amongst the people executed (<http://www.geocities.com/dutcheastindies/balikpapan.html>, accessed 12 November 2005).

events with the invading Japanese Army cut short the time I would have liked to grieve properly for him.

Between the occupation of Kalimantan and the Japanese invasion of Java a few weeks later in March 1942, everyone grew increasingly anxious. Eddie was in the city of Solo attending high school when the Japanese launched heavy air raids on main cities and military installations across Java in preparation for their invasion. Solo was one of the cities bombed. The next day he rode around the city on his bicycle to inspect the damage which was mainly to the airfield, only to discover that the few Dutch defenders had evacuated during the previous evening and that no-one knew where they had gone.

The city was now defenceless. A rumour spread like wildfire through Solo that the Japanese had already landed and would arrive in the city at any moment. Panic seized the city and people started fleeing in their thousands. In fact the small Dutch garrison had been sent to reinforce defences elsewhere and the Japanese would not invade for another fortnight, but nobody knew that at the time. It was a scary time for everyone but it was very exciting too with an overwhelming sense that great events were unfolding during this period of extreme uncertainty.

The Dutch had assumed that the Japanese would invade Java through the two major port cities of Surabaya and Jakarta and therefore concentrated their defences in those locations. They were taken completely by surprise when, on the night of 1 March 1942, the Japanese launched simultaneous amphibious landings along the poorly defended north coast of Java instead. From these beachheads the Japanese quickly spread out across Java before the Dutch could react and within days had surrounded the Dutch forces, still struggling to reorganise themselves out of their port cities. It was a hopeless situation, reminiscent of the method used to defeat the Allies in Malaya and Singapore. The expected Battle of Java was effectively over before it had begun and the Dutch Colonial Government officially surrendered on 9 March 1942.

The prevailing mood was one of stunned disbelief that the Dutch in Indonesia had capitulated so quickly. The Dutch had been in Indonesia for over 350 years, but they surrendered unconditionally to the Japanese within a week or so of their invasion! I just could not believe it but Eddie informed me later he had long harboured a suspicion the Dutch were going to lose. His father had told him weeks before the invasion that the Dutch "loved their wives and families, whereas the Japanese loved their country and Emperor". In the coming showdown between the two countries, the

Japanese would win "as they would sacrifice everything to achieve victory, even themselves".

One of the first official orders of the Japanese, issued about three weeks after assuming control of Indonesia, was to close down all Chinese- and Dutch-speaking schools, sending their students home or in some cases into internment.[2] The Japanese had been in Salatiga for only a week or two but had already established their authority over the city. In the circumstances I felt I had no choice but to obey the order without question. I locked up the school buildings and wondered what I should do next. Saartje and her child returned to Kediri because she wanted to be with her extended family during this uncertain time. As there was nothing for her to do in Salatiga, she was effectively leaving my employment permanently. I gave her a considerable severance bonus to start life again in Kediri.[3]

Japanese soldiers entering Salatiga in March 1942. (KITLV # 25449)

---

[2] Indonesian-language schools stayed open, but formal education for the Dutch and Chinese would not resume until late 1946, a year after the Japanese defeat. An refused to teach in any "village school" as it would have meant learning Japanese to communicate with the authorities and this she would not do.
[3] According to a later conversation with An, Saartje purchased a small beancurd factory in Kediri and made enough money to live comfortably.

While still in Salatiga, I heard that my old Headmasters Penn and Lange together with their wives had been interned in a prisoner-of-war camp hastily constructed in Ambarawa, a small town about 17 kilometres from Salatiga and next to Danau Rawapening where I had taken young girls camping while I was a teacher at Salatiga. This was a large camp for the Dutch in central Java and housed up to two thousand people in two adjoining camps. The men were accommodated in one camp with women and children under fifteen housed in the other. I was relieved that they were all alive, especially Mr Penn who had been called up to join the KNIL and must have fought against the Japanese.

I prepared parcels of food, groceries and medicines which I was told were already in short supply at the camp and without a thought to my own safety journeyed by horse and cart to Ambarawa. I was not allowed to enter the camp but managed to spend a pleasant afternoon talking firstly to the men at the barbed wire fence line, then with their wives at the adjoining camp. There did not appear to be any problems in passing some of my gifts through the fence to the men and the rest later to the women. The Japanese soldiers seemed casually disinterested.[4]

I am glad I caught up with the Penns and Langes at that time because I would soon depart Salatiga forever and return to my family home where my father forbade me to have anything more to do with the Dutch for fear of Japanese reprisals. He was shocked that I had personally gone to an internment camp to supply the Dutch with food and provisions and could not believe that I had not been dealt with as a collaborator. In any event it would prove impossible for me to see these people again during the occupation because travel passes were extremely difficult to obtain. Much later I heard that Mr Penn and Mr Lange had been transferred further away to the island of Ambon and that put the matter of visits completely out of the question for inter-island travel was strictly prohibited.

Meanwhile in Solo, Eddie found himself also without a school to attend and decided to return to his family in Balung. As this town was near Tanggul, he took it upon himself first to journey by *andong* the 50 kilometres or so to Salatiga, where he asked me if I wanted to return

---

[4] An's recollection of the camp is complimentary. According to her, the Japanese merely erected a perimeter fence around an existing township, crammed the Dutch inside in two camps separated by gender and left them to organize their own lives as long as they did not attempt to escape. An's visit to the camp was in the first few months of the Japanese occupation when Ambarawa was only lightly secured and at that point may have been used principally as a holding centre.

to my family as well. It did not need much persuasion to convince me that I should accompany him back to the security of my family, so we left on a train together the same day he arrived. The train was so crowded that we had to climb through the windows to get in.

It seemed that everyone in Indonesia was travelling back to their home villages as well. After two days of travelling with little sleep and several stops along the way, we finally made it to my family's town. We rushed down the road from the railway station the few hundred metres to the rice mills and I gratefully fell into the welcoming arms of my father.

It was during this trip to our respective homes that our relationship began to change. I was in a vulnerable state and Eddie began to see me as a person he could look after and protect. A year earlier, Eddie's long-term girlfriend of four years, Caroline (the grand-daughter of my mother's sister), had rejected him for a more settled man who owned a house and was wealthy.

He was informed quite coldly and impersonally via a letter from Jakarta while he was in Solo. I could not understand why she — or anyone else for that matter — would want to reject Eddie. I saw many admirable qualities in him, such as his frugality, good character and capacity for hard work that more than made up for his lack of wealth. I knew he had the potential to make something out of his life and it was during this time that I decided I would help him to become successful.

Occupation

After the capitulation of the Dutch, but while the Japanese occupying forces were still consolidating their presence in the hinterland, my father hastily rented a house in Darungan, a small out-of-the-way kampung about five kilometres from Tanggul, where he deposited my mother and several younger relatives for safekeeping. My father knew that the Japanese would probably commandeer the rice mills under his control, which meant that they would come to his house, and he did not want my mother to suffer another and possibly fatal heart attack when they eventually arrived. My brother and I both had Dutch degrees and the entire family had close ties with the Dutch.

My father was worried that the invading Japanese might see our qualifications and our intimacy with the Dutch as a threat, so he destroyed every document and every photograph the family possessed that might have incriminated us. Having just returned home, I was preparing to join my mother, half-sisters, nieces and nephews in their out-of-the-way location when the Japanese finally arrived.

It was only about a month since the Japanese had first landed in Java when a small detachment of armed soldiers drove up to our house in a truck, efficiently searched the building and brought my father and me to the front room.[5] We were the only family members present. I had seen many Japanese soldiers in the preceding weeks, so that when I entered the room I immediately recognized three soldiers reporting to two officers. Unlike the other soldiers who wore cloth puttees, the two officers had brown leather leggings and wore leather belts as well, but the two notable features were that they wore pistols and swords while the ordinary soldiers carried rifles. One officer was a lieutenant and interpreter, who also spoke fluent Bahasa Melayu.

Later we found out he could speak English too. He had spent time in Indonesia before the war, when he had studied the language and gathered intelligence for the Japanese Army under the guise of being a trader. The other officer was a captain, whom we were to shortly discover was in charge of the Japanese detachment that would be responsible for Japanese administration over the Tanggul area.

The Japanese officers quickly established that my father was in charge and that I was his daughter. When they were satisfied that no other member of the family was present, the interpreter told my father that a detachment of eleven soldiers were going to be billeted in the township of Tanggul. He went on to say that their purpose was to secure the rice mills under my father's control to guarantee that a certain proportion of rice always went to the Japanese Army. My father would stay on as the civilian supervisor to the mills as the Japanese needed his expertise. He would be paid for the rice that the Japanese wanted, but he had new responsibilities too. My father would be responsible for feeding the Japanese. The officer interpreter said, "Obey our orders without question. To ensure your family's absolute cooperation, your daughter is personally responsible for feeding ourselves and our soldiers from this point on. If anyone of us gets ill through food poisoning, your daughter will be executed. Is that perfectly clear?"

I was petrified and so was my father. It was all he could do to muster enough presence of mind to agree totally with whatever the officers wanted.

---

[5] By the time interviews were conducted with An Sudibjo for this book, she had no specific memory of her first meeting with the Japanese at Tanggul. What follows is a reconstruction by the author derived from casual comments made by her during the previous fifteen years.

Later during the War my father confided to me that he wished any other member of the family had been chosen rather than me.

Ironically, I was the only member of the family who could not cook, but at the age of 30 I now had to prepare food properly to stay alive. Concerned that I could not cook at all, my father made immediate arrangements to hire a full-time chef. The family had eaten several times at a restaurant in Kediri, which had a good reputation for serving European and Chinese meals (uncommon in east Java at the time). My father went to the restaurant and immediately hired its chef, who had particular expertise in East Asian food, to work exclusively for us and cook for the Japanese.

Her name was Ijem (pronounced "eeyum") and she knew how desperate my father was to secure her services. In the end my father had to pay almost double her salary before she agreed to come and work for us. It was chef Ijem who actually prepared the meals for the soldiers, even though I was still responsible. One unintended consequence of having a trained chef amongst us was that the quality of our own meals also improved and people eagerly accepted an invitation to the occasional dinner party we were allowed to have. Chef Ijem did try to teach me to cook and I certainly showed some interest in the activity, but I found out that I was better at supervising other people in the kitchen rather than actually doing the cooking myself.

With no school to teach at, I remained with my family for the duration of the war, serving the Japanese and home-tutoring my younger brother and relatives who were placed under my father's protection. Despite a terrifying introduction, my family's relationship with the Japanese from this point on improved immediately.

The daily routine of the Japanese troops involved motoring out each morning in vehicles seized from the Dutch Colonial Army to travel to the various rice mills and guard them throughout the day. Two soldiers were posted to guard each of the rice mills and each evening they would return to have their dinner. As my father also had his car confiscated by the Japanese for use elsewhere, he was occasionally allowed to accompany the Japanese on their route to inspect the rice mills.

Roostien arrived in Tanggul soon after the Japanese took control of the mills to leave her son Adolf (aged 15) and her two daughters, Ida (about 13) and Evy (about 11), with us for an indefinite period while she returned to Jakarta to be with her husband. From time to time, Eddie and his best friend Willem Liem would visit from Balung and stay several days at a time. To help distract everyone from all the surrounding upheaval, my father and I organized long afternoons of swimming and having fun in the nearby big river. He ordered workers to clear and dam part of the river to create a swimming pool. My nieces had observed how gracefully the native women would slip out of their sarongs as they entered the river to bathe. After perfecting this technique in their rooms, these young girls enjoyed skinny-dipping in the river.

Some of the games I saw the children play involved throwing one spider into another's web to watch the ensuing flight; catching fireflies and keeping them in muslin bags to twinkle in their rooms; or capturing crickets and fashioning harnesses and carts out of cassava leaves to race them. The children played bridge also, which I used to determine sleeping arrangements because there were not enough beds for all of them. The one who lost had to sleep on the slippery dining table. After some months the situation with the Japanese had settled enough for my mother and younger relatives to return from their little "hideaway" in Darungan, but my mother refused. She did not want to have anything to do with the Japanese.

Because my father's three-bedroom house at the rice mill was too small to accommodate all the family and friends who had gathered under my father's protection and mother did not want to return in any event, my father got permission to relocate everyone to a huge house in Mangisan, located closer to Tanggul about three kilometres away. Before the War it had been the house of the local manager of the British-American Tobacco company, but had since been confiscated along with all other foreign property.

The Japanese allowed my father to move everyone, about ten of us including servants and myself, into the vast six-bedroom mansion. It was too far away for the Japanese to use themselves because they had to stay closer to the strategically important rice mills, so they were glad to have my father's family accommodated there. My father arranged for everyone to move from Darungan about three months after the Japanese settled in the area and my mother was quite happy to see out the rest of the war in this fine house without ever having to see a Japanese soldier face to face. She did not return to live with Dad at Tanggul until the Japanese had left the area after the War in late 1945.

Even when Dad suffered a stroke in late 1943, my mother was so fearful of the Japanese that she refused to come and see him. There were no medicines or doctors available because of the War, so my father was given herbal remedies from a local faith healer. But still my mother steadfastly refused to come. In the end I relocated Dad to her house in Mangisan, where he stayed for some weeks convalescing.

My usual daily routine over the period of Japanese occupation dealt with organizing Ijem to prepare the food for the Japanese in my father's kitchen. I would then take it to them in their billet at the edge of the town a few hundred metres away. Afterwards I would cycle in the dark along small bush tracks to the big house at Mangisan, where I would sleep and look after the children and my mother. I prepared a program of activities which the children had to follow, involving academic and fun activities.

Some months after we moved into Mangisan, Roostien arrived to collect her children for her husband's job with PTT was secure for as long as the Japanese could not find someone to replace him. This left only a few children in the large house at Mangisan, but I still maintained the schedule I had established earlier at Darungan for the next three years until the end of the war.

For the Japanese soldiers, duty in Tanggul became a very comfortable existence. When they were not guarding the rice mills in the district, they would while away the days, often playing tennis on the court opposite our house and sometimes inviting locals to play against them. They taught the chef how to prepare Japanese food such as *sashimi* and *sushi*, but I was also allowed through Chef Ijem gradually to introduce them to Chinese

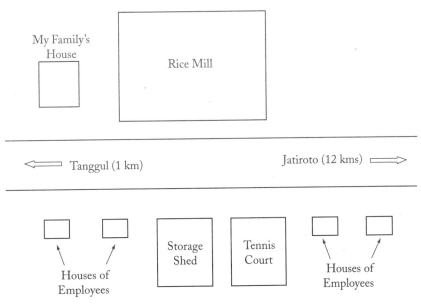

My family's house near Tanggul during the Japanese Occupation (1942–45).

and Indonesian cooking. Sometimes, in appreciation, they would give us items that were in short supply, such as cloth.

Nine Japanese soldiers plus the two officers were billeted a few hundred metres away from us in two houses they had commandeered on the outskirts of the small town of Tanggul. These eleven people, augmented at times by an officer from the dreaded *Kempeitai* (Military Police) who stayed occasionally from Jember, were my direct responsibility with regard to their food. During their occupation they treated my family well and were respectful of me.

Throughout the course of the war we grew close enough for them to tell us about their wives and families back in Japan. They would also share with us stories about Japanese life and customs and occasionally they would ask me to organize a special dinner for major events such as the Emperor's Birthday or to celebrate a national holiday. One officer, Lieutenant Suzuki, became particularly friendly with the family. He was not present at the traumatic first encounter and arrived only a few weeks later after everyone had overcome their initial shock.

Lt. Suzuki was more cultured and educated than the other soldiers and treated us in a genuinely caring manner. Over the course of his three-and-a-half year stay with us in Tanggul, he told us that he originally came from Kyoto, where he lived with his wife and daughter in comfortable circumstances. Before the War he had been employed as a middle-ranking member of staff in a large bank, but had been conscripted into the Army during 1939 when Japan was rapidly building up its military forces.

My niece Evy (Roostien's daughter) was about the same age as his own daughter. The first time they met — some weeks after he arrived — he burst into tears. Afterwards he told us that he had not seen his own daughter for over two years and missed her greatly. From that point on, he gave Evy and the other children I was looking after some chocolate and sweets on a regular basis whilst the children stayed with us. If he could not give special treats to his own daughter then I guess some other children of a similar age would have to suffice.

The Fate of the General Population under Japanese Rule

The Japanese treated the Dutch, Chinese and indigenous Indonesians very differently. The Dutch were the defeated former masters and they became prisoners; the Indonesians were promoted as the "true owners" of Indonesia

Billboard on a street in Jakarta during WWII showing Japanese victories in the Pacific, including Pearl Harbour at upper right. (Image courtesy of <www.gimonca.com/sejarah>)

who would become masters of their own country "some time in the future"; and the Chinese were tolerated as long as they continued to manage the economy and produce material required for the Japanese war effort.

The Japanese produced a great deal of propaganda directed at the indigenous Indonesians while they were in occupation. It was all designed to convince the native Indonesians that they would eventually become an independent country within a Japanese Co-prosperity Sphere, a type of Commonwealth, with Indonesia and other countries as junior partners.

It was hard to reconcile the fact that at the same time that the Japanese were promoting the Indonesians as the true inheritors of the archipelago, they were stripping Indonesia of all its resources to support their war effort and treating the natives harshly.

In October 1943 the Nationalist leader, *Ingenieur*[6] Sukarno, was made personally responsible for organizing a labour workforce for the Japanese,

---

[6] Also abbreviated to Ir, literally "Engineer" but denoting a university graduate with a technical degree.

Japanese propaganda poster promising Dekati Merdeka (Approaching Independence). Note the inclusion of the Japanese soldier in silhouette holding the Japanese flag. (Image courtesy of <www. gimonca.com/sejarah>)

called by its Japanese name as *romusha* (forced labour). Sukarno actively promoted the organization as one supposedly utilizing unemployed workers on public infrastructure projects such as irrigation, roads and the like, but by mid-1944 many people realized that the scheme was nothing more than a slave labour program.

In our area, one persistent report alleged that hundreds of workers in West Java had been forced to dig underground tunnels for the storage of food and munitions, after which they had been summarily executed to maintain the secrecy of the tunnel's location.

The Japanese military increasingly demanded more of everything, such as food, textiles, and especially petrol, while the Indonesian citizenry began to starve. For the first time in living memory, we began hearing rumours of people in the cities literally dying in the streets from extreme malnutrition. We were much better off in the country than people in the cities and towns. At least we had land, and servants who helped us grow food and raise animals. What we could not buy, we traded or bartered,

Sukarno posing for propaganda photograph to promote *romusha* (forced labour) under Japanese Occupation. (Image courtesy of <www.gimonca.com/sejarah>)

and in this regard the special rewards given to us by the Japanese proved especially valuable.

One member of the Kempeitai who had the rank of Captain visited us regularly from the district headquarters nearby at Jember, where the main bulk of hundreds of soldiers were in barracks.

While the infantry soldiers busied themselves protecting assets of value to the Japanese war effort, including our rice mills, he took charge of the civilian administration in our district. He assumed control of the existing system of colonial administration and the *Wedana* (District Head) reported directly to him. He also quickly established a network of paid informers to report to him on any anti-Japanese activities. Being both investigator and adjudicator in one, he had unlimited power to punish individuals, families or entire communities. Punishment ranged from fines, withdrawal of privileges such as food rations and imprisonment to, in extreme cases amputation or execution.

Our Kempeitai officer favoured occasional public displays of violence to maintain order. He was not interested in minor forms of punishment. Being the only man responsible for civilian order in a population of hundreds of thousands, his preferred method of operation was the occasional amputation, strangulation, or decapitation. Yet he was kind to us. We looked after him every time he visited and he could see we were treating the billeted soldiers very well, never provoked them, and always ensured that an agreed amount of rice was delivered to the Army.

The regular presence of the Kempeitai officer did produce one unexpected benefit. Previously, our rice mills had experienced losses due to grain theft. In fact, most mills across Indonesia suffered similarly. However, with the arrival of the Japanese, the overall crime rate dropped dramatically, including theft of grain from rice mills. For this action alone, most people including my family were grateful.

Because there were more Chinese in Indonesia than Dutch — two million compared with about a quarter of a million — the Japanese could not arrest and intern all Chinese. Moreover, they needed our expertise to run things just as the Dutch had done before them. The majority were allowed to continue working as they had before, but were now answerable

Japanese pamphlet (1944) directed specifically at the Chinese in Indonesia saying that they have nothing to fear from the military if they cooperate with the occupying Japanese forces. The pamphlet clearly shows that overwhelmingly military force will be used against those Chinese who do not cooperate.
(KITLV # 51 Z–2)

to new masters. The unstated rules in our household were simple and rigidly adhered to: respect the Japanese, treat them well, and do as they say without question. Then, hopefully, they would not harm you.

Nevertheless, the treatment of the Chinese was purely arbitrary and was entirely dependent on the local Japanese commander. In some regions of Indonesia I heard that the Chinese were brutalized, tortured, and even killed, but around Tanggul we made sure that the Japanese were treated well and we never had any problems. The family heard that my brother Tan Swan Bing, who before the war had been promoted to a senior position with Kian Gwan Trading Company in Semarang, had been interned and his house ransacked. We were all worried about his safety and that of his wife Huguette, who had just given birth to their third child.

We were told later that, by a strange twist of fate, a senior officer of the Kempeitai came across my brother when Tan Swan Bing had been imprisoned for about six months and learned that my brother spoke fluent Dutch, German and English. The Kempeitai officer was busy pursuing a PhD, which required the translation of German documents. He released my brother on the condition that Tan Swan Bing would help him complete his thesis. From that point on, my brother and his family received preferential treatment and they lived out the duration of the war without coming to any further harm.

Like me, my younger brother, Siauw Djie, returned to Tanggul from Semarang when all the Dutch schools were closed by the Japanese. He married his long-term girl friend, Khouw Mi Lien, in 1942 and turned to my parents for financial support. He said he could not find any paid work, did not know what to do and expected our father to help him. This dependent attitude was so unlike that of my sister and older brother, who never asked for parental assistance, even though they suffered much hardship on their own, including internment. I found this particularly weak of Siauw Djie but my father, who had always spoilt him, gave Siauw Djie a paid position in the rice mill to help him.

I never thought for one minute that the Japanese actually liked the Chinese. There had simply been too much bloodshed in the decade-long war in mainland China for that to happen. In Indonesia, I guess they tolerated the Chinese out of necessity. However, in our specific circumstances in Tanggul we managed to cultivate a friendly relationship with the Japanese that was like being a good and faithful servant. We were never equals, but at least the Japanese were kind and pleasant towards us, as long as we never did anything wrong.

The Closing Period of Japanese Occupation

In 1944 the tide of war turned after the Japanese had suffered several disastrous battles but in Indonesia the extent of these losses and the inevitable consequences of defeat for the Japanese Empire were kept hidden from the general populace. Those Indonesians who could read kept up with events mainly through the newspapers, but as the print media was heavily censored the Japanese were able to maintain a general tone of confidence. While there were items about Japanese defeats as well as victories, they were presented in such a way as to diminish the former and exaggerate the latter.

All pre-war radios had been confiscated but if you could afford it you could replace them with other radios that were "sealed" in such a way that you could listen only to Japanese-approved radio stations with their inevitable drone of propaganda, similar to the newspapers. However, there were a few brave people who managed to hide their pre-war radios and were therefore able to pick up enemy broadcasts from overseas. The possession of an "unsealed" radio was prohibited by the Japanese right up to the end of the war, but as long as these radios were kept out of sight the Japanese did not actively search for these devices. Because my family had such close contact with the Japanese, my father would not allow a prohibited radio in the house, but some other friends and relatives we knew did possess them and they informed us quietly about the true course of the war from these foreign broadcasts.

Despite Japanese propaganda of ultimate victory that persisted right to the end, by late 1944, it was obvious to us and to a growing number of others that the Japanese would inevitably lose this war. Coincidentally, Eddie and I knew about the atomic bombing of the Japanese cities of Hiroshima and Nagasaki from overseas radio broadcasts, which we listened to on an illegal radio while staying with Eddie's aunt, Tante Siem, in Jember.[7]

While some indigenous Indonesians looked forward to the eventual return of the Dutch, many more were prepared to throw their lot in with the Indonesian nationalists who wanted independence. Meanwhile, we Chinese predictably tried to sit on the fence. But as the Second World War came to an end, the penchant for Chinese Indonesians to change

---

[7] Tante Siem's maiden name was Tee Swat Siem and her mother was the sister of Eddie's adoptive mother, Ong Hwat Nio. She had married Tan Oen Khing, a baker, and established a *toko roti* (bakery) in the city of Jember which is still operating today.

their allegiances as readily as a chameleon changes colour was coming to an end. For two million or so Chinese living in Indonesia at the time, sitting on the fence was about to become unacceptable. In simple terms, we had to choose between supporting an independent Indonesia or the return of the Dutch.

During the last year or so of occupation the Japanese hastily prepared some native Indonesian units to resist the return of the Dutch and assume power in their own right. At the end of 1943, the Japanese provided arms, equipment and training for this embryonic force known as *PETA* (Pembela Tanah Air, Defenders of the Fatherland). Many native Indonesians enthusiastically supported this initiative, which was widely seen as their best chance of nationhood. These PETA soldiers were trained by the Japanese soldiers to defend Indonesia against the allied invasion that the Japanese feared would inevitably come. However, when it was obvious that the Japanese would lose the war, some PETA soldiers like those in the mountains behind nearby Pelalangan turned against the Japanese. In the last year of the war, these Pelalangan rebels would occasionally conduct guerrilla raids against Japanese soldiers garrisoned in the nearby cities of Jember and Bondowoso.

When the Japanese surrendered in late 1945 they came down from the mountains and were treated as heroes, but when the Dutch arrived a year later they returned to the hills and resumed fighting.

My Relationship with Eddie

After returning from Solo via Salatiga to collect me in early 1942, Eddie stayed with his family in Balung for a few months and then, at my instigation, worked as a clerk for my father in the Balung rice mill for ƒ12.50 a month. However, his father believed that Eddie was worth more and persuaded him to resign after only several weeks. By this time in late 1942 our family had not heard from Roostien for a number of months since she had brought her children to leave with us in Tanggul and my father was getting quite concerned.

We were starting to hear disturbing rumours about food shortages in the major cities so my father secured a travel pass for Eddie from the Japanese billeted locally and asked Eddie to journey to Jakarta to check on her. He took several parcels of food with him and upon his return reported that Roostien and her husband, Liem Sing Giap, were safe. Liem Sing Giap had been made a Dutch citizen years earlier for the essential role he was performing in the telephone system and my family feared that he might have been interned by the Japanese along with the rest of the Dutch community. Eddie reported that the Japanese needed his expertise just as much as the Dutch in maintaining the telephone system and for the time being everything appeared to be secure for them.[8]

While in Jakarta, Eddie's old girlfriend, Caroline, caught up with him and begged him to take her back. Her intended marriage had been cancelled at the last minute by her fiancée's father.[9] Eddie thankfully declined. When he told me about this incident upon his return I was somewhat jealous and realised that my feelings for him were growing stronger. Eddie went back to assist his parents in Balung about 30 kilometres away, but I continued to urge my father to organize some work so that we could be closer.

The local Wedana and my father were close friends and in casual conversation he informed my father that a nearby coffee plantation had become available for rent.[10] My father seized on the opportunity and arranged for me to lease the plantation in late 1942. He then wrote to Eddie asking him to come and look after it for me. The coffee plantation was located in the village of Pelalangan in the mountains behind Tanggul. It was a small estate of about 19 hectares that was in a poor condition and did not have any buildings. The property was mainly cultivated for coffee production but it also had a number of coconut trees as well as durian trees that produced a uniquely fragrant, sweet fruit.

The property had been leased for the usual period of seventy-five years by a Taiwanese businessman who was resident in Indonesia. The island of Taiwan (or Formosa as it was then known) and its citizens had been under Japanese rule for many years and when World War II broke out in December 1941, the Dutch confiscated all Japanese property and interned all its citizens, including the lessee of the Pelalangan estate. However, this

---

[8] In late 1944, the Japanese replaced Liem Sing Giap with one of their own and he was immediately interned. However, his period of incarceration lasted less than a year until the end of the war in August 1945 and did not involve Roostien, who was able to go on living in the family home at Jalan Jogja 7, Menteng without severe difficulties.

[9] Caroline may have been showing symptoms of a mental illness. A few years later she was committed to a psychiatric institution.

[10] The Wedana for Tanggul district was Muhammed Kafrawi, who later became the Secretary General in the Ministry of Religion in the early 1950s. He was dismissed in 1956 when he objected to President Sukarno taking a second wife.

person did not return to his former leasehold as expected after the Japanese overran Indonesia. The local people never knew what happened to him, but the rumours claimed that he either died while in Dutch custody or on his return journey to resume his tenancy.

In 1942 the village elders of Pelalangan did not know whether the War would end in a victory for the Japanese or the Allies but, as the abandoned estate was starting to fall into disrepair, they decided someone should take over the property on a short-term basis. They requested the district Wedana to make all the necessary arrangements. After he had informed my father about this opportunity, a short-term lease contract was quickly signed between the Wedana and me.

Eddie took up the challenge and relocated to the coffee plantation. He brought in some labourers from the island of Madura, because they were cheaper and harder working than local labour, and with their help built a one-room hut out of bamboo for them all to live in. He purchased six cows and released them into the plantation to graze on the undergrowth, which was threatening to choke the coffee plants. With his workmen, Eddie planted a small market garden to live off and sold the surplus to the market in Tanggul. Gradually, the plantation was put into good order and the seasonal produce made enough to pay the rent, but it was fairly primitive living and required a lot of hard work.

There were no vehicles and hardly any roads. If Eddie wanted to come down to Tanggul to see me or bring produce to the market he would ride a horse, but as it was over 12 kilometres away it was still an hour's ride. As a practical joke, he once rode his horse right into our house in Tanggul while I was asleep. I woke up startled with the horse breathing and slobbering all over my face!

While Eddie worked the coffee plantation at Pelalangan, he became friendly with some of the Indonesian PETA rebels who were located in the surrounding mountains. They offered to "protect" the estate if he supplied them with produce from the plantation, such as hundreds of coconuts. Of course, this was outright extortion as the plantation did not need protecting from anyone, but it has always been prudent to keep on the right side of men with guns in Indonesia.

Soon a comfortable relationship developed between Eddie and the PETA soldiers. Occasionally, he would borrow a rifle from the rebels and shoot wild pigs to take down to my family in Tanggul for food was now becoming scarce. It was about this time he declared his love for me, but it was never a passionate romance. It was more like two adults gradually realizing that they had more to offer each other as a couple than if they remained individuals.

By systematically rebuilding and renovating the plantation, Eddie had hoped to negotiate a much longer lease over the property at some point in the future. Unfortunately, in late 1944 as the War was turning in the favour of the Allies, the village elders felt confident enough to take over the estate completely. Presumably they wanted to plant more food for the village. The Wedana reluctantly told Eddie of the decision by the village elders to resume the property and he departed the estate for good in early 1945. Years later, I heard the plantation had again fallen into disrepair and was allowed to return to its original condition of tropical forest.

We remained friends with the Wedana, Muhammed Kafrawi, for many years. He had an infant daughter born about the same time as our son. Because we had a milk cow but he did not, we supplied him with fresh milk on a daily basis.

Wedding Bells

During 1944, Eddie sought his parent's counsel regarding a possible marriage between us. His mother was concerned about the nine-year age difference between me and Eddie, but his father thought the marriage would be a good union for both of us, especially his son. I think he understood that Eddie needed the "guiding hand" of a more mature and successful woman to develop his son's potential. A humorous exchange took place when Eddie's father came to discuss the prospects of a wedding with my parents. Because of the age difference, my parents at first thought Eddie wanted to marry my younger sister (Erna), who was about his age. After several awkward moments the situation was clarified and in the end both families agreed to a wedding.

The only condition my father had was that the two of us had to first obtain the approval of my older brother (Swan Bing) and older sister (Roostien). We wrote away to both of my siblings and received the necessary approval. Because Roostien knew Eddie well, her reply was instant and effusive. Swan Bing however, did not care a great deal whom I married. He was just grateful that at the age of thirty two I was marrying anyone at all!

We were married at the vacant administrator's house of the rice mill that was situated on the eastern end of Tanggul, known as Karanglo, on 15 December 1944. The Wedana provided Eddie with his own chauffeur-driven car to bring him the short distance from west Tanggul to the wedding.[11] It was a most difficult time because the Japanese were stripping Java bare to feed their armies and there was no money to buy anything. Eddie borrowed a suit from my father and I wore Roostien's wedding dress.

The administrator's house was owned by my uncle Tjioe Sien An, who had originally made my father Superintendent of the rice mills. It was a large house that had been recently renovated for Tjioe Sien An's son, but was left empty after this person changed his mind about living there. We had to borrow furniture from family and friends to make it presentable. It was a small civil wedding attended by about a hundred people. As times were tough and no one had cars, some guests had to come by train and others by dokar. Some people just could not afford to come at all. One of Eddie's uncles, who was the head of a pig cooperative, gave us a live pig as a wedding gift. This we slaughtered and fed to thankful guests, many of whom had not consumed meat for a long time.[12]

My bridal bouquet was donated by my previous boyfriend (the dentist, Oei Hok Tjwan), which may seem a little strange but he was still very fond of me. Nevertheless, he declined to attend the wedding.

After our wedding and at the end of the lease on the coffee plantation in late 1944, Eddie and I lived in one of the empty employee's houses across the road from my father's house next to the rice mill. When we knew that the lease was coming to an end, Eddie had the presence of mind to make a lot of charcoal from dead wood at the plantation and from the surrounding mountains to provide future income. He made so much charcoal that it filled up the large storage shed at the rice mill in Tanggul.[13] Over the next few months after he left the plantation he gradually sold off this stockpile of charcoal to merchants in Surabaya. The sale of charcoal and also of salted duck eggs, a skill I had learnt from my mother, provided us with the only source of income.

---

[11] He was the only non-Japanese person in the district to be given permission to retain his government car.

[12] By this stage of the War, some Muslims in the district would eat any form of meat they could — even pig meat, which is prohibited by Islamic Law — to avoid hunger or starvation.

[13] Kerosene, which had been one of the major fuels for cooking and lighting, had all but disappeared from the shops and markets during the War due to the Japanese confiscating all petroleum-based products for the war effort. As a result, many forests and teak plantations were plundered to produce charcoal (*arang*) for cooking purposes.

It was in August 1945 that we heard the Japanese had unexpectedly surrendered. It should have been a period of joy and celebration, but that is not what happened in Indonesia. The Indonesian people had cooperated with the Japanese and it was under the authority of the Japanese that the independent nation of Indonesia had been created. What would the victorious Allies, which included the Dutch, make of this?

The Japanese soldiers in Tanggul were withdrawn immediately after the Japanese surrender and control of the district passed back to the Wedana, who may have also relied upon the assistance of the PETA soldiers based in the mountains. When the Japanese soldiers and their officers received orders to withdraw, they asked me to organize a special farewell dinner. Many speeches were made and much liquor consumed, including the last of their *sake* (rice wine) which they had been hoarding. Over the three years they had been with us they had grown quite fond of my father and at the farewell dinner several of the Japanese hugged my father and wept openly. Some were still crying the next day as they drove off to uncertain futures.

Our special friend, Lieutenant Suzuki even gave details of his Kyoto address to my father along with an open invitation for any member of my family to visit him any time after the War. This was a kind and respectful gesture, but one that none of us ever took up.

7

Revolution (1945–49)

The End of the War

We knew about the Japanese surrender (15 August 1945) and the declaration of Indonesian Independence (17 August 1945) through the newspapers as well as the radio. We also knew that Ir Sukarno and his deputy, Dr Mohammad Hatta had used, or been forced to use, the suddenness of Japan's capitulation and the absence of any Allied forces in Indonesia as an opportunity to seize control. However, Japanese preparation for indigenous government had barely begun and the unexpected announcement of Japanese surrender had not given Sukarno sufficient time to establish a viable Government. He had no apparatus of state and no effective army to defend it. The newly declared government was weak and vulnerable and virtually non-existent outside Jakarta.

Almost as soon as Sukarno had declared independence, the countryside was rife with rumours that he had actually been forced to do so. Years earlier Sukarno had formed the *Partai Nasional Indonesia* (PNI), so it was only logical that he declared Indonesia's independence on behalf of a Nationalist Government. The rumours alleged there had been a rift at the top of the Nationalist party between younger radicals (Wikana, Subardjo and Chairul Saleh) insisting on an immediate declaration of independence and the older, more conservative elements (Sukarno, Hatta and Sjahrir) wishing to adopt a more cautious approach. The issue was brought to a head when the radicals kidnapped Sukarno and Hatta, who were taken to a place outside Jakarta and persuaded to draft a Declaration that was read out publicly next day.

On the morning of 17 August 1945, Sukarno read the declaration of independence to a small crowd outside his house in Jakarta. The red-and-white (*merah-putih*) flag was raised and the national anthem, Indonesia Raya (Great Indonesia), was sung.

The news about the Declaration of Independence spread quickly and within days even the smallest kampung throughout Indonesia knew about it. I was told there was much singing and dancing throughout the land, but I saw no evidence of that in our district. In Tanggul the announcement was greeted with silence. The Chinese, the indigenous Indonesians and even the Japanese in our town were all too thoroughly exhausted by the War. No-one had any energy left to celebrate the birth of the Indonesian nation. Everyone just wanted life to return to normal as quickly as possible.

I have read histories of this chaotic period but much of it is romanticized, revolutionary nonsense produced by the Indonesian Government after the event to convince the masses of their righteous and heroic struggle for Independence. I even taught the so-called official version to trainee teachers for years when I was Principal of the Teachers' College in Jakarta. In my opinion, there was no heroic struggle for Independence, just one long struggle for survival!

Sukarno's cooperation with the occupying Japanese had been at best naïve, at worse criminal collaboration. The hastily cobbled together Declaration itself was opportunistic as Sukarno attempted to salvage something out of the unexpectedly early defeat of the Imperial Japanese Government.

The British forces, which had overall command of the Allied War effort in Southeast Asia theatre against the Japanese, arrived in October 1945 to take temporary control of Indonesia. The Indonesian people were convinced that the true purpose of British intervention was eventually to hand the country back to the Dutch, which gave rise to much antipathy towards the British. Open conflict broke out in several cities such as Semarang, Surabaya, Bandung and Jakarta between the British troops, which included Indians and the feared Ghurkha soldiers, and Indonesian Nationalists.

It was the PETA soldiers that faced the British soldiers in these cities and their rallying cry to gather popular support was "*Bersiap*" (stand ready). When they yelled this in the streets, hundreds of ordinary citizens would arrive to attack or defend a particular location. In early 1946, the first Dutch troops began arriving and, as their numbers increased, the British departed. This activity further convinced Indonesians that the true reason for Britain's involvement was to return Indonesia to Dutch colonial rule.

During this period I was in the later stages of pregnancy and my condition would unintentionally cause me to witness some of the turmoil of the *bersiap* period. The wife of my cousin, Tjioe Swie Hian, was pregnant with her second child at the same time that I was expecting my first. Living in Surabaya and being wealthier than our family, she could afford to be under the care of one of the few doctors available in the region trained in Obstetrics. Knowing that I was expecting my first child at the age of 33, she organized for me to be his patient too.

Once a month during my pregnancy, my husband and I would journey to Surabaya by train from Tanggul, stay a few nights with the Tjioes and have my regular check-up with the doctor. I wanted to have the close support of my family when I gave birth. As Surabaya was about 200 kilometres away from them in Tanggul, the doctor agreed that I was healthy enough to deliver in the smaller district hospital at Jember, about 30 kilometres from Tanggul. Unfortunately, my doctor informed me from the outset that his practice in Surabaya prevented him from physically attending my delivery, so arrangements were made for the most qualified midwife in the Jember district to assist instead. My monthly check-ups with the doctor in Surabaya were to ensure that no medical complications upset these arrangements.

About three weeks before the anticipated birth date, my husband and I went to Surabaya as usual for my last medical check up. When we arrived, the city was seething with revolutionary activity and was so tense you could feel it. The Japanese were actively supporting the Indonesian Nationalists with weapons and training and their leader, *Bung* (brother) Tomo, was creating fanatical revolutionary enthusiasm throughout the city of 750,000 people in preparation for a battle with the Allied Forces, which everyone knew were about to arrive.

Barricades and defensive positions were being constructed, while young indigenous Indonesians were marching or running all over the streets shouting revolutionary slogans and working themselves and the populace into a frenzy. The walls of the main streets were adorned with nationalistic graffiti and the Merah-Putih revolutionary flag was hanging everywhere. I did see some people carrying Japanese rifles and machine guns but thousands more only had machetes, swords, or home-made spears fashioned out of bamboo.

Between 10,000 and 20,000 Dutch men, women and children were still being held nearby in the Surabaya suburb of Darmo in the largest Japanese internment camp in East Java. I heard that they were slowly being

A passionate Bung Tomo urging the citizens of Surabaya to defend the city against the impending arrival of British troops in November 1945. (Image courtesy of <www.indonesianembassy.org.uk/photo_history>)

Photo of graffiti on the streets of Surabaya in November 1945 warning the British soldiers, in poor English, that the citizens of the city are prepared to fight. (Image courtesy of <www.indonesianembassy.org.uk/photo_history>)

starved to death by the Indonesians. My husband and I knew carnage would follow the moment Allied troops arrived and, as they were expected any day, we were anxious to leave. As soon as my appointment with the doctor was concluded sometime during the third week of September 1945 and he had given me a clean bill of health, we got out of the city as hurriedly as we could.

We returned home to Tanggul and a week or so later travelled by train to Jember where, by prior arrangement, Eddie would stay with his aunt, Tante Siem, in a room at her bakery shop and I would enter the maternity ward at Jember hospital. In those days you could not book your accommodation in the delivery ward in advance as you can now. You just had to take your chances. The maternity ward had about fifteen beds but when I arrived they were all occupied by the mistresses of Japanese soldiers, who were given preference to stay there as long as they wanted.

I was worried that I would not have the baby in a hospital as I had intended, but Tante Siem appeared quite sanguine about the news. She merely shrugged her shoulders nonchalantly and insisted that I deliver the baby in a spare room that she would prepare at her house.

Under the instructions of Tante Siem and with the approval of the skilled midwife, servants quickly prepared the spare room and I readied myself for the imminent birth. There, I gave birth to my first child in Jember on 9 October 1945 and we named him Kang Tjay Djien (meaning "gift of wisdom"). Later, he would be known simply as John. It was a difficult birth and I was in labour for over twenty-four hours.

After the birth of John and a week's convalescence, we returned to the quieter and much safer surrounds of Tanggul to carry on life as new parents as normally as possible. In April 1946 we heard that the Dutch had arrived back in Jakarta with the intention of restoring their authority over Indonesia and we decided to seek out their protection as soon as we could, but it would still be another year before we could make the journey to the capital.

It was not safe outside British and Dutch-held territory at that time in Indonesia. In fact it was probably best described as anarchy. We continually heard about massacres of the Dutch and the Chinese. Several of my relatives near Kediri and Ngronggot were killed by Indonesian rebels who were based in the Communist stronghold of Madiun in central Java. In the kampung of Prambon, near Kediri, Tan Tik Loen (the husband of my cousin Tjie Hwie) was murdered by Indonesian Communists. In Ngronggot, another group of Communists suddenly arrived one day and rounded up all the

Chinese males in the kampung, including Kwee Soen Sian (the husband of my father's younger sister, Aunt Kira) and his son. They were taken away and murdered in the jungle and their remains were never located. The few remaining Chinese in the town fled in terror.

These horrendous activities were happening all through central Java and prevented us from reaching the capital city of Jakarta. We had no choice but to wait in Tanggul for almost two years after the war ended before it was safe enough to travel.

In my opinion, the Indonesians saw *merdeka* (freedom) as more than a political aspiration. For them it was an opportunity to rid Indonesia of the political and economic influence of both the Dutch and the Chinese. The average Indonesian is a proud individual, particularly if he or she is Javanese. The Javanese culture is strong, rich and historically long for it has its roots going back many, many centuries. Before foreigners came to this part of the world, Java was the dominant power in Southeast Asia. Then Europeans came and soon after the Chinese. Within a century the whites had come to dominate politics and the Chinese controlled the economy.

For the average Indonesian, these two groups of interlopers had usurped power and there was much resentment. Therefore there was a strong determination to expel the Dutch and the Chinese and take back control of their country. For example, it was widely believed at the time that the Chinese held 70 per cent of Indonesia's wealth but represented only 3 per cent of the population. Variations on this sentiment are still used to this day to justify violence against Chinese Indonesians.

Often, however, even the ordinary person in the street saw through the political rhetoric and wanted to get back to some form of normal life. I can remember our regular greengrocer complaining loudly one day, "When is this so-called merdeka going to be over?" We were horrified at his public outburst of cynicism and for his own safety told him not to repeat the comments.

Struggling Nation

At the end of the War the concept of an independent nation as declared by Sukarno in 1945 was not welcomed by everyone in Indonesia. The Dutch, numbering 250,000–300,000, overwhelmingly yearned for the return of Dutch colonial rule and their sentiments were shared by a million or so intellectuals and former public servants who were Dutch-trained, Dutch-educated and "Dutch thinking".

As the independence movement was promoted heavily by the Javanese, large numbers of non-Javanese Indonesians saw independence as a thinly disguised grab for Javanese hegemony over the entire archipelago. In particular, the people of the outer islands of Ambon were violently opposed to the notion of independence and enlisted in their thousands to fight for the Dutch colonial army. The Ambonese have always had a deserved reputation for being fierce fighters and their participation in the revolution as elite commando troops on the side of the Dutch had significantly prolonged the war. Similar break-away movements opposed to the (Javanese) Nationalists flared across the islands in areas such as Aceh, West Sumatra, South Maluku, Timor, Sulawesi and Kalimantan. In all, possibly a fifth of the Indonesian population or around 15 million people opposed the Independence movement, or at least the Javanese version of it.

The Javanese independence movement was mainly supported by the working man in the street and the rural peasantry of Java. They had everything to gain in this struggle and the pro-independence propaganda reinforced this by promising them riches, position and power for their cooperation.

Even though the pro-independence movement had vast numerical superiority, their victory was not a foregone conclusion. The Nationalists were only lightly armed with guns and traditional weapons, while the Dutch were equipped with superior transport and heavy weaponry, including tanks, aircraft and naval vessels.

Even within the 80 per cent of people who wanted independence, different groups pursued their own versions of what independence meant and often they were in conflict with each other. It was anarchy at the beginning of the Revolution in Indonesia. Communists, Dutch, Nationalists, Socialists, Christian Youth Groups, and Islamic Republicans were killing each other all across the archipelago. Despite armed resistance, the Dutch quickly regained control of much of Indonesia but they could not crush all opposition. There were pockets of resistance and areas of the countryside that the Dutch did not even attempt to subdue. By early 1947, the Dutch had reoccupied between 60–70 per cent of Indonesia, but they had become over-stretched and a stalemate ensued.

In West Java, the Javanese mystic Kartosuwirjo declared himself head of a new Islamic state that was known as *Darul Islam* (Abode of Islam). It was centred on the city of Bandung and the town of Subang and advocated the formation of an Islamic Republic. It fought both the Dutch and the

Nationalists, but even though it was initially suppressed by the Nationalists in 1949 it continued to survive for decades.[1]

Similar religiously motivated rebellions sprung up in Aceh, Kalimantan and Sulawesi and would continue to be a thorn in the side of the Indonesian republic for years. In the case of Aceh, an Islamic independence movement remained active to the present day.

During the entire Revolutionary period (1945–49), not one of our relatives supported the pro-independence movement. Most were either neutral or pro-Dutch, but definitely no-one was pro-independence. Our families spoke Dutch, were Dutch-educated, and owed their livelihoods to Dutch-run commercial enterprises. Privately, we referred to the Nationalists as "rebels", just like the Dutch did, though we were careful not to use this expression in public.

Relocation to Jakarta

We had an infant boy and our physical safety was under threat in Tanggul. Even though the Dutch controlled some of the major cities, much of the countryside still remained in the hands of various groups of people vying for control over their area. Nevertheless, I still believed that the Dutch would eventually prevail.

Apart from my relatives being murdered by Communists, one of my former colleagues, an indigenous Indonesian, was killed by a radical Islamic *Pemuda* (Youth group) because he was a liberal-thinking intellectual. That is why I wanted to get to Jakarta and safety as soon as possible. Besides, we had no income to live on. So I decided to get my old job back with the newly returned Dutch colonial administration. After a surprisingly uneventful three-day train journey through terrain held by the Nationalists, we arrived in Jakarta in July 1947. I then went directly to the Department of Education seeking a return to teaching.

To my relief I found that there was an acute shortage of qualified teachers. Some had fled Indonesia, while others were dead or still held in internment camps and could not return to Dutch-held territory. Therefore, I was immediately re-instated and sent to a combined Junior and Senior High School in the Jakarta suburb of Pegangsaan, where I started

---

[1] The Darul Islam movement and its leader Kartosuwirjo survived for years controlling much of the countryside of West Java until 1962, when Kartosuwirjo was finally captured and executed.

teaching mathematics again. The School had about nineteen teachers and I commenced as the Subject Head of Mathematics and Physics. I was quickly promoted to Deputy Principal under a Dutch Headmaster.

In 1948, when that Headmaster resigned to leave Indonesia along with many other Dutch citizens when the recognition of Indonesia's Independence seemed inevitable, I was promoted again to the position of Principal of the combined schools.

During the latter half of 1947 there was still intermittent street fighting in the suburbs of Kota, Senen, and Matraman in Jakarta against the Dutch, but by early 1948 the Dutch had prevailed and a peculiar calm settled over the city. Meanwhile fighting still raged in other parts of Indonesia. During this period we stayed in Jakarta without ever venturing out of the city, thereby avoiding areas not under Dutch control. I was paid in guilders, which was a currency recognised by all sides in the revolution as it was backed by the Dutch and therefore stronger than the rupiah (the currency of the Nationalists).

For accommodation, the Dutch authorities agreed we could stay in the government house at Jalan Jogja 7, Menteng that my sister and brother-in-law were currently renting.[2] Menteng is one of the older, centrally located suburbs of Jakarta where the Dutch had built a number of sizeable residential houses because of its proximity to nearby embassies and government departments. Our house was large enough to accommodate three separate families plus their servants. After a few weeks, my brother-in-law told Eddie that he had to find a job in the public sector or else we would lose our eligibility to stay in a government house. Even though I was a public servant, only male public servants or employees of state-run enterprises were entitled to government-subsidized family accommodation.

Thankfully there were considerable shortages in every area of work for the Dutch and Eddie had no trouble securing employment, initially

---

[2] The name of the road, which runs just south and parallel with Jalan Diponegoro, was changed in the late 1950s to Jalan Mangunsarkoro, after a Hero of the Revolution. However, not one member of the Sudibjo family has ever used the altered street name. They explain that the previous name was shorter and therefore more convenient to use. In deference to the continued usage of the older street name by every member of the Sudibjo family, the name Jalan Jogja is used throughout the memoir.

An's brother-in-law, Liem Sing Giap, was a senior public servant working for PTT and had been a tenant at Jalan Jogja 7 from the early 1930s.

L-R: Ida Liem (now Karyadi), Tjay Djien (now John Nielsen), and Evy Liem (now Tan) with their dog in the front yard of Jalan Jogja 7, Jakarta, c. 1947–48.

Eddie holding John standing in front yard of Jalan Jogja 7, Jakarta, c. 1947.

as a clerk for the Dutch shipping company KPM (*Koninklijke Paketvaart Maatschappij*) for two months, then with the Royal Dutch Airline KLM (*Koninklijke Luchtvaart Maatschappij*), where he had greater prospects. KLM operated both domestic and international routes in Indonesia.

At first Eddie performed shift work as a cargo clerk at the airport in Kemayoran, Jakarta, but after a year he organized a transfer to KLM's office in the city. There he worked normal business hours so that he could attend night classes to further his career. Eddie passed a Custom's course conducted by KLM's own training staff and completed a separate English-language course as well, but when he then wanted to undertake the company's Manager's course he was informed that he was ineligible. Eddie had almost completed MULO (Junior High School) when the War came and Dutch-speaking schools were closed, but this level of schooling was unfortunately insufficient for him to attend the course.

Eventually, Eddie persuaded his Director to give him a chance and in 1949 he started at night the one-year part-time Manager's course that would significantly change his life. This was an important undertaking for my husband and I supported him in every way I could. I kept the household free of noise and distractions, made sure the servants constantly supplied him with small meals to study by, and even helped him through the more difficult mathematical content of the course. By the time he completed this program, the part of KLM he was working for — the domestic operations in Indonesia — had became *Garuda*.[3] In 1950, some months after the Dutch formally relinquished sovereignty over Indonesia, the domestic operations were taken over by a newly-created Indonesian company called *Garuda Indonesia Airlines* (GIA), which was originally a joint venture between KLM and the Government of Indonesia.

My older sister Roostien and her husband Liem Sing Giap left for Holland on sabbatical leave with their family during 1949. Their tenancy in the house was taken over by the army which sent Captain Subroto Hamijoyo and three lieutenants to be quartered there. They were all single. The remaining space at Jalan Jogja 7 was occupied by Jan Nielsen, a Dutch teacher who would be joined a year later by his wife Gerda and children.

Roostien and Liem Sing Giap eventually returned to Indonesia and moved to Bandung, leaving behind their son, Liem Sian Hong, to complete

---

[3] Garuda is a fabled phoenix-like bird inspired by ancient Hindu mythology.

his degree in Holland. At the time I was receiving a small allowance in guilders to purchase teaching materials from Holland. The allowance, called *boekendelegatie* was held in an account in Holland. I used this money to support my nephew's studies and to defray some expenses incurred by my sister while they were in Holland.

Photo of An, John (aged 3) and Eddie outside the Hotel Lembang at Lembang near Bandung in about 1948.

While I was teaching mathematics and physics at the high school in Pegangsaan, I became pregnant with my second child. When my pregnancy was advanced and I was no longer able to teach in front of a class, the Department asked me to join a special task force translating school text books from Dutch into the new national language of Bahasa Indonesia.

Fortunately, I had maintained close communications with the Department of Education since my return to Jakarta. Frequent visits to Head Office and my membership of the Teachers' Union had put me in good standing with Departmental directors. Fellow teachers would translate other subjects but my responsibility, if I accepted, would be to translate the mathematics and physics textbooks and associated teaching materials. It was a considerable honour and I readily agreed to the challenge.

In the meantime, on the rainy day of 10 January 1949, I gave birth to a daughter, Kang Tjay Ing (meaning "gift of joy") in Jakarta Hospital. From this point on I regarded myself as a "complete" woman. I had given birth earlier to a son and now I had delivered a beautiful baby girl. In my mind, a male and a female had come together to produce another male and a female to replace them. There was a delightful symmetry to this and I was pleased to have had it happen.

The translation exercise took some time and I completed much of it from home after the birth of my daughter. Every week I was required to attend progress meetings at the Department's head office to discuss various aspects of the project such as terminology, grammar, and use of local content in the exercises. For example, instead of questions like, "Jacob and Frieda have ƒ7.50 to buy bread and chocolate from the local shop in Amsterdam", I would replace the text with "Mohammed and Kartini have Rp3.50 to buy rice and durian from the local warung in Medan".

There were constant spelling revisions too because the Indonesian language was being standardized in parallel with our translation efforts. Several times we were told that the official spelling of a particular word had altered, only to find that it had changed again before the task had finished. Finally, the process was completed by the end of the teaching year in June 1949. Even though this was prior to the Dutch handover of Government, I think the Dutch were trying to appease the Indonesians by granting them their demand that all teaching should be conducted in Bahasa Indonesia, except at Dutch-run schools.

At the start of the next school year (August 1949) I returned to active teaching as the Deputy Principal of a newly built senior Teachers' College (SGA — *Sekolah Guru Atas*) in Setiabudi, Jakarta, where I also taught mathematics and physics to trainee teachers using textbooks that I had translated only a few months before. The College had a staff of seven or eight teachers and we graduated around 30 new teachers every year. Within a few years the Teachers' College had tripled in size and this coincided with my promotion to Principal. I now had a staff of 25 teachers and we were graduating about 100 new teachers every year.

I stayed at the SGA until I resigned from the Indonesian Education Department by letter from Australia in 1967, after a total of eighteen years.

Dutch soldiers escorting citizens on the road from Surabaya to Jember during the 1st Police Action against Nationalist rebels in July 1947. (KITLV # 33250)

Parents

At the same time that Eddie and I moved from Tanggul to Jakarta, my parents moved from Tanggul to Kediri. It was just too unsafe to stay in the countryside with marauding Communists, Nationalists, and lawlessness bordering on banditry. The larger cities at least offered a higher degree of protection.

My father, now in his late sixties, retired from the Superintendent's position at the rice mills he had resumed after the war and took his wife to live in their house in Kediri. The mills were still owned by Tjioe Sien An and he appointed another relative to take over father's position of Superintendent.

The house in Kediri to which my parents fled was where Oma Njoo had lived until her death and Father's second wife Kasminah still resided. There were no objections this time from my mother to living in the same house as Kasminah. Times were far too serious for such petty differences. I guess my mother and Kasminah reached an accord. All three people lived under the same roof for the rest of their lives with my mother continuing to sell salted duck eggs as she had done for decades previously.[4] This meagre income was augmented by my parents continuing Oma Njoo's original ice business. These two small businesses were sufficient for them to live comfortably until they died.[5]

Unfortunately Eddie's parents remained trapped in East Java after we had moved to Jakarta. Thankfully they were freed a few months later by the first Dutch military offensive or "Police Action" and put into a camp for their own protection. After a month or so, it was safe enough for them to travel and they came to Jakarta, where Eddie rented a house for them in the nearby suburb of Cikini. They stayed there until their three-year lease expired in 1951 and came to live with us in Jalan Jogja 7 in Menteng.

[4] According to Tan Liem Nio, An's parents did not reside with her mother Kasminah all the time, but looked after the house opposite for their relatives the Djie family (related through Oma Njoo) for over fifteen years until these relatives eventually returned in the early 1960s. After this, An's parents lived out the remainder of their lives with Kasminah.

[5] From discussions with a number of relatives, it is clear that this statement is incorrect. It was Kasminah who continued to operate Oma Njoo's business of ice, syrups, and salted duck eggs for years before and after An's parents came to live in Kediri. An's parents lived off the charity of family members — including Kasminah — until they died. This may be the real cause of a falling out between An and Tan Swan Bing as she wrote letters to her older brother in Holland demanding more money to support their parents. Finally, Tan Swan Bing's wife, Huguette, had had enough and severed any further contact by letter in the 1980s.

8

Independence and Faltering Nationhood (1949–59)

The End of Colonial Rule

While the military situation was not going well for the Nationalists at home, it was another matter entirely on the international stage. There, the Nationalists held the political advantage. From the end of World War II the mood of international politics had radically changed. Empires were now considered to be a thing of the past. The Japanese, Germans and Italians had their colonies stripped from them and the Americans and British were at the forefront of a pro-independence movement within the newly-created United Nations. Only the French, Portuguese, Spanish and Dutch resisted this new attitude, but the anti-colonial momentum was growing so strongly that it seemed only a matter of time before these countries would have to grant independence to their colonies too.

In the case of Indonesia, the stalemate was broken when the American Government threatened to cut off Marshall Plan aid to Holland if the Dutch did not get out of Indonesia. But we never heard about that at the time in Indonesia. In fact the history of independence taught to all Indonesians has continually emphasized that it was the Nationalists alone who eventually forced the Dutch to the negotiating table, without any outside assistance. To this day, I am puzzled and perplexed that it may have been the Americans and not the Nationalists who finally convinced Holland to recognize Indonesia's Independence.

Independence, At Last

In 1949, despite strenuous Dutch opposition, the United Nations (UN) voted overwhelmingly in favour of Indonesia becoming an independent nation. Later that year an international Round Table Conference was organized by the UN in Holland to work out the details of the handover.

Meanwhile, back in Jakarta President Sukarno still resided at Jalan Pegangsaan 56, protected by his troops, while the Dutch Governor, van Mook, resided at the official Palace. Finally on 27 Dec. 1949 the new nation of Indonesia officially came into being with the formal signing over of power by Queen Juliana of the Netherlands. Indonesia was now truly independent and the next day I remember Sukarno receiving a tumultuous ovation in Jakarta to celebrate the event. He moved into the Governor's residence, immediately renaming it the Presidential Palace.

A crowd in Jakarta jubilantly heralds Sukarno at the formal announcement of the Dutch handover of power in December 1949. (Image courtesy of <www.gimonca. com/sejarah>)

When the Dutch Government finally handed over power at the end of 1949, all the Dutch people who held senior positions in the Department of Education were replaced by Indonesians. I am sure this happened in other government departments too. Prior to this, no indigenous Indonesian had ever held a top position such as director within a government department but the incoming Nationalist Government made certain that a level of professionalism remained by replacing only the very top echelon of employees. Some Dutch were encouraged to remain, but they were mainly people in the middle or lower ranks of the bureaucracy such as teachers or clerks. Their roles were to help the new administration become proficient and professional as quickly as possible.

One outcome of the handover of power was that many Dutch — and Indonesians sympathetic to the Dutch cause — left Indonesia, mainly to Holland, but also to Australia. Once started, the exodus would continue for a decade. By 1960 very few of the original 250,000–300,000 Dutch citizens remained in Indonesia.

However, many of the big Dutch companies remained in Indonesia after 1949 and continued to operate more or less as normal until the end of 1957. Even though the Government had changed with Independence, business remained essentially the same. The public and private sector still operated the same way as it had done previously under the Dutch. The only two things that changed were the language (from Dutch to Bahasa Indonesia) and power (from the Dutch to the native Indonesians).

Inflation

Sometime during 1950 the Indonesian Government did something very strange regarding the currency. Inflation was beginning to show itself and the Government asked all citizens literally to cut the bank notes in two. The right-hand side of the bank note could be exchanged for a government bond; the face value on the left-hand side of the note was immediately devalued by half. If the original note was 100 rupiahs, then the halved note became Rp 50 overnight.

It was a bizarre feeling transacting everyday business with only half a bank note, but people seemed to get on with everyday life without much comment. Within a few months the Government had issued fresh, full-sized, banknotes and quickly withdrew the old currency from circulation. Everyone was given only a few days to exchange their half notes for the new before the old currency was declared worthless.

The PETA Soldiers

Immediately after the Revolutionary War, the new Government of Indonesia faced the problem of creating a modern, professional army out of the estimated 120,000 PETA soldiers who had been fighting Japanese, British and then Dutch troops for the previous several years. These troops were regarded by the general population as heroes but the problem for the Government was that they were ill-trained, uneducated and, unfortunately, heavily armed. Any solution would require delicate handling.

The Government came up with a proposal to offer free high school education to every PETA soldier so that they could either go on to university or secure better jobs with their new educational qualifications. The trouble was that many PETA troops regarded this offer as a reward for their efforts without the need to actually study, and most people knew it.

Soldiers in their tens of thousands went about their daily tasks without bothering to attend the classes which had been specially provided for them. Two years later, as the time neared for them to sit their final high school exams, many teachers became uncomfortable with the prospect of marking their examination papers. It was even rumoured that some soldiers were still illiterate, having never attended any schooling in their young lives or any special classes provided by the Government, yet they were expecting automatically to receive a high school certificate. Senior Government officials in the Department of Education approached a handpicked number of teachers, including myself, to set the special exams for the PETA soldiers.

We examiners were never told outright to set an easy exam but we clearly understood that the easier the exam, the better it would be for everyone. My personal quandary was that I had never set an unduly easy exam before in my whole teaching career and I did not want to compromise my standards now for the political expediency of the Government. Yet the prevailing fear was that the soldiers, who had not been disarmed in the two years since the end of the war, would resort to violence against us teachers, or the Government, if they did not get the exam results they expected.

I told the Department officials that I would set the mathematics and physics exams according to my usual standards, but only if my anonymity could be assured. Other teachers who were asked to prepare the remaining subjects bravely asked for the same condition. The Departmental officials agreed and we prepared the exam papers together with the answer templates a few weeks before the exam date and handed them into the Department for safe-keeping.

A short time later a stranger arrived at my house in Menteng, dressed in a PETA soldier's uniform, and offered me the considerable sum of 50,000 rupiah for the exam results. I was shocked but had the presence of mind to plead ignorance. I convinced the man that I had not set any papers, did not know who had and that his approach to me was a case of mistaken identity.

I never told the authorities about this incident as I did not want an official investigation that might identify the person, for then he would probably return to my house armed with a weapon to intimidate or kill me.

Some weeks later thousands of PETA soldiers sat for their exams across Indonesia and, not surprisingly, almost all of them passed. I say "not surprisingly" because even though the papers had been prepared to the usual high standard, I knew that once in the hands of the Education Department anything could happen. Either the exam questions and answers were leaked in advance, or the examiners were prevailed upon to pass all but the most undeserving. Either way, my conscience was clear. I had not compromised my integrity and I could not be held responsible for what happened to the exam papers after I had prepared them.

Modes of Transport

Though surrounded by family and servants who could drive a motor vehicle, I have never had to learn to drive in my life. My husband first learned to drive a motor vehicle of any description when he was 29 and we were visiting his oldest brother, Kang Hoo Tjong, in Jember in 1950.[1] At the time our two children were young, Ingrid, the youngest being just a baby, and Eddie decided that we needed an automobile to transport the family around. His brother gave driving lessons in his Chevrolet convertible and Eddie had no difficulty obtaining a driver's licence from the local Police.

Back in Jakarta, even though we could not afford to buy a car, Eddie used his driving licence as proof of competency to obtain a motor-cycle licence without the need for testing. He purchased a 125cc Vespa scooter in 1951 and a 200cc TWN motor-cycle followed in 1953. Meanwhile the children were growing and becoming too big for a motor-cycle, so my husband used it for himself or to take me on long trips, such as to Bandung. The following year, he purchased another, slightly bigger motor-cycle (a 250cc Czechoslovakian-made Jawa motor-cycle) and then in late 1954 our first car, a second-hand Skoda from a relative in Bandung. The car was a rust bucket of inferior manufacture from communist Czechoslovakia but we used it on and off over the next six years.

---

[1] While Eddie was "adopted" by his father's brother and wife and raised as a single child, he was one of five children, a fact unknown to him until his adulthood.

Jalan Jogja 7, Menteng

We rented part of the house, sharing it with officers from the army. They were all single and from 1949 to 1955 we pleasantly co-existed — except for one incident involving our chickens — and even had some very happy times together sharing the joy of three of the officers getting married and moving out to their own homes. Being tenants, we paid our rent to the *Huisvesting Organisatie van Batavia* (HOB – Housing Organization of Batavia), which managed a large number of properties on behalf of absentee Dutch owners.

In 1953, with Ingrid soon to join her brother at a privately run Dutch school in Jakarta, we were looking at paying expensive school fees for both our children. My husband started a small chicken farm in the backyard of our home to augment our income and help pay off the expenses of the children's education. These were not the scrawny chickens you would typically find scratching around in a village.

Eddie purchased internationally recognized breeds, rarely seen elsewhere in Indonesia, such as Rhode Island Red, Australorp and Leghorn obtained

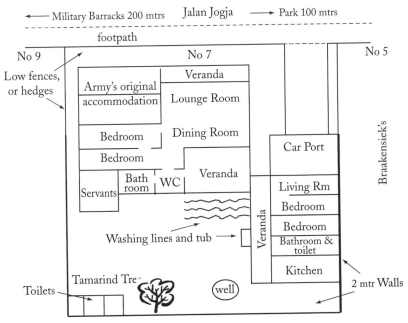

Home at Jalan Jogja 7, Menteng in Jakarta, where I lived from 1947–67.

from the only licensed importer we knew about in Bandung. The chicks were hatched by incubation and for the first few weeks were occasionally hand-raised by our children before being released into the yard. Eddie was buying commercial seed pellets from the same importer in Bandung, who was also the only source of commercial poultry feed in Indonesia, and as a result produced excellent plump chickens. This commercial feed was so popular that my husband purposefully bought more than we needed to sell on to other farmers in the Jakarta area for profit.

Tengku (Prince) Halim was an important and wealthy person who was a junior member of the royal family in Medan, known as the Sultanate of Deli. Eddie met Tengku Halim in 1953 when my husband was working for Garuda as a Sales Manager and in charge of training all new sales staff, of which the young prince was just one of many. We invited the prince to our home in Menteng and he was impressed by the big fat chickens my husband was raising at the time in our back yard. Tengku Halim said that Medan had no commercial chicken producers and wanted to know if Eddie would be interested in starting a commercial chicken farm there to produce thousands of chickens on land he owned in North Sumatra. My husband declined the offer, without offending Tengku Halim of course, and eventually the prince returned to Medan, where he ran the sales office for Garuda. For some years afterwards we exchanged parcels of seasonal and local fruit to each other. My husband continued profitably to raise chickens and sell their eggs from our house until they were all poisoned in 1954.

One of the Army lieutenants at Jalan Jogja 7 had objected to the dust and noise associated with the birds, especially the roosters crowing at dawn, and told us to get rid of them — or he would. A few weeks later, I awoke one morning to find that all our birds had died overnight. The Veterinarian we called performed several autopsies and confirmed that rat poison was the cause.

As we did not want to antagonize our fellow army tenants with whom we had generally a very good relationship, we ceased commercial chicken farming at our house from that moment on. Thankfully, Eddie was soon able to take a more highly paid job with a timber company and we did not need the extra income. For my husband though, it had been more than just a source of money, it was a hobby that he loved and was good at. However, he never raised chickens again.

In early 1956 Captain Hamijoyo was replaced by Captain Said Pratalikusuma at Jalan Jogja. From the moment he arrived, the domestic atmosphere turned dramatically for the worse. The political climate between

Holland and Indonesia also deteriorated during 1956 and the Indonesian Government made it clear that, if the situation did not improve, any remaining Dutch would be expelled from Indonesia and all Dutch property would be confiscated. We had known for some time that Jalan Jogja 7 along with several adjacent properties was owned by Mrs Ogilvy who, despite her English-sounding name, was a Dutch national residing in Holland.

We feared that the Army might simply kick us out if the properties were confiscated, so we wrote to the owner offering to purchase the individual land and house we were renting and asking them to set a reasonable sale price under the circumstances. After some delay we received a reply from Mrs Ogilvy's son, who obviously thought that the Indonesian Government was bluffing about the threat to seize Dutch property, because he asked a staggering f10,000 for the land and house. It was the equivalent of almost five times my annual salary as an executive public servant and approximately ten years annual salary for an average wage earner.

Of course we could not afford this figure, but before we could reply with a counter offer the Dutch were expelled, and true to their word, the Indonesian Government confiscated all Dutch assets in the country without any financial compensation.[2] Afterwards, we sometimes wondered about Mrs Ogilvy in Holland and how she must have felt about losing all her property investments in Indonesia worth a fortune in today's terms. If only her son had taken the Indonesian government threats more seriously, we both might have achieved what we wanted. We would have owned a valuable piece of property in the middle of Jakarta and he would have received a reasonable figure for its sale under the circumstances. Unfortunately political events deteriorated faster than landlord and tenant could manage.

After confiscating Dutch private property, the Indonesian Government determined that the longest serving tenants across Indonesia would have first option to purchase the former Dutch landholdings. In Bandung, my sister Roostien and her husband Liem Sing Giap took up this offer and purchased the property they had been previously renting in that city, but in Jakarta my husband and I were never offered the property. As it turned out, the property was offered to and purchased by the Army, even though they had become

---

[2] The seizures began in December 1957 after the United Nations had rejected Indonesia's call for sovereignty over Dutch New Guinea. Nationalization was not formalized until 1960 and negotiations over compensation dragged on for many years. Dutch nationals who did not wish to become Indonesian citizens were expelled in 1958.

co-tenants after us. From that point on in mid-1956, we knew we were living there on borrowed time. Sometime in the future, we knew we would be evicted and that there would be nothing we could do about it.

Pratalikusuma's wife gave birth to their first child not long after taking up residence in 1956, but it was a sickly baby and intolerant of noise. In October that year, we had a party at home to celebrate John's eleventh birthday and a half a dozen school friends were present to celebrate. Halfway through the party while the children were noisily playing games, Pratalikusuma burst into our living room. He made some heated complaints about the noise and worked himself up into a rage. He suddenly started to punch Eddie repeatedly in the head. A signet ring he was wearing caused deep lacerations, profuse bleeding and a depressed cranium. My husband still bears the marks of that assault, having a noticeable dent in his forehead to this day. My mother-in-law was present and pleaded with Captain Pratalikusuma in Madurese dialect to stop hitting him. The Captain broke off the attack and walked away still fuming, leaving my husband dazed and badly beaten.

I was hysterical. I knew that we could not report the matter to the authorities for one just did not accuse military personnel, nor seek hospital treatment because Captain Pratalikusuma would hear of it and retaliate further. In short, we could do nothing about the assault. We were powerless, so I directed my anger at Eddie, shouting at him such things as, "Do not provoke him. Do not upset him". I realised that Eddie had not incited the confrontation, but nevertheless I was so afraid for our family that I yelled at my injured husband, "If he can do this to you, then he can get away with killing any one of us whenever he wants and no one will care. Is that what you want?" But Eddie was not listening; he was beaten so badly he just moaned in semi-consciousness.

With the help of our servants and my mother-in-law, we cleaned up Eddie's wounds as best we could, but more than forty years later I still see that depression in his skull and shudder at the thought of what might have happened if Pratalikusuma had not stopped.

Good Neighbours — Braakensiek

Our next door neighbour at Jalan Jogja 5, Herman Braakensiek, was the owner of a gold-refining business in Jakarta. His company produced high-quality bullion in a factory protected by armed guards in Jalan Hayam Wuruk, Kota, in the old part of Jakarta. The company was one of only a few that had Government permission to smelt gold and the gold ingots bore the company stamp, not a Government stamp, to attest to their purity. They were very wealthy people and had been living at No. 5 for some years before we arrived as their next-door neighbours in 1947.

For the next decade we very much enjoyed each other's company and our children, who were about the same age, regularly played together. They had three children Herman (Junior), who was about the same age as our John, Meikel (Margaret), who was a year older than Ingrid, and Corina, the youngest. The family left Indonesia hurriedly for Holland in early 1958 after his business was nationalized and their home confiscated by the Indonesian Government.

My Husband's Work

In 1950 my husband passed the demanding Commercial Airline course with the recently renamed Garuda Indonesia Airlines (GIA) with the second highest marks in the class of twenty students. He was immediately rewarded by being elevated to the position of Sales Promoter in Garuda's sales department at the head office in Jakarta. It was only a small office of five people but it had the responsibility of generating all the company's commercial and government revenue from firms and public sector agencies which had located their head offices in the capital. The preferred method of selling was through establishing a strong network of business and personal relationships in the various companies and government departments. Although firms in Western countries know of this practice and have even given it a name — relationship selling — it is not the West's preferred form of doing business, but in Asia it is.

My husband was exceptional at relationship selling. He was empathetic and quickly created strong relationships out of a genuine desire to please.[3] Over the next five years he worked his way up the promotional ladder until he was second-in-charge of the Sales Department. In the process he had established an extensive network of mainly Dutch contacts throughout the capital.

---

[3] Part of Eddie's method of building a network of business contacts was to entertain the senior personnel of client companies. He would arrange dances, take clients to a rarely performed opera in Jakarta, and lavish expensive meals on these people. Over time, many business contacts became friends and Eddie developed personal relationships with numerous senior company executives.

In 1953 Eddie was offered a promotion as Garuda's regional manager for South Sumatra, based in the river city of Jambi. The position involved maintaining close business ties with the agricultural community in the region, particularly the valuable rubber plantations, and carried with it a significant pay rise. However, we discovered that there were no Dutch schools in Jambi for our children, so reluctantly Eddie declined the offer and continued to work in Garuda's main office in Jakarta office until 1955.

Eddie was happy enough in his job, but after Garuda was nationalized by the Indonesian Government in 1954 he felt that he could do better elsewhere. That opportunity came in December 1955 when he was lured across from Garuda to work as the Sales Manager for a family-owned timber trading company called Sioe Liem Kongsie. This was at the personal request of its owner Go Ing Hoe, who was related to us through my father's cousin, Tjioe Sien An.[4] Go Ing Hoe needed an honest and trustworthy manager and offered my husband a significant pay rise to work for him. Shortly after, Go Ing Hoe relocated to Rotterdam in Holland, leaving Eddie in charge of much of the day-to-day operations of the business in Indonesia out of its head office in Jakarta.

Returning home from his first day at work with Sioe Liem Kongsie in December 1955, my husband had a slow-speed collision with a truck on Jalan Diponegoro, which was near our house. He had ridden his motorcycle that day as he did not trust the unreliable Skoda to ensure that he got to work on time. The next day when Go Ing Hoe saw the cuts and bruises on Eddie's face and hands he said, "That's it. You're not going to ride a bike any more. I'll give you a company car instead." That afternoon I was very surprised and pleased to see Eddie arrive home in a dark green Fiat 1100 car. My husband drove the Fiat for the next three years while he was employed at Sioe Liem Kongsie and used it for both company and personal purposes, as was the normal custom.

My husband's predominantly Dutch network of commercial contacts built through years of hard work at KLM/ Garuda appeared set to expand Sioe Liem Kongsie's business. As a major timber supplier, Sioe Liem Kongsie earned revenue from export as well as domestic sales. It was about

---

[4] Sioe Liem Kongsie was a Surabaya-based firm owned by three brothers: Go Ing Tjwan (eldest), Go Ing Hian, and Go Ing Hoe (youngest). Go Ing Hoe had married Jeanne Tjioe, the daughter of Tjioe Sien An who had earlier appointed An's father to the position of Superintendent of the rice mills in East Java. Decades later the Tjioe, Tan and Kang families were still very close and continuing to help each other out.

this time that our neighbour, Herman Braakensiek, successfully nominated Eddie for membership of the exclusive Tanjung Priok Yacht Club. Of course my husband did not sail, but that was not the point of membership. Up to that time the club had been the exclusive domain of the Dutch, but with so many Dutch people leaving Indonesia, membership was in severe decline. Club officials needed more members and more revenue to maintain the very high level of service for which the club was renowned. Meals were served on tables covered with white starched linen by a battery of servants offering food on silver platters. A band played western music every Saturday night at a dance where members and their guests were obliged to wear formal attire. It was living at its most indulgent level and we felt very privileged to be welcomed into this world.

My husband used the club mainly to socialize with family and friends, but occasionally it was put to great effect as a venue for a business luncheon or dinner. Eddie's clients were always impressed by the club's atmosphere and my husband's membership to it, as many thought it was still off limits to Asians and native Indonesians. Whenever my husband took clients to the Yacht Club, he felt that he was able to negotiate a better business deal.

While the export business still relied heavily on mainly Dutch contacts overseas and was doing well, the domestic side of the business relied upon indigenous contacts and was suffering. It appeared that indigenous Indonesians were increasingly conducting business directly between themselves in the domestic marketplace and no longer needed Chinese traders to act as brokers. Eddie began to realize that he would be better off in a purely export-oriented business where indigenous Indonesians would have to rely upon him rather than other Indonesians. Eddie did manage to build up domestic sales for Sioe Liem Kongsie but it was a struggle. He was much better at exporting timber overseas.

During late 1958, somewhat disappointed with years of frustrated effort and wanting to return to the one export-oriented industry he knew and liked — airlines — Eddie readily accepted an invitation from a friend to meet the Territory Manager of an international airline who was looking for a new Sales Manager in Indonesia. The company was TAI (*Transport Aériens Intercontinenteaux*) and its Territory Manager in Indonesia was Daniel Richez, a French national.[5]

---

[5] TAI eventually became UTA (*Union de Transports Aériens*) in October 1963 and subsequently Air France in 1993.

When they met for the first time, Daniel Richez told my husband that the company had only recently set up in Indonesia but he had already had a bad experience with a dishonest employee whom he had to dismiss. He needed to hire a new Sales Manager who not only had extensive business contacts but, more importantly, was someone Richez could trust. Eddie found out later that Richez had already conducted some informal background checks on my husband and had been impressed by what he had discovered. My husband was indeed reliable and had worked diligently over the previous three years to build a new network of business contacts with the indigenous leaders of the Indonesian public and private sector, including knowing the Manager of Jakarta Airport whom Eddie classed as a close personal friend. My husband and Daniel Richez struck up a friendship from the very first meeting. Richez felt so comfortable with Eddie that he offered my husband the position of Sales Manager on the spot!

Eddie accepted the position, but did the right thing with Sioe Liem Kongsie by handing in his fortnight's notice to the timber company and clearing up unfinished business before he started at TAI two weeks later in September 1958.

My husband was quite aware that TAI then only had a small presence in Indonesia, but he believed he could significantly contribute to its growth. TAI only had one office, located in Jakarta, for the whole of Indonesia. Apart from my husband as the newly appointed Sales Manager, there were only two other employees, Daniel Richez, the Territory Manager for Indonesia, and Michel Priou, the Station manager in charge of operations at Jakarta's airport. Unusually, for companies operating in Indonesia, there was no clerical or administrative staff apart from a driver for Richez's car. Eddie would soon change that by bringing in a great deal of business.

A company motor vehicle was not included in his employment package with TAI, so Eddie started driving our old Skoda again, apart from a brief two week period at the beginning when Richez left to attend a company meeting in Paris and we had access to his car and driver in his absence. However, the Skoda was never a satisfactory solution for it was in poor condition and Richez was embarrassed to see my husband use it to attend business meetings and convey clients to the airport.

Luckily, a few months after Eddie started work, Monsieur Michel Priou was transferred back to France and Richez sold Priou's car to Eddie at a very attractive price. The Peugeot 203 was a beautiful car with internal wood-grain finish and a sunroof which everyone enjoyed. When we went to Bandung to visit our relatives, Ida and Ban Kong Karyadi,[6] their children wanted to ride in the Peugeot all the time and to stick their heads through the open sunroof, even though Ban Kong owned a more expensive Mercedes at the time!

After Independence, KLM had continued to service most of Indonesia's overseas air requirements while Indonesia's own company Garuda had supplied the domestic market. When KLM hastily pulled out of Indonesia to avoid confiscation of its assets by the Indonesian government in late 1957, Garuda was left to take over the international business as well. However, KLM had taken its planes and pilots with it and without long-haul planes and skilled pilots to fly them, Garuda found the task near impossible. One of the more important and lucrative routes KLM had previously serviced involved taking Indonesians to Mecca for the pilgrimage or Haj.

For people wishing to travel from Indonesia to Mecca for the Haj, citizens needed a special travel permit from the Department of Religion as well as the normal requirements for a passport and visa. While most pilgrims travelled by ship, each year a few hundred rich and influential Muslims were allowed to travel by air, which since the early 1950s the Department had organized through chartering planes from KLM. The Department would then act as travel agent in granting permits to fill the number of seats and charge a handsome price for the privilege. The destination was the port city of Jeddah on the Saudi coast, from where pilgrims would travel overland to Mecca to join the Haj ceremonies.

Now that Indonesia's own airline could not fill this demand, Eddie saw a huge business opportunity for TAI from the very moment he joined the company. TAI was a charter airline that was using Indonesia as a stop-over for planes flying to French Polynesia and Australia. My husband believed that if he could get the Indonesian Government to charter TAI planes for Haj pilgrims, it would get the Government out of trouble and provide a substantial new source of revenue for his new employer.

Eddie ran his proposal past Monsieur Richez who, although doubtful of my husband's ability to succeed, nevertheless gave his full support to go ahead. The person in the Government whom Eddie had to approach with his proposal was the Secretary in the Department of Religion. Thankfully he knew this person from his days with Garuda. Apart from rekindling a past friendship, the timing could not have been better because the

---

[6] Ban Kong Karyadi had married Roostien's eldest daughter, Ida.

117

Photo of DC-6B with TAI company livery in 1961.
(Image from <www.chez.com/utawebfan/html/new/UAT_TAI>)

Department was desperate for a solution. Some influential Muslim leaders, frustrated at the Government's inability to organize air transport for them, were getting increasingly agitated.

My husband and the Secretary struck a deal immediately in American dollars to charter two DC-6B planes for the then considerable sum of US$27,500 each. Of course, what Eddie did not tell the Secretary was that TAI would make a total of US$10,000 profit out of the entire contract. This was an enormous sum at the time. When converted to Indonesian currency, Eddie's ten thousand dollar profit was worth a staggering forty million Indonesian rupiah!

By chartering planes from TAI, the Indonesian Government not only got itself out of a political bind but also made more money than it expected. The DC-6Bs chartered from TAI carried 80 passengers, whereas the previously chartered planes from KLM were Lockheed "Constellations" carrying only 55 passengers. The Department was delighted to fill more seats for a greater profit than before. Eddie rushed back to inform Monsieur Richez of his coup and the entire office of only three people spent the rest of the day getting drunk! It was one of the only times I have seen my husband intoxicated but I did not mind at all. He had pulled off a remarkable deal for himself and his new company and Richez was ecstatic. He later told me that Eddie had sold more business in one day than Richez had been able to achieve in the whole previous year!

As a reward, Monsieur Richez resolved to pay Eddie his wages surreptitiously in American dollars from then on. It was illegal to possess, transact business, or pay wages in a foreign currency without Government approval, but nevertheless some did and there was a thriving black market to convert foreign currency into Indonesian rupiah. Black marketeers were so anxious to get their hands on American dollars that they were willing to pay many times the official exchange rate. My husband was paid US$390 per month and, as was the normal custom at the time, he received thirteen months wages every year, the extra month's payment being a bonus for good work.

The arrangement with his company was that my husband would receive the equivalent of US$40 in Indonesian currency every month to live off and the remaining US$350 per month would accumulate and be paid into a foreign bank account once a year in arrears.

Forty American dollars per month may seem a paltry amount but, when converted to local currency on the black market, that US$40 produced enough rupiahs to pay for everything we needed. Occasionally, Eddie would take the US dollars to a contact in central Jakarta and return with a briefcase full of rupiahs. At the time I was earning a good salary too, having been promoted to Principal of the Teachers' College from 1953, so between us we started earning a small fortune every month from 1958 on.

Family Connections

Around 1952 Eddie's father, who along with his wife had been living in Jakarta for almost five years, yearned to return to the country where he had lived all his life and to start a rural business again. Leaving his wife behind in Jakarta, he travelled to East Java to try his hand at business again, but before he got started he had a serious fall and broke his hip. Eddie helped him convalesce in the hospital at the Jatiroto sugar mill until he was well enough to travel and then brought him back to Jakarta. He never left again and stayed in Jakarta until his death sixteen years later.

My father's cousin, Tjioe Sien An, who figures so prominently in my father's life, was forced to sell his rice mills in East Java by a piece of Government legislation directed against Chinese Indonesians and other foreigners. In 1954 the Government issued a regulation restricting the ownership of rice mills to Indonesian citizens only. I suspected this relative of mine, like so many other Chinese Indonesians, had not taken up Indonesian citizenship years earlier at the time of Independence and now was being forced to relinquish ownership of his rice mills because he was technically an alien resident.

Tjioe Sien An arranged to sell his mills to a buyer who promised him payment in American dollars, but the exchange had to take place in Singapore as it was illegal to conduct foreign currency transactions inside Indonesia. He intended to convert the US currency into rupiah in Singapore and return to Indonesia so rich that he would be regarded as a plutocrat, but when it was time to go the authorities would not grant him a visa and he had to send his daughter instead. Unfortunately, she was not as adept at business as her father and was duped into accepting the agreed price in rupiah, not US currency. The amount was still large, but if my Uncle had been paid the agreed figure in American dollars as expected he would have been 4,000 times richer.

Even though the sale of the rice mills made Tjioe Sien An wealthy, he nevertheless became depressed at being cheated out of the huge sum of money he had expected. He relocated his family to a smaller house in Surabaya, where he continued to fret over the loss of such an enormous fortune. We had not seen him for a few years when he visited us in Jakarta in the late 1950s. He had aged visibly and was now gaunt, but his behaviour had altered too. Though it may seem like a small thing, he kept washing his hands obsessively whenever he ate. In Indonesia, individual fingerbowls and towels are usually provided with each meal, but Tjioe Sien An would wash and dry his hands after every mouthful and constantly leave the table to replenish the bowl with fresh water, or wash his hands even more thoroughly under the tap with soap. We thought this behaviour a little strange and even my daughter, Ingrid, remarked on it, but we did not know at the time that it was related to clinical depression. He returned to Surabaya and died a short time later in the late 1950s.

Raising Children

When Ingrid was a little girl, I taught her the same games I had learned when I was a child such as *bikkelen* (jacks) and *touwtje springen* (skipping). Ingrid was taught to cook by Eddie's mother who was living with us in Menteng for most of Ingrid's childhood. My mother-in-law and I had both grown up in households that had servants and a cook but, unlike me, my mother-in-law had taken notice of what the cook was doing and learned how to cook. She derived great pleasure in teaching this skill to Ingrid.

When the children were small, Eddie purchased a number of ready-made kite kits from a local warung as the kite-flying season approached and helped John to assemble them.[7] Then we went down to nearby *Bisschopsplein* (Bishop's Park, renamed Taman Suropati after Independence) and instructed both children how to get the kites aloft and keep them in the air. Over weeks John became quite competent at this activity. Ingrid, who was only five at the time, was too young to manage the intricacies of kite-flying. She would run around all over the park, trailing her kite behind her and expending a lot of energy, but never managing to get a single one aloft. In the end, she watched adoringly as her brother grew more confident and more skilful.

The next season, my husband graduated John to the level of "fighting kites". First he taught John how to apply glass-powder to the strings so that his kite could cut the control lines of competing kites and over weeks we would regularly attend the park while John honed his skills. John enjoyed the activity greatly, but it takes years of experience to become an expert. Kite-flying in Indonesia is a serious business and at the elite level is performed by master kite-flyers with decades of training behind them. Nevertheless, for some years afterwards John and Ingrid would go to the park each kite-flying season and take much pleasure out of this hobby.

There were a number of foreign embassies in the streets around our home, including the Norwegian embassy which was directly behind us over the back fence. They would periodically host outdoor parties and film nights in their rear garden. Sometimes Ingrid would climb up the tamarind tree growing in our rear yard and use it to scuttle across to the two-metre high back wall and watch the activities in the embassy's back yard. Being a little girl of between eight and ten in the late 1950s, she would pretend that she was a guest at the embassy's party and even fantasize about finding her Prince Charming among the invited gathering.

Sometime later in the early 1960s, when the political environment was becoming unstable, the Norwegian embassy topped the wall with broken glass and barbed-wire to deter undesirables from climbing over it and

---

[7] The kite-flying season in Jakarta is signalled by the arrival of on-shore trade winds that blow constantly across the city for about two months each year during September and October.

entering the Embassy grounds. However, by then Ingrid was an adolescent and those tree-climbing and fairy-tale days were already behind her.

Tengku Halim's offer to start a commercial chicken farm in North Sumatra was the first time that I had thought about the city of Medan, but the first time I actually visited the regional capital was in 1955 when we took the whole family on a holiday to the Sumatran resort of Prapat on Danau Toba. We flew into and out of Medan and stayed overnight there on our way to and from the resort by taxi. Medan was a lovely city of a million or so inhabitants with wide boulevards and a real cosmopolitan atmosphere. Danau Toba was stunningly beautiful with silica beaches around the edges of this inland fresh-water lake with the finest white sand I have ever seen. It was as fine as crystals of castor sugar and glittered at night from the moonlight like a cache of diamonds!

Eddie learnt to water ski and John, then ten, took to canoeing. I whiled away the time with Ingrid, then six, building sandcastles and taking walks together. Each morning we would take the family for a walk along the beaches and observe the fishermen stringing out their previous evening's catch on bamboo poles to dry. We were introduced to the soft, succulent taste of freshwater carp during this trip. It was like nothing we had ever eaten before.

I took some of the sand back with me in a large jar for our aquarium at home and on our return journey we were stopped at the airport to have our bags searched. Under the Government at the time, imports were severely restricted. Because Medan was regarded as a haven for smugglers the authorities in Jakarta had taken the unprecedented step of searching all luggage from people arriving on domestic flights from that city. When the inspection officer discovered my jar, he thought it was contraband sugar and opened the jar to taste it. He ignored my warnings that it was only sand and scooped up a small quantity into his mouth. He immediately spat out the contents in disgust and waved us though without inspecting any more of our luggage.

Breakdown in Dutch–Indonesian Relations

By December 1957 the relationship between Holland and Indonesia had reached a point where President Sukarno ordered the repatriation of Dutch residents remaining in Indonesia and nationalized all the Dutch companies that were operating in Indonesia. No compensation or assistance was offered at all and the Dutch residents had just three months to put their affairs in order and leave. By March 1958, Indonesia proudly announced that it had nationalized over 500 Dutch firms and expelled the last remaining 30,000 Dutch residents, out of a Dutch population in Indonesia of between 250,000–300,000 twenty years earlier. In 1958, my brother Tan Swan Bing, having been a Dutch citizen for over twenty years, left for Holland with his family, joining the Dutch exodus.

The majority of indigenous Indonesians were in favour of this dramatic action as finally ridding themselves of the last vestiges of their colonial past. We Chinese viewed it differently. Most Chinese Indonesians considered the move to be commercially stupid and likely to threaten the economy even more. Not only was the Indonesian Government removing the very people they desperately needed for future economic growth and political stability; if they could do it to the Dutch, we feared that it was only a matter of time before they did it to us Chinese Indonesians.

My Own School

When the Dutch schools were officially closed by Presidential Decree in December 1957, I decided to teach my son John at home. There were many bright, intelligent students who were having difficulties adjusting from the Dutch education system to the Indonesian one, the main problem being the different languages of instruction. Other parents of students at the Concordante School, which John and Ingrid had attended, asked me to teach their children too. As I had sufficient qualifications and could easily obtain Government approval, I decided to start my own private school, called *Harapan Kita* (Our Hope).

I had developed good relations with the Department of Education going back over a decade by setting the exam papers for mathematics and physics for both junior and senior high school students across all of Indonesia and coordinating the marking of them afterwards. I chose the name because I believe that our children are our future, our hope, and that the greatest gift we can give them is education.

The school was located in our home at Jalan Jogja and I commenced classes in December 1957 with only three students: my son John, Liem Tjie Hwa and Ong Kiem Sian. At the start of the next teaching year in July 1958, they were joined by Lie Mu Lhan, a family friend and swimming club member, and Liem Giok An. Her father had a chemical factory and he was recommended to enrol his daughter by the Lie family. Lie Mu Lhan's mother had a florist business which she operated from her home and during busy periods, such as Christmas and Chinese New Year, Eddie and I would help fill out her orders. By July 1959, the enrolment numbers had increased to eleven and each year Harapan Kita continued to grow until it reached a total of about eighty students in 1967.

From 1958, we parked the Skoda permanently in a specific part of our driveway at Jalan Jogja to create space for assemblies and recreation behind it. We did this as a deliberate strategy to prevent Captain Said Pratalikusuma from parking his car there and depriving Harapan Kita of using the space. It stayed there for another two years, continuing to fall apart, until Eddie replaced it with a bus from TAI which he arranged to garage at Jalan Jogja. Finally, in 1960 he abandoned the Skoda on a nearby street outside Taman Suropati, where a neighbour recognized it as ours and asked our permission to take it.

9

Political Instability and Personal Consequences (1959–67)

Citizenship and Growing Anti-Chinese Discrimination

Under the provisions of the Round Table Conference which decided the terms of Indonesia's Independence, the sensitive matter of citizenship for its 70 million inhabitants was also resolved. Native Indonesians automatically became Indonesian citizens while Eurasians could accept Indonesian nationality or the nationality of their European forebears. Likewise, *peranakan* Chinese, that is Chinese born in Indonesia, had a choice between Indonesia or China, but *totok* Chinese, that is Chinese born outside Indonesia, were ineligible for Indonesian citizenship.

In reality it was not that simple. I believe the Indonesian Government wanted to rid itself completely of Chinese, so they structured the arrangement in such a way that everyone who had not accepted Indonesian citizenship by December 1951 was automatically regarded as an "alien" and therefore liable for expulsion. In practice, however, most Chinese in Indonesia (peranakan and totok alike) ignored this government direction and continued living in the country with their nationality unresolved.

Throughout the 1950s the Government imposed progressively harsher legislation to force the issue of nationality and Indonesia became increasingly more difficult to live in if you were ethnically Chinese. After 1954, a succession of discriminatory government decrees officially sanctioned anti-Chinese prejudices which had never been far below the surface. Priority was given to financial and other government support for *pribumi* (native) enterprises at the expense of Chinese businesses. New laws prevented Chinese from purchasing rural property (1954), owning rice mills (1954), or studying at University (1955) and in 1957 Chinese-operated schools were forced to close. In 1958 newspapers and magazines printed in the Chinese language were banned.

Then there was a Presidential Order (*Peraturan Presiden* No. 10 of 1959), instigated at the insistence of some Muslim politicians, which banned Chinese from participating in any form of retail trade in rural areas. This latest edict was catastrophic! Chinese in their hundreds of thousands earned their livelihoods from trading, just as many Chinese before them had done so for centuries, but this decree suddenly denied many Chinese in Indonesia a right to earn a living. The only way out was for Chinese traders to bring indigenous Indonesians into the business at senior levels or else the Government would shut them down. For many Chinese firms, having Indonesians "freeload" as board members or senior management was a very unpalatable demand. A large number of firms decided to cease trading and leave Indonesia. These included one of the wealthiest trading houses in Indonesia at the time, Kian Gwan, which anticipated nationalization by sending my older brother to organize the transfer of some of its assets to Holland.[1]

In 1960 Indonesian and Chinese governments belatedly ratified their Dual Nationality Treaty of 1955, giving the estimated 2.5 million Chinese Indonesians two years to decide their nationality. The Indonesian Government accompanied the directive with enforced name changes and other anti-Chinese measures. If the Chinese did not take up Indonesian citizenship and change their names, essential services and government pensions would be denied them and life would become even more difficult. Through these measures an estimated 1.25 million Chinese living in Indonesia were classified as Chinese citizens in the early 1960s and approximately a tenth of that number actually departed.[2]

For Indonesians however, this plan was less than a complete solution. Over a million people of Chinese ancestry living in Indonesia thereby became Indonesian citizens and with their new nationality became safe

---

[1] Kian Gwan continued trading in Indonesia until its local assets were seized and nationalized in 1961. Later it was re-incorporated as P.T. Rajawali Nusantara Indonesia (<http://www.nusindo.co.id/menu.cgi?2>, accessed 22 August 2007).

[2] Mackie, *The Chinese in Indonesia, Five Essays*, University of Hawaii Press, Honolulu, 1976.

from expulsion, though certainly not safe from further discrimination. Chinese Indonesians were issued with new identity cards that included their racial origins. People frequently used these new identity cards to discriminate against the Chinese, such as placing restrictions on travel inside and outside Indonesia and having to notify authorities when guests stayed in your house. Chinese Indonesians, like us, were becoming prisoners in our own country.

People who held on to their Chinese names found their utilities, such as electricity, phone, gas, water and garbage collection, suddenly cut off. The emergency services of fire, ambulance and police would not respond to calls of assistance. Then they found that they could not get a job or, in a growing number of cases, could not keep their jobs if they persisted with their Chinese names. All in all it was becoming burdensome to sustain a Chinese name, which of course was exactly what the Government wanted.

We felt that we had no choice. If we were to exist in Indonesia, we had to accept Indonesian citizenship, which also meant renaming ourselves. For many others this was the last straw and they chose to leave instead. During the early 1960s over 100,000 Chinese departed overseas, with the People's Republic of China being the main destination. The resultant loss of commercial expertise sent the economy into a dramatic downturn. My husband and I discussed these developments quietly amongst ourselves as public comments often resulted in the loss of one's job or even arrest. We had a real sense of sadness and concern. First the Dutch had been forced out of Indonesia causing instability and now the Chinese were being forced out, which was causing more instability. For us and many others who thought likewise, Indonesia appeared to be on a downwards spiral towards political and economic ruin.

Our friend and spiritual guide, Mas Djon[3] selected new indigenous names for us, choosing An Utari for myself and Slamet Sudibjo for my husband. An is short for Sian and means "angel" in Chinese and Utari means the same in Javanese. Slamet means "safe" in Arabic and Sudibjo is likewise in Javanese. Therefore our new names meant "Angel Angel" and "Safe Safe", like a double blessing. Ironically, our new Indonesian names did not improve our position. We still looked Chinese and our identity papers officially confirmed our racial origins. Thus discrimination continued.

---

[3] More details of Mas Djon follow later in this chapter.

It is not the custom with indigenous Indonesians to use surnames or family names like Europeans or Chinese. For example, it is not uncommon for every member of the same family to have a completely different name. This practice often led to many humorous episodes with us when we travelled to Europe on holidays and later when we emigrated to Australia. Hotel managers would become suspicious when we checked in under different names and once my husband was even accused of sleeping with another man's wife! In Australia we have naturalization papers in separate names and to this day we receive two individual pensions rather than one combined pension as a couple. Despite our repeated attempts to convince the Australian authorities that we are a married couple, I am sure that they still believe that we are two individuals living under the same roof rather than husband and wife.

Family

In December 1963, my parents celebrated their 60th Wedding Anniversary in Kediri. It was not a hugely attended affair as the adverse political climate worked against Chinese Indonesians gathering in large numbers for any reason. Nevertheless we did manage to assemble the two dozen family members present in the country to celebrate their anniversary. My older brother Tan Swan Bing and his family unfortunately could not attend as they were now living in Holland and he was afraid his return would result in his arrest.[4]

Also present at my parents' wedding anniversary was my recently divorced younger brother who, after at long period of estrangement from the family, had reconnected with us in 1962. After the War, Siauw Djie had eventually moved with his wife and two daughters to Bandung in West Java, where he continued teaching. Unfortunately, he became increasingly isolated from the rest of the family.

When Siauw Djie's marriage to Mi Lien broke down in 1961, he came to live with us in Jakarta along with his youngest daughter, Tan Sian Ien, who was about ten years old at the time. For the next five years he continued

---

[4] As General Counsel for the immensely wealthy Chinese trading house of Kian Gwan, Tan Swan Bing had overseen the relocation of some of the company's financial assets offshore to Holland in the early 1960s. Tan Swan Bing believed that if he ever returned to Indonesia he would be arrested by government officials for diverting assets out of the country.

60th Wedding Celebration of Tan Ting Bie and Njoo Hing Tjie (parents of An Sudibjo) in Kediri, December 1963.

Children in foreground L–R: Bing Karyadi, 2nd son of Liem Sing Boen and Flora, Ruby Karyadi, Eddie Karyadi. L–R (front row): An's daughter Ingrid (kneeling), Ida Karyadi, Njoo Hing Tjie, Tan Ting Bie, 2nd daughter of Flora and Liem Sing Boen (kneeling). L–R (standing): Tan Sioe An (husband of Evy), Evy Tan, John Nielsen, Ban Kong Karyadi (married to Ida), Tan Liem Nio (younger half sister to An), Tan Siauw Djie (younger brother of An), Roostien Liem, Liem Sing Giap (married to Roostien), An Sudibjo, Eddie Sudibjo, son of Liem Sing Boen and Flora, Liem Sing Boen (younger brother of Liem Sing Giap), Flora (wife of Liem Sing Boen), daughter of Liem Sing Boen and Flora, Kasminah.

to commute between his weekly teaching commitments in Bandung and Jakarta, where I had given him a job at my own private school, Harapan Kita. Whenever Siauw Djie taught in Bandung, he stayed with Roostien and in 1967 he returned to live there permanently.

My mother died in the mid-1960s with my father following a year or two later. The only asset they had left from all their years of hard work was one house in Kediri which passed into the possession of my father's second wife Kasminah and, subsequently, to her side of the family upon her death in 1971. Even though my parents had never fully recovered

Tan Ting Bie and Njoo Hing Tjie at their 60th Wedding Celebration in Kediri, December 1963. Celebrations held at a private house opposite Kasminah's residence (former Tan household) in Kediri. "Peringetan Kawin Inten" means Diamond Wedding Anniversary.

financially from their sugar crisis of the mid-1920s and the succeeding ravages of War and Revolution, they had tried to rebuild their lives and their fortunes several times, finally retiring on income from selling salted duck eggs and small ice blocks. However, it appeared to me that every time they looked like succeeding, a new political or economic disaster demolished their accomplishments. It must have been heart-breaking for my parents to see every attempt at prosperity thwarted so many times. It was certainly heartbreaking for me to watch them endure these tribulations.

Eddie and the Airline Industry

After KLM departed from Indonesia in late 1957, Garuda attempted to fill the vacuum and become an international airline in its own right. However, being financially overstretched and lacking enough trained pilots to fly long-haul overseas flights, the company soon faced bankruptcy. KLM resumed flights to Indonesia in 1963, but not before other companies, such as my husband's TAI, had taken the opportunity to establish profitable businesses in Indonesia.

The office of TAI in Jakarta in early 1959. L-R: Elizabeth, Secretary; Anwar Gozali (Go Djoen Sian), Assistant Station Manager; Ollie, Clerk; Eddie Sudibjo, Sales Manager is on the phone.

My husband and I had a wonderful life while he was working in the airline industry. All our trips were free and we mostly travelled first class everywhere. During the nine years he worked for TAI/UTA (1958–67), Eddie must have taken over forty international trips. I accompanied him on half of those trips and one or both of our children came along on about a third of them.

Our travels took us to North America, three times to Europe, and once to Japan and South Korea, but most of the trips — maybe as many as twenty — were to Australia to visit our children in Sydney as often as twice a year. Not all the flights were with Eddie's company. Because TAI/UTA was affiliated with the International Air Transport Association (IATA), our unlimited free flight privileges could be redeemed on any other affiliate airline. Over the years we also travelled on Garuda, KLM, Swiss Air, SAS, Thai International Airlines, Japan Airlines and Air India.

During the Sukarno's Guided Democracy regime (1959–66), imports were restricted because of the acute shortage of foreign reserves. Highly-prized overseas luxury items were especially scarce, so we even went once or twice on shopping trips to Singapore and Hong Kong! Having a double weight allowance to 60 kilograms per person, we filled up our bags with perfumes, radios, clothes, watches, alcohol and tobacco that our friends and relatives had paid for in advance. In addition Eddie would always buy gifts for some of his business contacts and surprise them upon our return. Even after we gave some items to Indonesian customs officials by way of the usual bribes to get the goods into the country, we still had plenty of gifts left over to make us very popular with our friends, relatives and business acquaintances.

Whenever Eddie travelled overseas on business for conferences, seminars and training, he received a travel allowance to pay for all his living away from home expenses such as accommodation, food and drink. However, when we travelled for personal reasons we had to pay for those items ourselves. As this was very expensive, we restricted ourselves to only a few family holidays in Europe and North America. When we travelled to Sydney after purchasing our home there in 1964, everyday expenditure was kept to a minimum.

Life at Jalan Jogja

Captain Said Pratalikusuma, the last Army person billeted to Jalan Jogja 7 in 1956, was an ignorant, rude, aggressive man who often resorted to threats and bullying to achieve what he wanted. And what he most wanted was for us to leave the house. He was Madurese and, like so many others from the island of Madura, was considered less cultured and more uncouth than the Javanese. I was told later that a very senior person in the Army coveted the house and purposefully chose Captain Pratalikusuma to bully us out of it.

First he fully occupied the space in the house allocated to the Army for himself and his wife. It was supposedly meant to accommodate four army officers in total, but after Captain Pratalikusuma arrived the other officers who left were never replaced. Over time he took over the rooms behind the car port vacated by our son and parents-in-law, filling them with his own servants and family members. And he continued to pick fights with us. On one occasion in early 1960 my husband politely asked him to move his car which was blocking the driveway and he responded by yelling and hurling abuse at Eddie. Thankfully this time it did not degenerate into a violent assault as it had during another incident some years earlier, but there was always the threat that Pratalikusuma would become violent any time there was an argument.

We had to share the toilet and bathroom facilities between us, but one day he locked our internal access to these conveniences and forced us to go outside to gain entry. From then on we had to wait until he and his family had finished with their ablutions before we could use them. He also controlled the mains water supply into the house and deliberately turned the flow off at will, sometimes for days at a time. This forced us to store clean water in large 44 gallon drums, but we also had to use the unclean water from the well, which we had to boil to avoid illness.

Not only was the house unsafe from within, but there were disturbing incidents with some of our neighbours as well. In 1963, when Ingrid was about 14 she was startled by a young man from next door (a Batak from North Sumatra) who had scaled the side wall to watch her undress in her bedroom. She shouted out, "What are you doing", but he disappeared from view back into the house. Some time later when Ingrid was out on the street with a school friend, she noticed him and said to her friend, "There goes the pig who spies on us in our bedrooms!" The man overheard the remark and, because any reference to being a pig is considered a grave insult in Indonesia, he exploded. He chased her down the street and slapped her around when he caught up with her a short distance away.

Fortunately some local *becak* (pedicab) drivers intervened and Ingrid fled home crying. I took my frustrations out on Ingrid, telling her to be careful because Chinese do not have any rights in Indonesia, where using grossly insulting language was considered far more serious than either assault or being a voyeur. It now became more of a priority to get my daughter out of Indonesia to prevent her from being the subject of further assaults and injustices.

In the early 1960s with the rise of the *Partai Komunis Indonesia* (PKI), weapon searches were held regularly on the houses of many Chinese Indonesians. Even though Captain Pratalikusuma now occupied much of the house and observed us closely, our section was nevertheless searched at least once by a group of soldiers. Even though we had nothing to hide, it was still a very uneasy feeling having armed soldiers enter our part of the home and roughly go through our possessions. The soldiers did not have a warrant or any other document officially authorizing the search, as in those days they did not have to. I followed the soldiers from room to room, just in case they thought they could use the opportunity to steal something of value. My husband and I suspected that the search had been organized by Pratalikusuma to harass and intimidate us into leaving, but we had no proof of his involvement.

A year later soldiers suddenly arrived to search our part of the house for foreign currency. Again, my husband and I believed that Pratalikusuma had instigated the action. It was illegal for citizens to hold foreign currency at the time and Pratalikusuma, who knew my husband worked for a foreign company, could have easily organized the search to further his campaign of intimidation. The soldiers did not find any foreign currency as my husband was too smart to keep it at home and the soldiers departed angry and disappointed.[5]

Spiritual Guidance

Following Captain Said Pratalikusuma's arrival in the house and the deterioration of our relationship, one of our near neighbours, Henk Soeleiman, in 1958 introduced us to a person whom he thought could help us restore good relations within the house, namely Raden Mas Soedjono.[6] He was a high-ranking official with the Department of Transport and Telecommunications, but in his spare time people would come to him seeking his counsel and advice on personal issues. He performed this through meditation. We came to know him as Mas Djon.

We soon became close friends and he meditated with us to help with our domestic troubles. Mas Djon helped us in a spiritual sense so much over the years that to this day we still have a photograph of him on our wall at home to remind us of him, even though he died almost two decades ago.

In the early 1960s, while attending meditation sessions at the home of Mas Djon, my husband and I met an air commodore by the name of Soedjatmiko. We became good friends and in the natural course of evening meditations exchanged details about our respective employment. Soon Eddie was selling him charter flights on behalf of UTA. Soedjatmiko was in charge of travel arrangements for *Angkatan Udara Republik Indonesia* (AURI, the Indonesian Air Force) and he commissioned UTA to provide

---

[5] The author doubts An's explanation of a ten-year campaign by the Army to force the Sudibjo family from the property. As owners, the Army could have simply terminated the Subibjo lease at any time of their choosing. They did not need to resort to threats or violence, nor did they have to wait ten years. Therefore it seems probable that the intimidation was a personal campaign by Pratalikusuma.

[6] Raden Mas literally means Golden King in Javanese, indicating a relative or descendent of royalty.

air travel for the young pilots attending training programs in Europe. At the time the Indonesian Air Force was being equipped with planes from the Soviet Union and the pilot training was held in Moscow, Prague and other major cities behind the Iron Curtain. Over the next few years Eddie arranged round-trip tickets for up to one hundred pilots several times a year to journey overseas. I also coached Soedjatmiko's children in mathematics and physics. They attended their own schools but would come to me for extra coaching after school.

Soedjatmiko was not the only person of influence meditating with Mas Djon. The political adviser and Secretary to President Sukarno, Pak (father) Wahab, was part of the meditation circle. Through Pak Wahab we were introduced to another spiritual leader of importance, Pak De, who was the President's personal spiritual guide and would sometimes lead meditation sessions at Wahab's home. This network of friends formed from these various sources were all high-ranking officials in the Sukarno Government, which historians now say was highly influenced by Javanese mysticism.[7]

We were so impressed by Mas Djon's powers that we introduced a number of our relatives and friends to him, including my niece Evy's husband, Sioe An. He had told us he was having marital problems at the time. Mas Djon lived in a small suburban house with a large living room that was filled with many people awaiting an audience with him. I ushered Sioe An into a small backyard where Mas Djon sat alone with a smoking fire nearby to repel mosquitoes. Mas Djon meditated for a short time and then said to Sioe An, "The problem is not with your wife but with your child. She is sick." Sioe An appeared shocked but did confirm that his eldest daughter was indeed suffering from an unknown illness and that her condition was serious.

---

[7] According to An and Eddie, Javanese mysticism is a unique synthesis of the spiritual or mystical elements of Animism, Hinduism, and Islam. There are ghosts, spirits, gods and "life forces" at work in a mysterious world that is parallel to the real world. Sometimes these beings interact with the real world on their own, and sometimes people with significant psychic powers can summon them. These people are held in very high regard and become a vital part of the community. Some offer advice, others heal people, and yet others tell fortunes or invoke spells. They have Indonesian names to describe what they are, such as *kiai* (religious teacher) or *dukun* (native healer).

The characteristics of Javanese mysticism include repetitive prayer or meditation, fasting, sleep deprivation, and isolation, all designed to produce a purified "altered state" of consciousness to contact the "other" world.

Mas Djon gave Sioe An a small bottle of water with the instructions that the sick daughter should drink the contents. He also directed that Sioe An bury an egg in the rear yard of the family home. There was much consternation later at Sioe An's house as Evy, who had previously converted to Christianity, regarded this matter as the work of the Devil. Evy's mother and my sister, Roostien, did not have any qualms. She intervened and administered the water and buried the egg herself. The child's health immediately improved and coincidentally so did their marriage.

Mas Djon and his followers occasionally went on pilgrimages to Pelabuhanratu on the Javanese coast facing the Indian Ocean. It was a location of much spiritual significance as it was believed to be one of only two places where the ancient Goddess of the Southern Seas, *Ratu Loro Kidul,* resided, the other being Parangtritis, on the Indian Ocean coast near Yogyakarta. Both these places were regarded as sacred sites and it was believed that spiritual energy accumulated there, offering solutions to any problem we may have had with our lives, such as with love, health, career and happiness. We would meditate overnight on the beach and travel back the three or four hours to Jakarta in time for work the next day.

Harapan Kita

When I started my own school, Sekolah Harapan Kita, I ran it in parallel with my commitments as Principal of the Teachers' College. There were no conflicts of interest and very few clashes of time. In fact the two institutions complemented each other.

I found the best teachers possible out of my alumni at the Teachers' College and asked them to work for me at Harapan Kita. In turn, these teachers produced top graduates every year from students who were enthusiastic and intelligent.

During my tenure as Principal and owner of Sekolah Harapan Kita, not one student failed their final exams and in fact many, many pupils passed with the highest marks possible out all of Indonesia.[8] The curriculum was divided into morning and afternoon sessions of four classes, each

---

[8] An is very proud of her school and its academic record which she attributes to her continued use of Dutch teaching methods. In a nation where everything was rapidly being Indonesianized, Harapan Kita, in spite of its Indonesian name, was one of the last examples of the Dutch education system left in the country.

held in the dining room, bedroom, veranda and car port of our house. One of the reasons for locating the school at Jalan Jogja was to protect the tenure of our accommodation for myself and my family. We thought that Captain Pratalikusuma would not dare to expel us while the house was filled with students whose parents were very influential people. Some were Chinese, others Indonesians but they all had one thing in common — they had previously worked for the Dutch administration and many still spoke Dutch as their prime language. I had the children of senior civil servants, three former Indonesian Ambassadors (for Belgium, France and Holland), wealthy business people, royalty, and even the top echelons of the armed forces.

One of my students was the son of the ruler of the Balinese kingdom of Gianyar, Raja (King) Ide Anak Agung Gde Agung (1921–99), who had been the former Minister for Foreign Affairs (1955–56), Internal Affairs and was currently an Ambassador in Europe. In 1962, he was recalled suddenly without explanation and upon his return was placed under house arrest in Jakarta for allegedly plotting to overthrow the Sukarno Government, though he was never charged. I had to spend a lot of time counselling his son, Prince Agung, as he was so angry and upset at his father's treatment. Restrictions were eventually lifted against his father and he was fully rehabilitated later during the Suharto regime, when it was shown that the allegations against him were completely without substance. Prince Agung went on to become Raja after the death of his father in 1999 and in the same year became Minister of Social Affairs in the Cabinet of President Wahid.

In Jakarta, Harapan Kita quickly earned an enviable reputation as a school delivering excellence in sport and academics. The quality of the teachers and the academic results of the students rapidly gained the interest of many new parents, who rushed to send their children to the school as well. As several of my students were already competitive swimmers, including my son John, the school ended up gaining a reputation for promoting champion swimmers. In truth the school did little to deserve this sporting accolade, except to allow the children time off for morning and afternoon practices, but nevertheless a growing number of people believed that Harapan Kita was intimately involved in fostering both sporting excellence as well as academic excellence and I did nothing to disavow them of this belief. Each new swimming record by one of my students and every new top mark at a national exam reinforced the school's growing reputation.

137

Poster advertising the 1962 production of Djoko Kendil by Harapan Kita students.

One other activity of the school resulted in much positive publicity and praise. In 1960 and again in 1962 the students put on public performances of plays to raise money for an orphanage in Kebayoran, then an elite outer suburb of Jakarta. There were three or four public performances each year at Gedung Kesenian, the main Performing Arts Centre in Jakarta (formerly known under the Dutch as the *Schouwburg* or Theatre) and in both years the school managed to raise over Rp 100,000 as a donation to the orphanage, which was a great deal of money then. Under adult supervision the students were responsible for lighting, sound, direction, sets, raising advertising revenue and even promoting the plays to the general public.

At each of the biannual performances the students acquitted themselves superbly and one year even managed to attract some good press coverage from an inquisitive journalist interested in school children doing a good deed for orphans. Unfortunately these productions were not continued after 1962. They were becoming too elaborate and too complicated and if the school had put on a third play in 1964, it would have taken on the proportions of a major commercial play. In the first few years while the school had under thirty students or so, producing a play involving all students was manageable, but by 1964 when the student numbers had risen to over sixty, the prospects of involving all the pupils in a new play was simply too much.

The two plays were adapted from common children's stories, one Dutch and one Indonesian, and co-written in Dutch with Mr Lange[9] my old School Principal twenty years earlier in Jember. Years later, all I had to do was translate the plays into Indonesian and then produce and direct the performances, but if I was to put on a third play in 1964 I would have needed to write a new play first and I just did not have the time for that. I am sorry I had to discontinue the productions, but I simply found the task too much.[10]

Property Investments and Inflation

In 1960–61, with our new Indonesian names and identity papers we were at last entitled to buy property. My husband purchased three vacant blocks of land in a new suburb of Jakarta called Tebet, not far from Kebayoran. The reason for purchasing the land was two-fold. First, the domestic situation at Jalan Jogja was continuing to deteriorate and we knew that eventually we would have to leave. Better to build our own house than continue to rent elsewhere. Secondly, the remaining two properties could be sold later and hopefully make us a healthy profit.

Over the next year or so we supervised the construction of a house on one of my husband's the three properties in Tebet. As soon as it was completed in 1962, Eddie's parents moved to the new house in Tebet from Jalan Jogja, which was just as well because life for them there had become intolerable. Nevertheless we stayed in the government-owned house at Menteng for another five years.

---

[9] Mr Lange was interned by the Japanese on the island of Ambon for the duration of the War and returned to Holland after Independence. He died of natural causes in Bandung around 1976 while conducting a Dutch tour of Indonesia. He would have been in his mid-seventies when he died.

[10] The first play, *Si Ragil Mendapat Tugas* (The Youngest Receives a Task), involved the school when it had eleven students. The second play, *Djoko Kendil* (Prince in the Urn), was performed when the student body had grown to about thirty pupils.

In 1963 the Government developed a parcel of land in the then rural outskirts of Jakarta at Depok on the way to Bogor. Shortly afterwards I received an offer of public housing at this location, to which I was entitled as a public servant. The land was owned by the Department of Education and set aside exclusively for teachers to purchase for Rp 250,000 per block (less than US$100). The arrangement was that the land could be paid off over time from regular deductions out of our wages. I was entitled to two blocks of land, one as a teacher and a second as a principal. I took up my full allocation and then a few months later took over the ownership of a third block from a fellow teacher who urgently needed some money to assist his sick mother. For about a year I made regular payments on all three properties. My husband paid off the outstanding amount in total in 1964 when he converted the equivalent of only a few hundred American dollars into rupiahs on the black market. By the mid-1960s, we had personally accumulated a total of six properties and stood to be a beneficiary in a seventh, my father's house in Kediri.

General Decline

The social, political and economic cohesion of Indonesia was coming apart during the early to mid-1960s. Inflation as rapid as 700 per cent a year was destroying the savings of the middle class. Food shortages were common.

The rule of law had been replaced with the rule of powerful men with guns — including the Armed Forces and Police — who acted corruptly and with impunity. It was said that even President Sukarno had secret Swiss bank accounts where he was depositing millions of dollars that were being siphoned from the national treasury.

In 1959 President Sukarno decided that Western parliamentary-style democracy was an anathema for Indonesia and he replaced it with Guided Democracy (*Demokrasi Terpimpin*) with himself as the Great Leader of the Indonesian Revolution and Commander in Chief of the Armed Forces.

On the international front, Indonesia befriended the Soviet Union and China on the one hand, as well as the USA on the other, and tried to walk the politically dangerous tightrope during the Cold War of not declaring allegiance to either the East or the West, but playing them off against each other.

Sukarno was antagonizing the Dutch by demanding that Irian Jaya, the only part of the former Dutch colony not yet incorporated into Indonesia,

Amidst growing political uncertainty in the 1960s, the Sudibjos still found time to dance at the most exclusive nightclubs in Jakarta. This picture was taken during Christmas in 1960 at Kemayoran Airport Restaurant.

be handed over to Indonesia immediately. He sent in commando troops to dislodge the Dutch by force (1960–62). Then as soon as the Irian Jaya crisis was over, Sukarno started a guerrilla war, known as *Konfrontasi*, against the newly-formed Republic of Malaysia (1963–66). In the process he claimed in 1965 that Singapore "would be destroyed".

In August 1965 he cut off ties with the International Monetary Fund (IMF) and the World Bank, thereby depriving Indonesia of critically-needed financial aid. Earlier in 1965, he had withdrawn Indonesia from the United Nations, claiming the organization was only a pawn of the West.

There was also an idea by Sukarno — which I thought simply crazy — that Communist China would give Indonesia a nuclear weapon! Perhaps most threatening of all to Indonesia's internal security was the re-emergence of the Indonesian Communist Party (PKI). Rising out of the ashes of the crushed rebellion in Madiun in 1948, the PKI had rebuilt itself into a popular and powerful movement. Communists had infiltrated

141

and influenced the trade unions (including my own Teachers' Union), the civil service (again, including my own Department of Education), and the everyday lives of indigenous Indonesians down to the village level.

By successfully recruiting village elders and chiefs, the PKI would control who got irrigation water, seed and patronage, who got work and who did not. This increased the desire for others to become party members and sometimes resulted in entire villages and towns joining the party en masse. By June 1965, the Communists party boasted that about one-fifth of Indonesia's 105 million people were members of the PKI or its affiliates.[11] It was said that the PKI was the largest Communist party in the world outside the Socialist bloc.

Sukarno had organized the purchase of more than 100,000 weapons from the People's Republic of China to be distributed to a vague new entity

Communists celebrate 45 years of the PKI in Indonesia. "45 Tahun PKI" with large banners across main street in Jakarta in 1965 displaying Marx, Stalin, Mao, and Sukarno is added for political expediency. (Image courtesy of <www.gimonca.com/sejarah>)

---

[11] Paul Hampton, *Communism and Stalinism in Indonesia*, Article No. 61 Worker's Liberty.

he described as the "fifth force".[12] Many suspected that these weapons were secretly intended for the Indonesian Communists instead. Meanwhile President Sukarno was spouting slogans, building grandiose monuments, and internationally flirting with the Soviets, the Chinese and the West at the same time. It was a precarious time and even Sukarno knew it. In a famous speech in late 1964 he called it "the year of living dangerously".

What we needed desperately was strong stable leadership, instead we were getting chaos. Throughout 1965, rumours of possible coups, insurrections, and rebellions were rife throughout Jakarta. Most of us thought that it was only a matter of time before something dramatic would happen.

The Attempted Coup d'Etat

In late September 1965 our friend, Air Commodore Soedjatmiko, and his adjutant arrived unannounced at our home in Menteng and offered my husband a machine gun, ammunition and several grenades. I was away in Holland at the time. He said he could not tell Eddie exactly what was about to happen, nevertheless it was something so serious that he might need the weapons for his protection when it did. This was very alarming. The Defence Forces just did not hand out military weapons to civilians.

Fearing Captain Pratalikusuma's reaction if he discovered weapons in the house, my husband declined the offer of firearms. Soedjatmiko left him saying that if Eddie ever needed protection in the near future, for whatever reason, he was to go immediately to Soedjatmiko's house about five minutes walk away, where he would be safe. At the time, my husband did not have a clue what Air Commodore Soedjatmiko was talking about.

Three days later the purpose of his warning became absolutely clear. It is obvious that Soedjatmiko had some prior knowledge of an attempted Coup, though he never discussed the matter with us again. All we know is that the officer he served under directly, Air Marshall Omar Dhani, was later found to be a central figure in the attempted overthrow of the Government. For his involvement the Air Marshall was initially sentenced to death, which was later commuted to life imprisonment. Dhani spent the next thirty years in prison until finally released in 1995 as a broken, old man.

---

[12] Sukarno described the "fifth force" as some kind of people's militia, but never defined it — the other four forces were the Army, Navy, Air Force and Police (Ricklefs, M. C., *A History of Modern Indonesia since 1200*, 3rd Edition, 2001).

What transpired is that during the night of 30 September/1 October 1965 there was an attempted coup d'etat. Elements of the Army, supported by part of the Air Force and some members of the Communist Party, abducted six generals from their private homes in Jakarta and killed them. As we were told later, this was to be only the first step towards overthrowing the Government. However, General Nasution, the most senior Army officer escaped capture and another general, Major General Suharto, Commander of the Army Strategic Reserve Command (KOSTRAD) was not even on the conspirators list of targets.

At this time I was in Holland for medical reasons and desperate to be with my husband back in Indonesia. When I returned, he told me that early on the morning of the coup he was driven to work along the usual route which passed near the Presidential Palace, where he noticed large numbers of soldiers with automatic weapons positioned at important intersections and along the main road half-hidden behind trees. This was very disturbing and he did not know then what was happening. When he reached his office building a short distance away, one of the company watchman hurriedly approached him and told him, "*Tuan, Tuan* (Sir, Sir). Go inside. It is not safe. There are many soldiers trying to attack the Palace." Once inside his office my husband tried to call the airport to ensure UTA's operations and planes were safe but the phone system across Jakarta was shut down.

Later in the morning he was being driven out to the airport in an effort to contact staff there, when he was turned back by university students who were blocking the road. Back in the city, Eddie listened to the Government radio station — *Radio Republik Indonesia* — but found the broadcast gave confusing messages. Even though it seemed that the radio station had been taken over by the coup plotters, announcements were nevertheless ambiguous and sometimes contradictory. At first the broadcasts were revolutionary in nature, claiming that the old corrupt regime had been overturned and that all citizens should come out and support the new Government. Then the announcements became hesitant, stating that President Sukarno would not be harmed and remain in power. Only his corrupt advisers would be dismissed. People were now being urged to remain indoors.

In the afternoon the phone system was restored and Eddie made several frantic phone calls to try and find out what was going on. His staff at the airport told him that nothing had happened there and that everything was safe and under control. Eventually, he spoke to a friend in the Customs and Immigration Department who confirmed that a coup d'etat was indeed still in progress. He was also told that Lieutenant-Colonel Untung, Commander of the Cakrabirawa Regiment of Presidential Guards, was the leader of the coup and wanted to install himself as the next President of the Republic of Indonesia.[13]

However, the situation was not progressing smoothly for the coup-plotters. During the day General Suharto had assumed command of all loyal troops in the Jakarta area and had recaptured several government installations, including the radio station and the central telecommunications office. He then surrounded rebel troops who had taken over the Palace. Suharto had also assumed command of the Armed Forces in the absence of General Nasution who was grieving the loss of his daughter killed in the attempted abduction. Over the next day or so my husband heard that Suharto had swiftly gained the upper hand.

For a few brief days the situation appeared to return to normal, which is when I returned to Indonesia on the first available flight from Holland. My Deputy Principal at Harapan Kita, Ibu Kus, managed to keep the school open during my absence, except for the times when the students were away demonstrating. Ibu literally means mother in Indonesian, but is often used a title of respect.

Collectively, Indonesia breathed a sigh of relief that yet another dangerous incident appeared to have been averted. Then the Army discovered the bodies of the abducted Generals down a well at Halim Air Base near Jakarta. There was a massive public funeral with much outpouring of emotion on 5 October and it was then that the Army came out and publicly accused the Communists of organising the coup. A day or so later there was a huge demonstration in Jakarta, where over 100,000 people (mainly students) whipped themselves into a frenzy and burned down the PKI headquarters.

Clashes started between communists and anti-communists and riots started across Indonesia. Civil order broke down completely when Muslim religious leaders declared a *jihad* (holy war) against the Communists. Without warning the whole country suddenly erupted in a spontaneous orgy

---

[13] Although many details of the Coup are still shrouded in mystery, what is clear is that Lt.-Col. Untung appears to have been merely a pawn in the hands of other more powerful forces. When the attempted coup collapsed, Untung fled to the mountains in central Java, where he was eventually captured and subsequently executed after a trial in March 1967. The best analysis of this murky incident is John Roos, *Pretext for Mass Murder: The September 30th Movement and Suharto's Coup d'Etat in Indonesia*, Madison, University of Wisconsin Press, 2006.

of violence. It was as if a licence had been given to the people to commit murder and over the next three months a bloodbath ensued. There are no official estimates of the number of people killed but the accepted figures range from 300,000 to 800,000 dead. My husband and I never witnessed scenes like this in our life, and we never want to again.

Eddie's office was situated at Jalan Pintu Air besides a tributary canal that eventually runs to the port of Tanjung Priok and the Java Sea beyond. Many mornings he arrived at work to see the canal literally running red with blood and sometimes littered with corpses from the previous night's bloodbath. For weeks after my return, we passed houses where rioters had murdered the occupants and burnt the buildings. This insanity did not appear to have a focus. Chinese and indigenous Indonesians alike were being slaughtered, as well as Hindus, Christians and Muslims (both orthodox and liberal). It was havoc and I would describe this period as one of collective madness.

The only way we survived these horrific episodes was through meditation and prayer. Every night we would go to Mas Djon and meditate, sometimes to one or two o'clock in the morning, and we are convinced that Mas Djon saved us. Without his help we know we would have died. There were hundreds of disturbing incidents happening around us, but personally we felt cocooned in a protective force that prevented any threat to our well-being. When Mas Djon died in the 1980s, we gave one million rupiah (A$1,000) to his wife and relatives to spend on a new kitchen. It was our gift of thanks for his protection.

Bad as it was in the capital of Jakarta, the real violence occurred in the countryside. There not only did individuals murder each other, but sometimes entire villages would collectively slaughter the residents of neighbouring villages, including women and babies. We heard that the people of Bali committed the worst excesses of communal slaughter. I was told that on this beautiful Hindu island alone over 100,000 citizens were massacred.[14] After several months of uncontrolled carnage, the Armed Forces finally decided to assert themselves and order was gradually restored across Indonesia. During this period the last remaining PKI officials who were still alive were captured and the first treason trials commenced.

---

[14] Robert Cribb, "Introduction: The Problems in the historiography of the killings in Indonesia", in R. Cribb (ed.), *The Indonesian Killings 1965–1966: Studies from Java and Bali*, Centre of Southeast Asian Studies, Monash University, Melbourne, 1991.

Throughout this mayhem I was really concerned about my safety and that of my husband. First, I was Chinese and therefore automatically suspected of Chinese Communist sympathies. Secondly, I was a senior bureaucrat in the Education Department and a member of the Teachers' Union. Because both organizations had been infiltrated so effectively by the Communists, I was scared that the Army would accuse me of collaboration with the coup plotters.

In the first week after the attempted coup, when the political situation was still uncertain, a senior teaching colleague (Mun Wahyudi[15]) anxiously told me that high-ranking Communist officials in the Department of Education had prepared death lists of all principals and teachers with higher educational qualifications who were believed to be a threat after their takeover. The Communists employed a simple test to determine the political affiliations of government workers. During mealtimes or at office meetings, one party member would publicly boast about the latest achievement of the PKI while another would note the names of anyone who disagreed or, like me, simply remained silent. Either way, unless you loudly voiced your support, you were marked down as a potential enemy.

Mun Wahyudi informed me that both she and I were named on the list and that a mass grave had been prepared in the southern suburb of Kebayoran to receive us all. In 1965 there would have been only a few dozen senior bureaucrats and principals in the Education Department in Jakarta, so our elimination would have been a simple and easy task. Later, I was told by others that similar death lists had been prepared for many top people in other government departments as well. In retrospect this made sense because the empty mass grave I had seen in Kebayoran was designed to take hundreds of people.

With the murder of only a few hundred people across all the government departments, the Communists would have wiped out any public service threat to its new regime in one stroke because there were only about 3,000 top civil servants in the whole of Indonesia at this time. To be honest, however, I never actually saw any death list and I have no direct evidence about it. I did see an empty pit and was certainly convinced that other people believed it to be true. There were many rumours around

---

[15] Her first husband was killed during the Communist uprising in 1946 in Central Java and some time after the 1965 coup she was elected to Parliament.

147

at that time, but this one seemed so real I became convinced about its truth as well.[16]

After a few weeks or so when the Defence Forces gained the upper hand, they produced lists themselves to target people for arrest and questioning. The Armed Forces had obtained the membership rolls of the PKI, but had also added their own names and, so the rumour went, names supplied by foreign intelligence services, such as the American Central Intelligence Agency (CIA). Our old friend, Soedjatmiko, who had by now been promoted to Air Marshall of the Indonesian Air Force informed me that my name was not on this government list and he would make sure that it would not go on it either.[17] Air Marshall Soedjatmiko represented the Air Force's interest in the compilation and maintenance of this list. Even though Soedjatmiko said the named people were merely wanted for questioning, he may have known that the list was being freely circulated to radical groups and used to kill people instead.

About a week or so after the coup, my husband had to go to the city of Medan on the island of Sumatra on behalf of UTA to reassure the travel agents there. Medan was a very dangerous place as it was the centre of anti-PKI feeling, which had spilled over into anti-Chinese violence on the island. Eddie rang Soedjatmiko prior to his visit and the Air Marshall arranged for a permanent military escort to guard my husband for the three days he was in Medan. Air Marshall Soedjatmiko went on to become the Indonesian Ambassador to Singapore in the late 1960s.

One of the students of Harapan Kita was Hedi, the daughter of Admiral Martadinata who was the Chief of Staff of the Indonesian Navy. The Admiral was killed a month or so after the attempted coup when his helicopter mysteriously exploded while the Admiral, his crew and the then

---

[16] An Sudibjo went on the say that ever since she was a young girl, Indonesia has always been thick with rumours. Even when she and Eddie meet Indonesians today, conversation quickly moves on to discuss the latest conspiracy theory or rumour, usually involving senior government officials and some illegal act.

[17] An suspects that Soedjatmiko's unexpected and rapid promotion following the attempted coup was the result of his anti-Communist loyalties. Of the three branches of the Armed Services it is accepted that the Air Force was the most infiltrated with Communist sympathizers. In the preceding decades leading up to the coup, most of the Air Force's equipment and all of its training had been supplied by Eastern Bloc countries. Indonesian Air Force pilots spent years overseas under the influence of Eastern Bloc trainers and many became adherents to the Communist cause. It is interesting to speculate how much Soedjatmiko knew of the coup and whether his rapid promotion had anything to do with what he may have divulged in advance to Army authorities. Soedjatmiko was invited to comment for this book but did not respond.

Pakistani Ambassador were flying from Jakarta to the Admiral's mountain retreat in Puncak, about 100 kilometres from Jakarta. Hedi was devastated by the sudden and violent loss of her father and for some time afterwards she was inconsolable.

Martadinata's widow was lucky to have avoided death herself as she had been scheduled to accompany her husband on the helicopter. Instead she had stayed behind comforting a son who had been injured in a bicycle accident just before departure. She spoke to my husband to ask whether in his opinion the explosion was an accident. There was a growing rumour that a bomb had been placed on board and Eddie told Mrs Martadinata that he believed her husband had been murdered. Other rumours said that the assassination was carried out on the direct orders of President Sukarno because Martadinata reputedly had proof of Sukarno's complicity in the coup, but he had also made an enemy of the PKI by publicly advocating that party's destruction.

Even though we were sure that Martadinata's death had been the subject of foul play, we were never certain whether it was the Communists or Sukarno who were responsible and we never found out. Nevertheless, my husband and I suspected that it was Sukarno who had been behind the murder because there was never an official investigation into the explosion, nor was there a state funeral and the Government would have been the first to convene an inquiry if it thought it could uncover any criminal involvement by the Communists. In the highly charged and unstable environment after the attempted coup, it was critical for the government to find evidence against the Communists and Martadinata's murder would have provided a perfect opportunity — but only if the Communists were actually involved. The absence of any official investigation only added to the mystery surrounding the circumstances of his death.

It was only years later that the next President of Indonesia, President Suharto, finally took some steps to acknowledge and honour Martadinata by naming several main thoroughfares, a navy destroyer and even a naval college after him. However, for the surviving members of the Martadinata family and the Admiral's friends — including ourselves — the circumstances of his death left us all the more deeply suspicious of the authorities in Indonesia.

Economic Turmoil

All this political turmoil made the desperate economic situation even worse. Although the Army had taken control of security, the President

Sukarno and his unwieldy Nasakom Cabinet attempted to go on running the country. Embattled by rampant inflation, in mid-December 1965 the Government, decided to devalue the face value of the Indonesian rupiah by a massive 1,000 per cent! One thousand Old Rupiahs would have to be exchanged for one New Rupiah and a 10 per cent tax paid on the transaction. The Government tried to keep the announcement a secret but it always leaked like a sieve and word spread several days before the statement. People went crazy. They lined up to get their money out of banks and with the cash shopped for everything they could buy before the purchasing power of their money was obliterated.[18]

On the night before the announcement, restaurants across Jakarta were packed as patrons came out for one last orgy of spending. In one sense we were lucky: we had overseas accounts in American dollars so our financial situation was set to improve by a thousand per cent after the devaluation. Nevertheless, we did spend what little Indonesian currency we had, just like everyone else, to buy household items in advance of the proclamation. Looking back, it was probably one of the worse kept secrets of the late Sukarno regime. Even our servants knew about it!

The decision to devalue the currency by 1,000 per cent dumbfounded the average uneducated Indonesian. At first people just laughed the matter off as impossible. However, disbelief quickly gave way to disgust when prices soon started to rise again more rapidly than before. The very action the Government had determined would arrest inflation had actually fuelled it. People had to find 1,000 times the amount of money to buy anything, so they in turn demanded 1,000 times more in income.

This was not our first experience of inflation for it had been gnawing away at people's confidence for more than a decade. Nevertheless the absurdity of such a massive devaluation was very disturbing. The nation's confidence in government administration seemed to evaporate overnight. President Sukarno himself was never openly criticized. He was still the people's revolutionary hero, the man who personally had won us our independence, but it was a strange and somewhat frightening phenomenon to see the average person in the street losing faith in the Government

---

[18] According to D.H. Penny (1967), "Survey of Recent Developments", *Bulletin of Indonesian Studies*, Vol.3, Iss.6, pp. 4–5, the reform of currency was technically a revaluation of the domestic currency, not a devaluation of the foreign exchange rate. All existing currency would have to be converted at the rate of 1,000 old rupiahs for every 1 new rupiah.

apparatus as incompetent, corrupt and venal. Two months later, under pressure from the Army the old Sukarno Cabinet was drastically reshuffled, entrusting economic management to the highly respected Sultan of Yogyakarta, Hamengku Buwono IX.

Removal from our Home in Menteng

Captain Said Pratalikusuma was promoted to the rank of Major in 1964 but continued to reside in our house in Menteng. For several years our strong connections with admirals, ambassadors and senior government officials, plus the metaphysical support of Mas Djon had contained Pratalikusuma, which was exactly what we intended when we started Harapan Kita. During the attempted coup, Army troops under his command occupied the big former KPM building next to the Shell office on the eastern side of Medan Merdeka (Freedom Square) in central Jakarta.

Some years earlier, my husband had relocated his parents from our house in Menteng to a new house we had built in the suburb of Tebet. That left only the two of us and the school remaining at Jalan Jogja 7 from 1965 onwards.

Our children had already been relocated to Australia and now we told ourselves it was time for us to get out of Indonesia as well for we feared for our lives. Eddie first sought the support of a friend at the Chinese embassy to obtain visas for Australia. However, Eddie found out that Communist China at the time was not recognized by Australia and therefore could not process any visas for travel to Australia. Then my husband tried to get a company transfer to Sydney with UTA, but the head office in Paris refused.

We felt that we were alone and vulnerable in Indonesia, but Eddie thought he could still get us out of Indonesia by perhaps extending the duration of our visitor's visas. In mid-1967, we journeyed to Australia again and this time I intended to stay permanently. The law at that time allowed a visitor one three-month visa, plus three extensions of three months each. In other words, a non-resident could stay for a total of twelve months if the extensions were granted.

Through this device, I managed to stay in Australia for twelve months, living in our house in Chifley, while my husband continued to work in Indonesia and return to Sydney twice a year on leave.

In July 1967 during the annual school vacation while we were in Sydney on one of our regular trips to visit our children, Major Pratalikusuma finally decided to act. The house was empty except for Pratalikusuma's family and our servants. He organized a squad of his soldiers to rid the house of all our furniture. The school equipment and furniture was given to a school in a nearby suburb, while our personal furniture was dumped outside on the street. However, our faithful servants, who had also been expelled from the house, intervened and managed to relocate our possessions to my husband's house in Tebet. Everything that could not be hurriedly salvaged was left on the street by the soldiers and picked clean by strangers.

Being in Sydney at the time, neither of us was aware of what had happened. We found out only when my husband arrived back in Indonesia and was greeted at the airport by his regular driver from work who told him the bad news. Eddie did nothing about the situation — there was nothing anyone could do. Pratalikusuma's actions were illegal but the Army was the most powerful organization in Indonesia and actions by its officers — even unlawful ones — went completely unchallenged, especially when committed against Chinese. Eddie quietly swallowed his pride and his anger and meekly moved in with his parents in the house in Tebet, without ever visiting our old place in Menteng again.

Eventually Major Pratalikusuma somehow obtained legal title over the government-owned property and sold it almost immediately to a very senior Army officer, a general, I think. This general may have been the person behind the Major's campaign against us from the beginning ten years earlier, but we do not know. I was informed later by friends that the house was extensively renovated and expanded into an enormous home but my husband and I never visited the property again. The ownership of the house by the major and its subsequent resale to a higher-ranking officer was totally illegal, as I said before, but if you had enough money and guns to back up your actions then anything was possible.

Indonesian Property Investments Revisited

In 1968 Eddie's father died and his mother was relocated from our house in Tebet to relatives in Jember.[19] Eddie decided to sell his properties. The home and one block of land at Tebet was sold to a friend, Ong Kiem Ping (Ping Kadarusman). The remaining block of land in Tebet was intended for

---

[19] Eventually, Eddie moved his mother to a nursing home in Surabaya, where she died in 1982.

our faithful servant, Ratmi, who had served our family for over 20 years, but she died before this could happen. So the property was sold on the open market. After leaving Indonesia permanently in 1967, my husband occasionally urged me to sell my properties, but I refused. I wanted to keep them as investments and naively thought that I could sell the land anytime in the future if I needed the money. We actually do not know what subsequently happened to these last blocks, but we suspect that they were acquired illegally by an individual or confiscated by the state after we ceased being Indonesian citizens. Either way, we no longer own them.

To show how well entrenched this corrupt practice of illegally seizing property had become, I mention the case of a well known Jakarta businessman. I do not remember his name but he was a well-respected and immensely wealthy Chinese Indonesian who owned such a fabulous house in the southern suburb of Kebayoran that it was regarded as a palace. When he went overseas on a business trip in 1966, an Army general who had coveted the property for a long time, took possession of the house and its contents for himself. The house contained priceless antiques and art works which the general then started selling as if they were his own. It was straight out theft, but no-one objected and no-one took any action. The businessman never returned to Indonesia and lived the rest of his life overseas from that point on.[20]

A similar thing happened to our very good friends, the Winatas, whom we knew through the swimming club. The family was extremely wealthy and owned extensive property holdings across Jakarta, as well as a string of car dealerships called Mascot Motors. In about 1958-59 one of the young male members of the family punched an Army captain in retaliation for the captain insulting and spitting on the young man in public. He was immediately arrested, given a lengthy jail sentence and the entire family's possessions were confiscated. The rest of the Winata family left Indonesia hurriedly and re-established themselves in Thailand, where they live to this day.

If the military and their cronies could steal property from such highly visible individuals with impunity, imagine how much easier it must have been for people to illegally obtain ownership over mere vacant blocks of land from a non-citizen! Over the course of a few years we lost our title to all five of

---

[20] It is said that he still lived a prosperous life elsewhere as he had managed to withdraw a great deal of wealth out of Indonesia from his various business interests.

our remaining properties. It is difficult to quantify the loss financially, but in today's values it would have to be in the millions of dollars.

Swimming

Between 1956 and 1961, Eddie and I became involved in the Kuang Hua swimming club in Jakarta as a wholesome pastime for our growing children. I had been introduced to swimming during my years as a Girl Guide leader in Jember and found it to be a worthwhile exercise in childhood development.

Occasionally my husband and I would wake the children at 5:00 am and take them to the Olympic-sized pool at Manggarai, about 10 minutes away. On other mornings the servants would wake the children and they would cycle to the pool with their friends. There they would train for an hour and have breakfast together afterwards, usually *nasi goreng* (fried rice). Sometimes, each mother in turn would bring enough food to feed the whole team, but the swimmers liked my meals so much they wanted me to do it every day of the week! Of course, I declined. It was only because I was catering for the students at my school that I could feed another dozen or so swimmers a wide variety of meals without difficulty.

Group photo of Kuang Hua Swimming Club, Jakarta (circa 1957).

Several times a week our children would have more swimming lessons in the afternoons.

Swimming as a competitive sport was not well patronized in Indonesia. In the capital city of Jakarta there were only two Olympic-sized swimming pools, each with its own swimming club, and probably no more than a dozen pools and clubs across the whole of Indonesia. Compared to Australia, with its love of swimming and full-sized pools everywhere, even in small towns, Indonesia was a minnow in the swimming world. Nevertheless, my son was a very able swimmer and through hard work and training became National Junior Champion in the 1,500 metres freestyle for several years running and unofficially held National Junior titles for a variety of distances and strokes.

John continued this activity when he went to Australia. He found a very good coach, Sam Herford at the nearby North Sydney Olympic Pool who was at that time coaching the world-famous Olympic swimmer Murray Rose. Facing much stronger competition in Australia, John nevertheless managed to win several Club and District competitions finishing his career as a Junior Champion long-distance swimmer in two countries. He stopped swimming competitively in 1961 to concentrate on his academic studies.

Tobacco

I have only ever smoked tobacco when under stress and then only a few cigarettes in private. I have never had any desire to become a regular smoker because when I grew up in Indonesia it was not considered proper for a professional, cultured woman to smoke in public. Only peasant women smoked openly. Sometimes women chewed tobacco along with *sirih* (betel nut and leaf), which caused a characteristic reddening of the teeth, and occasionally other ingredients were added to the mix, including crushed lime and even opium. My mother-in-law chewed betel nut and tobacco, staining her teeth and spitting out great wads of black ooze.

I thought the practice revolting, but Indonesian society approved of it and surrounded this habit with containers and instruments that were often works of art. For example, my husband's mother had a special silver box with individual compartments for the separate ingredients and a special silver cutter with an intricate dragon's head handle to slice the beetle nut into thin slivers, plus a small spatula to mix the concoction.

There was quite an elaborate ceremony that accompanied the preparation of this mixture, but even though my mother-in-law enjoyed this pastime immensely, she never did it in public. However, there was a very different attitude when it came to smoking by men. It was entirely acceptable for them to smoke openly and the majority did so, but even here there were subtle class differences at work: males who were poor smoked *kretek* (clove) cigarettes or roll-your-own cigarettes; wealthier men smoked factory-made cigarettes; and the wealthiest of all smoked foreign cigarettes, imported cigars, or intricately carved expensive pipes.

My husband started smoking cheap domestic cigarettes while he was still at school in Solo in 1942, just before the Japanese Occupation. As his status grew over the next thirty years, he progressed to factory-made and then imported cigarettes. While he was working for TAI, he would smoke up to thirty cigarettes a day or forty-five packets a month, often giving packets of imported cigarettes away to clients and friends. He smoked *State Express – 555* and *Benson & Hedges* that were all purchased duty-free from overseas.

In February 1967 our children returned to Indonesia from a big international holiday by themselves through Japan and Asia. As they were both living in Australia, we had not seen them for six months and we stayed up all night talking. In the morning my husband looked at the ashtray which was overflowing with butts and announced emphatically that he would give up smoking from that point on. Nobody took him seriously, of course, and other employees in the office who smoked mocked him good naturedly, but true to his word he did stop the habit that day and has never smoked since. For months afterwards he would carry around a packet of cigarettes in his pocket for his customers and colleagues at work, but still he did not use them himself.

The Nielsens

Jan Nielsen became a tenant at Jalan Jogja 7 in 1948 and his wife Gerda joined him a year later in 1949 with the first two of their three boys. Jan was employed by the colonial Dutch Government as a teacher of *Wiskunde* (Mathematics) at a different high school to me in Jakarta. When his three-year teaching contract expired in June 1951, it was not renewed by mutual agreement.[21] The Nielsen family had a choice to return to Holland

---

[21] By this time the relationship between the Indonesian and Dutch governments was beginning to sour and the Indonesians had begun stepping up the pressure for the remaining Dutch citizens to leave the former colony.

or emigrate to Australia, and they chose Australia. We corresponded with them and as the situation in Indonesia continued to deteriorate we began contemplating getting our children out of the country.

Correspondence between the Nielsens and ourselves was infrequent and by post, happening about once or twice a year if you include Christmas cards. All the letters were written between Eddie and Jan. A very good friendship had developed between us and the Nielsens viewed my daughter, Ingrid, as the daughter they never had. When the Nielsens in Australia heard about the Dutch-speaking schools closing down by Presidential Decree in December 1957 and all remaining Dutch citizens in Indonesia being expelled, they wrote to us in sympathy.

Knowing that our children were at that time enrolled in Dutch Schools, Jan wrote inviting us to send them to Australia to receive a better education. He said that they would accommodate our children, but we had to arrange for their airfares out of Indonesia and pay for all incidental costs in Australia. However, we did not have sufficient funds at the time to get John and Ingrid out of Indonesia.

John and Ingrid had been attending the Dutch Concordante School in Jakarta, but with the enforced closures now had to relocate to an Indonesian school. Before we took advantage of this generous offer from Jan Nielsen, we wanted to see how things worked out with the children moving over to an Indonesian curriculum where the language spoken was exclusively Bahasa Indonesia. Unfortunately, neither child coped well with the new education system. Differences with the language, curriculum and teaching standards meant that both children became unsettled and fractious in an Indonesian school. For example, John's first language was Dutch and although he could understand and speak Bahasa Indonesia, he could not read or write it at all well.

My husband commenced employment with TAI in 1958, but it still took another year or so before he had sufficient sales commission points to afford a free family trip overseas. In the meantime, he had other trips to Europe and the US, but these were business trips which excluded family members. The trip to Australia in July 1960 was the very first opportunity to take the whole family overseas. Our major family trips before then had been to Lake Toba in Sumatra in 1955 and to Surabaya by ship in 1956.

The mail between Indonesia and Australia took a very long time to arrive. Even though Eddie posted off a letter alerting the Nielsens of our arrival months in advance, it was quite possible they did not receive the letter until shortly before we arrived. It had been almost ten years since we had last seen each other and over two years since Jan had made the offer to take care of our children, so our sudden appearance was a big surprise to Gerda.[22]

As far as we were concerned, even if we had not responded in writing, we believed the offer to have been genuine and until rescinded, could be acted upon at any point in the future. My prime motive was the safekeeping and future welfare of my children and I would have achieved that any way I could.

We stayed with the Nielsen family in their home at Manly Vale, Sydney and discussed our children's future with them, especially Jan's generous offer to educate the children in Australia. At first we wanted both our children to stay with the Nielsens, but as they had just taken on the foster care of two young girls together with their own three boys, it was agreed by them that John would stay initially and Ingrid would follow a few years later if she wanted to.

My husband and I discussed the matter with our children and asked them if they wanted to stay in Australia. John, who was 15 years old, accepted, saying the situation at our home in Jakarta was intolerable and he wanted to get out of Indonesia to start a new life elsewhere. Ingrid, who was only 11, declined as she wanted to return to Indonesia to finish her secondary school education. We had arrived with only a small amount of clothes sufficient for a two week vacation and no personal keepsakes for John, but over the next year we paid for a whole new wardrobe for him along with accommodation and education expenses.

To circumvent the restrictions imposed by the White Australia Policy on immigration,[23] Jan and Gerda suggested adopting our children, but

---

[22] Gerda Nielsen, who was widowed and still alive at the time this history was recorded, has a very different account of these events. According to Gerda, the Sudibjo family arrived in Australia with just three days notice and unexpectedly pressed the Nielsens into taking both of their children. She was initially taken aback by this audacious imposition but her husband, Jan (whom she accepts may have had prior discussions with the Sudibjo family on the matter), convinced her to agree. In the end, Gerda saw it as their Christian duty to help and reluctantly agreed to the Sudibjo request (see her full interview later in the book).

[23] Australia had adopted a racist immigration policy from the commencement of the Commonwealth of Australia in 1901. It was designed to prevent people with "black, brown, or yellow skin" from becoming citizens. A simple dictation test was the device used to exclude unwanted applicants by requiring them to pass a written test in a specific language with which they were not familiar. By the 1960s the policy was falling into disrepute and a growing number of Asians were gaining entry into Australia through legal loopholes and exemptions. Adoption was just one of the informal

none of us knew whether this was possible. However, our first priority was getting John's visa extended to stay in Australia as a student. Jan Nielsen, my husband and I went to the Immigration Office and asked the official behind the counter, "Is it possible for my son to stay in Australia to further his studies?" He smiled and said, "Of course. All you need is proof of enrolment and sponsorship for accommodation." It only took two days to put together the required documents and when we returned to the Immigration Office they checked our forms, had a brief interview with John, and endorsed his passport, allowing him to stay in Australia on a long-term student visa. It was as easy as that.[24]

We also caught up with the Braakensiek family, our former neighbours in Jakarta, who had settled in Sydney after initially returning to Holland when they had to leave Indonesia. They believed that Australia offered better business opportunities and had bought a modest home at Pymble on Sydney's North Shore. When the family first arrived in Australia, they tried their hand at running an import/export enterprise that Herman and his wife, Hetty, established in Milson's Point, Sydney, but business proved too difficult and the company was wound up some years later. From then on both Herman and Hetty worked as employees to other firms until they retired in the early 1970s.

The Braakensieks introduced us to a solicitor, Mr Henk Rutgers, who was a Dutch Australian. We could speak Dutch to Rutgers, as our English was not that good, and he took instructions to prepare the adoption papers for John. At the end of Eddie's two-week annual holiday, we returned to Indonesia leaving John behind in the care of Jan and Gerda Nielsen. The adoption application was lodged before the Court a few months later and was finally approved about a year later in 1961 without any problems.

When we arrived in Sydney in 1960, we brought with us a cheque from TAI for more than US$4,500, being Eddie's annual wage for the past year. We found a French bank in Sydney that would accept the French company's cheque and opened an account with them. When converted to Australian

---

methods used. The final vestiges of the White Australia Policy were quietly discarded in 1973. By then some 50,000 Asians had already arrived in Australia legally. By the year 2000, 8 per cent, or approximately 1.5 million Australians, were of Asian origin and a further 40,000 Asians were arriving each year to settle in Australia. (Main Reference: "The Evolution of Australia's Multicultural Policy" Australian Fact Sheet #6, found at <www.immi.gov.au/facts/06evolution>, accessed 10 October 2005.)

[24] See Gerda Nielsen's interview later in the book for her interpretation of these events.

currency in the pre-decimal system of pounds, shillings and pence we had over £5,000, almost enough to buy an average house at the time! Some of this money was invested with Rutgers in a solicitor's trust account and the remainder with a property developer, Ernst de Neve, another Dutch Australian, to whom Herman Braakensiek had also introduced us.

Apart from the investment money, there was still enough left over to pay for the adoption proceedings and give the Nielsens money for John's education (£900 per year) plus living expenses. However, while we were waiting for the cheque to clear we were without any other finances, so I had to sell some of my jewellery through the Braakensiek's contacts. Herman Braakensiek had been a gold bullion trader back in Jakarta and had already developed some contacts in the gold business in Sydney. It was enough for us to have a small amount of cash to live off before we could access our new account.

Between 1960 and 1964, when Ingrid also moved to Australia, my husband and I travelled to Australia twice a year to visit John and the Nielsens. For some part of that time, Indonesia and Australia were almost at war with each other over Sukarno's policy of *Konfrontasi* against the new nation of Malaysia. As direct flights from Indonesia were prohibited, my husband and I had to travel to Australia via a third country such as Thailand or the Philippines, which increased the travel costs. Each year we would bring another cheque worth about US$4,500. After clearing it through our French bank account in Sydney, a significant proportion would go to the Nielsens but most of it was added to the growing amount held in investment by Rutgers and de Neve. In four years our combined investments with these gentlemen would total more than £11,000.

The relationship between us and the Nielsen adults remained strong, but there was one area where it could have been better. That was with the issue of finances. On one occasion (possibly 1963) we paid the next year's agreed amount in advance. I no longer remember the figure, but it would have been a few thousand pounds. We were then shocked to receive a phone call from Gerda Nielsen a short time later informing us that the year's allowance had been fully expended in just three months. There were no extraordinary items that would have accounted for this sudden loss of money and we were forced to conclude that Gerda had an inability to manage large amounts of funds. Unfortunately, she told John that he was only living with them under sufferance and was in fact living off their charity. He got upset at this insult to us and threatened to run away from home. We had to fly to Sydney urgently to sort the matter out.

In the late 1950s, luckily my husband had set up a foreign banking account through Ing Hoe (the cousin who gave Eddie the job at Sioe Liem Kongsie timber company) in Holland as we had thought then of sending our children there to study. This money, the Australian equivalent of about 2,000 Dutch guilders, was transferred to Australia in 1963 to make up the shortfall in John's upkeep. But instead of placing any further sums of money in trust with the Nielsens, we asked Herman Braakensiek to continue this arrangement instead.

In 1961 we had taken Ingrid on a trip to Europe and in particular to Holland, where we hoped to find out if she was willing to be educated in that country. She did not like Holland at all saying it was too cold. Besides, her brother was already in Australia, so she now wanted to study in Sydney.

As Ingrid got nearer to completing high school in Indonesia, we discussed the matter of university education in Australia with the Nielsens. We all agreed that a degree from an Australian university was preferable and because only Australian residents could then access tertiary education in Australia, it was decided that Jan and Gerda Nielsen would adopt Ingrid in the same manner as they had with John four years earlier. In June 1964, Ingrid finished senior high school, and we journeyed to Sydney. Once again we went through Henk Rutgers, the same solicitor as before, and once again the process took about one year for approval. Like John's adoption application five years earlier, Ingrid's adoption was approved by the court without any objections or concerns from the authorities.

Even though she had completed secondary school in Indonesia, Ingrid had to obtain her Leaving Certificate from an Australian school before entering university. We felt it was better if Ingrid attended an Australian school as a full boarder because her brother was growing increasingly unhappy living with the Nielsens. John felt that Gerda was being unreasonable and demanded far too much of him while favouring her eldest son, Joe, who was excused from even the simplest tasks. We did not want to inflame the situation by asking the Nielsens to accommodate Ingrid, so we selected Monte Sant' Angelo Mercy College in North Sydney, where she attained her Leaving Certificate at the end of 1965.

When John began studies at the University of New South Wales in early 1964, he used the excuse of travelling long distances to University to leave the Nielsen household and lived temporarily in a flat in Cremorne. Ingrid however, always got on well with the Nielsen family. They had three boys of their own — four, if you included John as their adopted son

161

— and regarded Ingrid as the daughter they always wanted. Nevertheless, she did not ever live with them, except for short periods during her school holidays.

Living in rented premises in Cremorne, John put pressure on us to buy a house so that he could live in rent-free accommodation instead. In 1964, on one of our frequent trips to Sydney, we closed the investment accounts with the solicitor and the property developer and used part of the money to purchase a house at 55 Eyre Street, Chifley for £6,750. It was a modest three-bedroom brick-veneer cottage that was less than a year old.

We had a number of houses in different Sydney locations to choose from but John insisted that we purchase Chifley because it was the closest location, being only 5 kilometres away, from the University of New South Wales at Kensington.

The remaining money was held by Herman Braakensiek in trust for the children to draw down as needed for living and educational expenses added to which were now the extra expenses of household upkeep, such as electricity, water, gas and council rates which had to be paid regularly on the house. As the Braakensieks had been wealthy people and were used to handling large sums of money, we felt it was better for them to handle the distribution of monies to our children in our absence. Of course, they agreed willingly.

An and Eddie's first house in Australia in the Sydney suburb of Chifley. Photo taken soon after purchase in 1965.

Background to our Decision to Immigrate

Between 1960 and 1964 my husband, Ingrid and I journeyed back and forth between Australia and Indonesia, visiting John and the Nielsens on a regular basis twice a year. When our daughter Ingrid moved to reside permanently in Australia in 1964, Eddie and I continued the twice-yearly visits by ourselves, but by the late 1960s our personal circumstances in Indonesia had deteriorated so badly that we decided to get out of Indonesia too.

During 1966 my husband's boss in Indonesia, Monsieur Daniel Richez, retired with one of the most successful profit records of any of UTA's overseas offices. Most of this accomplishment, if not all of it, had been due to Eddie's wonderful salesmanship in securing an ever increasing number of charter flights from the Government, initially for pilgrims wishing to journey to Mecca on the Haj and then for other charter flights to Eastern Europe and China. From the initial two flights in 1959, Eddie was by 1966 regularly ordering up to fifteen charter flights a year for the Indonesian military, increasing the revenue of the Indonesian operations from US$50,000 to almost US$500,000 a year.

As Monsieur Richez's second-in-charge and Head of Sales, Eddie had his absolute trust and confidence. Whenever Richez left Indonesia for holidays or frequent business meetings overseas, my husband would be in total charge of the company's operations in Indonesia. Our two families exchanged gifts regularly. For instance, I can remember Ingrid getting an expensive gold watch from Daniel Richez for her 17th birthday in January 1966. But all that changed with Richez's retirement. Prior to his departure, he sold his Peugeot 403 to Eddie at a very cheap price, as he had done with the Peugeot 203 some years earlier. We were so pleased with the Peugeot 403. It was the most luxurious motor vehicle we had ever possessed up to that time, but our period of enjoyment was short-lived.

Two temporary managers replaced Richez in quick succession before Monsieur Girudy arrived in 1967 as the new permanent Territory Manager. Girudy was in the mould of an "old colonialist". He did not trust his Indonesian employees and assumed total control over every aspect of the business. Because there was no delegation of authority, the company quickly became indecisive and bureaucratic, waiting for the new manager to make a decision on every matter, large and small.

Later that same year, the lucrative pilgrimage charter flights were lost because Monsieur Girudy was too slow in ordering the planes from

France, a task Eddie had performed competently for years. Eddie became frustrated. The last straw was Girudy's decision to stop paying my husband in American dollars and remunerate him in Indonesian rupiah instead. Because of the long-standing arrangement with Monsieur Richez, my husband had up to then been the only Indonesian employee of the company paid in American dollars. Even if Eddie could transfer money out of Indonesia, the Indonesian currency was so devalued internationally by this time that it was virtually worthless in any other country.

A Legacy

From 1947 until I resigned from the Department of Education in 1967, I received a regular high rupiah salary for my teaching duties and when I was promoted to Principal of the Teachers' College in 1953, I was paid the highest salary possible. However, the school that I started, Harapan Kita, was a loss-making concern. I paid my teachers three times the normal salary for a government teacher and often waved the school fees for students of families in financial hardship. My costs were large and growing and my school revenue small and declining.

To augment my income, I ran a catering business as a sideline hobby. Because I already operated a small *rantang*[25] service to feed students living away from home, I took in orders occasionally to provide catering for outside events such as weddings and functions. It did not take up a lot of time, although when I had an order to fulfil there was certainly frenetic activity for a brief period. In the end all my income from teaching and catering went into Harapan Kita.

Even my husband financially supported the school whenever possible. We did not have expensive possessions or even a private car as was considered normal for people in our position. Although I had several blocks of land, I did not have enough money to build houses on them. To me, the school was not a business; it was an exercise in social engineering. I was taking problem children and turning them into model citizens who believed in themselves and had something worthwhile to contribute to society.

Harapan Kita was overseen by a Board of Trustees comprising senior and influential people in the public and private sector, including company

---

[25] Take-away lunchbox service where cooked dishes and rice are placed in small metal containers that can be stacked on top of each other to form a secure, portable cylinder.

directors and senior officials from the Department of Defence and Foreign Affairs. My normal custom was to hand over the running of Harapan Kita to my Deputy Principal, Ibu Kus, when I left for holidays in Australia. But in June 1967, when Major Said Pratalikusuma took over the house and displaced the school in my absence, Ibu Kus tried unsuccessfully to re-establish the school at another location in nearby Jalan Guntur, Menteng. Unfortunately, the school never flourished without my personal involvement and financial support and it ceased operating a few months later in 1967.

However, the school was highly regarded and had earned an enviable reputation over the years for producing students of superior quality. To this day ex-students still contact me personally from around then world to thank me for the head start they received at Harapan Kita. These students have gone on to become highly successful dentists, engineers, doctors, politicians, tradesmen and businesspeople in Indonesia, America, Holland and Australia.

I was therefore pleasantly surprised when I learned that Ibu Tien Suharto, the wife of the then President of Indonesia, had decided to use the name Harapan Kita to start her own school elsewhere in Jakarta later the same year (1967). She obtained a large site in the Jakarta suburb of Senayan on which she built a huge multi-storied school building. After investing millions of rupiah into the school, Ibu Tien Suharto some years later also started a maternity and children's hospital at the same location, which still bears the name Harapan Kita to this day. This hospital is the largest and best-equipped facility of its kind in the entire country and has earned an enviable reputation elsewhere in the world for the quality of its paediatric care.

I was so pleased that the name of my school was perpetuated by such a high profile person as the President's wife and I am very proud that my personal commitment to educational excellence over thirty years is the wonderful legacy I left to Indonesia. However, the truth is that for years my family had suffered much poverty, prejudice, lost opportunities, fraud and disappointment at the hands of others in Indonesia. Now that the children were already safe in Australia, it was time for my husband and I to escape this cycle too and leave Indonesia completely.

When my husband rang me in Sydney with the sad news of our forced removal from our home in Menteng, I decided that I had had enough. On a cold winter's day in Sydney in July 1967, I vowed to make Australia our home from that moment on.

10

A New Life in Australia (post 1967)

First Impressions

My family's first trip to Australia was in July 1960. Even though we stayed only in Sydney, which is a tiny part of that large country, I nevertheless formed a very strong first impression. In short, I fell in love with the place immediately. In Indonesia everything was unstable, unsafe, overcrowded, and as for its citizens of Chinese origins, subject to all levels of discrimination. But in Australia I felt safe straightaway. My husband's opinion of Australia was even more positive than mine. He said that Australia was not only safer but offered its people something more important again, namely freedom. Freedom to think and act, to pursue any desired ambition, and to practise any religion.

Despite the existence of the White Australia Policy, we were surprised at how welcoming Australia was to Asian visitors and students. An enquiry with the Department of Immigration to find the best way for John to stay in Australia resulted in the officials helpfully confirming that adoption by the Nielsens would be the swiftest and surest way of securing his residency.[1]

Even though the cost of living in Australia was many times more expensive than in Indonesia, we did not regard it as particularly high because Eddie was paid in American dollars. For every US dollar, he

---

[1] Read Gerda Nielsen's interview for a different interpretation of these events.

got one pound and two shillings in Australian currency,[2] so that for me Australia was a cheaper place to live than, say, the United States.

My husband and I have always liked fishing as a hobby. When Eddie took one look at the harbours and waterways around Sydney and saw how clean and full of fish they were, he decided then and there he could quite happily fish in Sydney for the rest of his life. When we dined out, I was impressed by how clean and well presented the restaurants were. The tables were wiped down and set with salt and pepper shakers, napkins and often tablecloths. In Indonesia, all of these items would have been stolen! Lastly, Indonesia was a very dirty place with rubbish and waste littering the streets everywhere, but in Sydney the streets were clean and tidy.

There was one negative impression, however, albeit a relatively minor one. We thought that Sydney was too quiet as there was no "night life" to speak of. In Indonesia we were used to shopping whenever we liked and going out at any time of the night to restaurants, functions, and nightclubs as well as visiting each other's homes. But in Sydney, shops closed early and most people retired to their homes directly after work, where they tended to stay in for the rest of the night. On this first visit we went into the central business district of Sydney one evening around seven o'clock and there was hardly anyone on the streets. It seemed deserted. Sydney apparently went to sleep after dark, whereas Jakarta was still a lively place all through the night to the very early hours of the morning. Forty years later Sydney has grown into a bright and bustling international city, but it certainly was not like that when we first saw it in 1960.

New Directions

Having no place to go back to in Indonesia after the Army took full possession of Jalan Jogja 7 in 1967 and being stranded in Australia with no possessions save a diminishing bank account, Eddie asked me what I wanted for Christmas. I showed him an advertisement for a coffee lounge that I had cut out of the paper and said, "I want us to buy this". Eddie objected, saying that I was only in Australia on a short-term visitor's visa and should not be buying a business, but my mind was made up.

---

[2] The exchange rate of US$1 = A£1/2. A£1/2 was the equivalent of A$2.20 for every American dollar in decimal currency. At the time of writing this biography the American dollar is worth only A$1.25.

I went to our bedroom and returned with our Australian bankbook showing my husband that we were continuing to withdraw money for education and living expenses, but had not made a deposit since his last foreign currency pay cheque six months earlier. I said, "We cannot go on like this. Soon we'll have no money left. I must start earning money." Eddie reluctantly agreed that we needed to improve our financial position and therefore we bought the Toby Coffee Lounge in January 1968 for $5,500. It was located in Piccadilly Arcade, off Pitt Street in the Central Business District (CBD) of Sydney.

I chose to buy a coffee lounge in Sydney for two reasons. The first was that I had some prior experience with managing a restaurant. Jakarta had been the host city for the IVth Asian Games of 1962 and two acquaintances of my niece (Ida Karyadi) whom we had known for more than ten years purchased a large restaurant nearby in Menteng that had been approved by the Games Committee to serve meals to competitors, officials and visitors. The owners (Njoo Dwan Poo and Tee Sik Hway) had been former students of the University of Indonesia in Jakarta, and we first met them when they chose to eat their meals at my place in Jalan Jogja 7 rather than eat the food served at the University cafeteria. I was running a small catering business out of my kitchen for other students, functions and restaurants at the time. We remained friends after they chose to finish University without graduating in 1960 and a year or so later decided to invest the restaurant trade by purchasing Cookie Restaurant.

Cookie had its own bakery and two full-time chefs: one to produce Asian dishes and, unusually for Indonesia at the time, another chef to present European cuisine. Even though it was a popular venue, it had not been well managed by the previous owners and the new owners were concerned that the Games Committee might "take over" the restaurant if it did not meet its standards. At the time the Indonesian Government was anxious to present Jakarta in the best possible light for its international guests and Cookie was one of the few venues that could provide both European and Asian cuisines.

The owners asked me to manage the restaurant for the duration of the Games and relied upon my catering skills as well as my general management skills (running a Teachers' College and a private School) to put the place in order. I did not ask for monetary payment, but my family could eat at the restaurant every night for free during the two weeks of the Asian Games.

One of the innovations that the owners appreciated was that I set up a small food concession alongside one of the Games' stadia at Senayan.

This proved very popular. I would ferry snacks and meals to the stall across town from the main kitchen. Through this innovation and better management at the restaurant, sales increased significantly. The owners valued my involvement so much that the next year when the Games of the New Emerging Forces were held in Jakarta, they asked me to repeat the exercise.[3] By now the owners had concluded that they needed to employ a professional manager to run the restaurant. They asked if I would be interested, but I had to decline as I was fully occupied with my educational commitments. However, I did agree to stay on part-time at nights until they found a full-time manager to replace me, which they succeeded in doing about two months later.

The second reason that I chose to buy a coffee lounge was that my English-language proficiency was poor — and still is. English is my third language and one that I started to learn only at Teachers' College in my twenties. I still prefer to converse in Dutch primarily, then Bahasa Indonesia and lastly in English. I knew my deficiency in English would prevent me from becoming a teacher in Australia and apart from managing a restaurant I had no experience in anything else. Through a simple process of choosing a business in which I had some prior experience and motivated by rapidly diminishing finances, I decided to enter the hospitality industry as the owner of a coffee lounge.

With personal circumstances for Eddie in Indonesia going from bad to worse, my husband resigned from UTA, gathered the few remaining possessions we had left and joined me in Australia towards the middle of 1968. However, he had been in Australia only a few months when his father died. Eddie therefore returned to Indonesia to pay his respects and take care of the funeral. He also took advantage of this opportunity to sell the home in Tebet and, after relocating his mother to relatives in Jember, used the proceeds of the property sale to pay for her care. When a Dutch nursing home opened in Surabaya in 1973–74, Eddie arranged for her to be moved there, where she stayed until her death in 1982.

---

[3] The Asian Games of 1962 had been politicized by Indonesia's last-minute banning of both Israel and Taiwan. As a result, Indonesia was expelled from both the Asian Games and its parent body, the International Olympic Organization. In retaliation, Indonesia established the alternate athletic organization Games of the New Emerging Forces (GANEFO) and the inaugural event was held in Jakarta during November 1963. GANEFO was moderately successful with forty-eight nations participating but the first occurrence was also its last. After the coup in 1965, Indonesia lost interest in promoting a rebel athletic organization and participating countries wanted to return to the Olympic movement (<www.internationalgames.net/ganefo>, accessed 14 March 2004).

Staying in Australia

At the end of the third three-month extension of my tourist visa in June 1968, I received a letter from the Immigration Department saying that no further extensions would be granted and that I had to leave the country. I closed the shop for a week, returned to Indonesia, obtained another visitor's visa from the Australian Embassy in Jakarta and travelled back to Australia to start the whole process of visa extensions all over again.

In the meantime my husband, who had also come to live in Australia, was embarking on his first twelve-month cycle of visa extensions to his temporary visitor's visa. In mid-1969, towards the end of my second twelve-month period of visa extensions and the end of Eddie's first, we intended to close the coffee lounge for a week and return to Indonesia to get yet another visa from the Australian Embassy in Jakarta. But I knew that we had to do something to get our visa status changed or at some time in the future we would not be allowed to stay. We could not go on renewing temporary visas for ever.

I was told through a friend that a certain immigration officer might be able to help us.[4] Eddie went to see him at the Department of Immigration, but instead of dealing with the matter there he asked my husband to visit him later at his private address. My husband became suspicious: why would this officer want to conduct official government business from his home? After thinking about it he told me he would not pursue the matter of our immigration status through this person. We later found out from other immigration officials that this person was corruptly arranging permanent visas for $10,000 per person.

As the deadline for departure to leave Australia and renew our visas overseas was looming, we started talking about our circumstances to several of our regular and trusted customers in the coffee lounge. One Dutch customer said he would introduce us to a friend of his who happened to be a Senator in the Commonwealth Parliament. The next day my husband and I went with this person to the Sydney Parliamentary offices of Senator Tony Mulvihill.[5] We did not know it at the time, but Tony Mulvihill had an abiding interest in the welfare of immigrants and was at the time Chairman of the Commonwealth Immigration Advisory Council that was playing a major role in liberalizing official policy.

---

[4] Name withheld by author.
[5] Labor Senator for the State of New South Wales in the Australian Parliament (1967–83).

Senator James Anthony "Tony" Mulvihill, New South Wales Labor Senator in the Australian Parliament 1967–83. Championed the Sudibjo application for permanent residency in Australia from the late 1960s. Died 2000. (Image courtesy of <www.workers.labor.net.au>)

After introductions and some preliminary discussions, Senator Mulvihill, said, "Where are your passports?" We handed them over and he continued, "You leave it all to me. You can go back to your coffee lounge and continue to run your business." We were stunned. Eddie replied, "We can not! You've seen the telegram from the Immigration Office. We have to get out of Australia." He picked up the phone and calmly phoned the Minister of Immigration, then Phillip Lynch in the Liberal Government. The two had a friendly chat over the phone and it was obvious that they knew each other very well on a first-name basis. After some minutes, Senator Mulvihill put down the phone and confidently informed us, "Everything's organized. Go back to your business and I'll see to it that you're granted long-term visas."

Within a few months in early 1970 we received a letter from Phillip Lynch as the Minister of Immigration stating that while he could not grant us a permanent resident's visa — we had no qualifications whatsoever and our business was too small — he would nevertheless grant us a two-year temporary visa because of the personal representations of Senator Mulvihill.

We were overjoyed. Over the next six years we were granted three further extensions of two-year's duration each while Senator Mulvihill continued to press relentlessly on our behalf for our permanent residency. Finally, in early 1976, we were granted permanent residency status. We wanted to confirm our new status by taking out citizenship (naturalization) straight away. Because this whole process had taken such a long time, the Department waved the usual two-year waiting period for naturalization and we became Australian citizens that same year in a quiet ceremony at the Sydney office of the Department of Immigration on a beautiful day in August.

During the many years we struggled for the right to stay permanently in Australia, we developed a very close relationship with Senator Mulvihill. He dined at our coffee lounge — and later our restaurant — as our guest several times a year. We were astounded that during this whole saga he never asked for any money to act on our behalf. Not one cent. We found this situation to be radically different to our experiences in Indonesia. There, we had to bribe officials and politicians all the time for everything, even the most inconsequential matters. But here in Australia, was a politician intimately involved with the most serious matter of all — our future — and he was merely doing his job without any thought of financial reward. We remained friends with Senator Tony Mulvihill for years, right up until his retirement from Federal Parliament (1983) and the closure of our restaurant (1990). We then lost contact with him and found out from a newspaper article about his death in 2000.

Our Businesses

We operated the Toby Coffee Lounge[6] profitably in the Piccadilly Arcade for two years until the end of 1971, when the owner of the building notified all the tenants to vacate because they wanted to redevelop the entire arcade. By the addition of Indonesian meals to the normal western fare to be found at a coffee lounge, we had increased the takings from $90 per week to around $300 per week. We were given an option to return to the site after redevelopment, but as this was expected to take a further two years we decided to start afresh somewhere else.

---

[6] In 1969 renamed *Warung Indonesia*, meaning "Indonesian eating stall".

My husband negotiated a three-year lease on a fish shop in Pitt Street, Sydney from a Greek friend from whom Eddie had been regularly purchasing seafood for the coffee lounge. Eddie had known for some time that his friend had wanted to sell, but no one had expressed any interest. After some discussion my husband bought the business for $4,500 at a discount for cash. The shop was located in a then unsavoury section of Pitt Street near Central railway station at the intersection of Campbell Street. I was not impressed by the surroundings and wanted something bigger and better elsewhere.

I soon found a restaurant in another location of my liking. It was called Happy Granny's in York Street opposite the Queen Victoria Building (QVB) and about a hundred metres away from Town Hall railway station, which is still the second busiest local station in Sydney. It was an American-style bar and grill that had fallen out of favour with the public, but it did have something that I was particularly looking for, that is seating for over one hundred patrons. The premises also had a liquor licence that the owners were willing to transfer. At the time new liquor licences for restaurants were very difficult to obtain. Transferring an existing licence to a new owner at the same premises was much easier and would certainly make the business more attractive to customers.

The bar at Warung Indonesia in the late 1970s with Sally Nielsen (left), Cotton (employee) and Peter Hestelow behind the bar.

Hundreds of public buses used the street outside the restaurant as a transport interchange and every day thousands of commuters walked past the restaurant's doors on their way to and from work. Within a radius of a few hundred metres, the restaurant was surrounded by hundreds of firms employing thousands of people. It seemed like the perfect location. All I needed to do was offer the public a cuisine that was more popular than the existing American-style brassiere. As Indonesian food had recently become fashionable, I was confident that the restaurant was bound to make a fortune.

The owners were anxious to sell. When I showed genuine interest, they sweetened the deal by immediately dropping the purchase price from $32,000 to $20,000. Even though the purchase price was more than the equivalent of a new house in 1971, I did not seek any legal advice or independent counsel. I wanted this restaurant and to me that was all that mattered. Despite my husband's strong objections, I prevailed upon him to counter-sign the contracts, as the $20,000 loan we needed from Westpac Bank to purchase the restaurant had to be secured against our home in Chifley, which was held in joint names.

There were several reasons why I was determined to proceed with this expensive purchase, even though my husband was independently purchasing another business. First, we had secured only temporary visas to stay in Australia and the major ground for rejecting our application for permanent residency had been that we did not have a substantial business. I felt that our legal status would be significantly strengthened if we owned a large restaurant rather than a mere fish shop.

Secondly, after losing everything we had worked for back in Indonesia, I thought that a big restaurant would build up our wealth more rapidly than the fish shop. Lastly, I wanted the prestige of owning a large restaurant in the CBD. We were fully aware each of us was negotiating to buy a separate business, but neither of us was prepared to stop. In the end, both businesses were purchased and opened within a week of each other.

I cannot remember for certain which opened first. My husband is of the opinion his fish shop was first, whilst I believe it was the restaurant. Either way, from early 1972 we had to operate two food outlets instead of one.

I immediately transferred the name Warung Indonesia to the new premises, and got our logo of a Balinese dancer painted on the front window. Thankfully that was all I needed to spend as the restaurant was already fully equipped and furnished. We did give the interior an Indonesian

Photo taken of An and her sister Roostien at Warung Indonesia restaurant in York Street, Sydney during one of Roostien's infrequent visits to Australia (possibly 1978).

flavour by hanging paintings and decorations and playing Indonesian music over the sound system. Later, I would organize Indonesian cultural events and evenings, but at the outset, these modest changes were sufficient to create an Indonesian atmosphere.

While my husband was content to commence trading in his fish shop without any opening celebrations, I was determined to open the restaurant with an impressive function to place the establishment "on the map". I prepared a huge banquet in the form of a *rijsttafel*[7] and invited as many members of the Dutch and Indonesian expatriate community as I could. It proved to be a very popular evening with fifty to a hundred friends

---

[7] Rijsttafel means "rice table" in Dutch and used to signify an Indonesian banquet, where numerous small dishes are served with rice.

and acquaintances enjoying themselves and promising to return as paying customers. However, the expatriate Indonesian community was then small and I knew that I had to reach the wider Australian community if the restaurant was to become a commercial success.

The next few years were a difficult time as neither my husband nor I would give up our respective businesses. Despite our differences, we would cross back and forth several times a day between our separate establishments to help each other, but the days were very, very long and tiring. Each day started with Eddie going to the fish and produce markets at 5:00 am and finished with the restaurant closing at 10:00 pm.

Occasionally, we had cross words to say to each other. Sometimes in anger or frustration my husband would say, "You stop this bloody restaurant. It is a nonsense", but I would snap back at him, "You stop your fish shop. My business is more important than yours". My husband knows how strong-minded I can be and in this instance I was determined to continue with the restaurant, no matter what the cost. If anyone was to give ground, it would have to be Eddie, not me. We continued this routine six days a week for almost three years until the building in which the fish shop was located was burnt down by an arsonist. There was a boarding house above the fish shop and one of the tenants deliberately set fire to the building after being evicted. Unfortunately, we had not insured the business against such calamities.

For the three years my husband operated the fish shop, its revenue was greater than the restaurant's and Eddie had increased sales considerably. To give one example, in the early 1970s leading up to the peak time of Easter he was taking over $3,500 a day, while the restaurant was taking only about $300 a day. In fact he had been heavily subsidizing my restaurant since the beginning, just as he had with my school in Jakarta, but he still managed to save thousands of dollars in a bank account. He had also won $12,000 from the State Lottery in 1975 — of which he gave me half — so he had accumulated quite a sizeable reserve for himself.

For a short time after the fire destroyed the building which contained the fish shop, my husband tried to continue in the seafood trade as a supplier. He had built up a substantial portion of his revenue from clubs and restaurants coming to his shop to buy large amounts of seafood, so he continued buying seafood at the fish markets and now took it directly to these other businesses. This practice lasted only a few months for he found the physical task of delivering many kilos of produce, sometimes up several flights of stairs, simply too arduous for a man in his fifties.

Dejected, he decided to throw his lot in with me and the restaurant, Warung Indonesia.

From the moment my husband fully committed himself to the restaurant in 1975, it started making money and the strained relationship between us eased. We worked closely together again and it was good to see our joint efforts result in a profitable business. At its peak in the late 1970s to early 1980s we were taking over $5,000 a week, employing 6 to 8 full-time and part-time staff and serving more than 800 meals a week.

Fostering Indonesian–Australian Understanding

Universities and high schools in Australia had started offering courses in Indonesian studies from the early 1960s but a decade later in Sydney there were still few opportunities available for teachers and students to practise their language skills and discuss Indonesian affairs outside the classroom. I became aware of this when I operated the coffee lounge and willingly arranged informal meetings and discussion groups to be held there. I

Indonesian dancers at Warung Indonesia (circa 1980). Daughter Ingrid is second from right (not counting the *raksasa* mask hanging on the far right).

continued this practice in the restaurant. We also organized batik fashion-shows, Indonesian cultural evenings featuring folk dances from various regions of Indonesia, school visits, and on busy nights an Indonesian band played Indonesian folk music (*kroncong*).

In the mid-1970s the Indonesian expatriate community living in Sydney was still small, comprising only a few hundred indigenous Indonesians and perhaps no more than a few thousand Dutch and Chinese who had previously lived in Indonesia. More importantly, the expatriate community was also starved of a meeting point. Apart from my restaurant there were only two other Indonesian eating places in Sydney — the Selamat Makan in the inner eastern suburb of Darlinghurst and the Java restaurant in Sydney's outer north at Dural — but mine was the only establishment large enough to offer cultural activities. The larger size of the restaurant allowed me to develop the informal gatherings of educators started earlier at the coffee lounge into something more structured for teachers and students alike.

University lecturers started having tutorial classes and primary and secondary schools in Sydney began arranging school excursions to the restaurant. There, students could converse in Bahasa Indonesia and learn about the history, culture and politics of Indonesia from someone who had lived there and listen to me relate my own personal experiences.

As my reputation as an educational resource quickly spread, schools beyond Sydney began arranging excursions to visit the restaurant. Classes of students came from high schools in regional New South Wales, such as Orange, Lismore, Bowral, Wollongong, and from as far away as Queensland and once even from Darwin in the Northern Territory. These formal visits occurred as often as four or five times a month over many years, during which more than 8,000 school students came to the restaurant to have an Indonesian cultural experience. The highlight of every school excursion was the partaking of a genuine Indonesian meal at the restaurant, for which I deliberately charged the students only half price. I willingly donated my time and insisted on subsidizing the cost as a form of community service to hopefully foster better understanding between Australia and Indonesia.

The place was full of Indonesian expatriates almost every day and with them came more and more Australians. We held political discussions with the expatriates and Australians and increasingly the restaurant was seen by many as a location for the general population to learn and understand more about Australia's most populous neighbour. On several occasions during the late 1970s my restaurant was honoured by the patronage of Gough Whitlam, who had been the Prime Minister of Australia between 1972 and 1975. I think he worked from an office nearby and he used the restaurant mainly to have lunch-time meetings with Labor Party colleagues. Even though he was no longer the Prime Minister, he was still a very powerful and influential figure on the Australian political landscape. Every time he visited the restaurant he would be accompanied by many advisers, staffers and sometimes Federal and State Labor parliamentarians.

I remember that on one particular occasion he requested exclusive use of a separate area in the restaurant for an important meeting. For several hours that day he led an intense discussion with a small number of people while my staff kept them supplied with plenty of food and drink. Afterwards, Mr Whitlam complimented me on the food and service — which he did every time he visited — and obviously appreciated my discretion, because he returned several more times for highly sensitive discussions over the next year or so.

Anzac Day[8] is a public holiday in Australia to celebrate the commitment and sacrifice of the military during times of war. The centrepiece of the day's commemoration is an Anzac Day march, when ex-service men and women from Australia and New Zealand and their Allies proudly march through the streets of cities and towns across the land to the admiration of millions of thankful Australians. Before one Anzac Day in the late 1970s, Dutch expatriates arranged to have Warung Indonesia opened on the forthcoming Anzac Day so that ex-soldiers from Holland and Indonesia could meet and celebrate amongst themselves and their families after the march through Sydney's streets. They had no eating place of their own to go to where they could consume Indonesian food. Of course, I readily agreed: nothing was too much trouble for the men and women in uniform who had defended Holland and Indonesia against German and Japanese aggression. For years afterwards, it became a tradition for these people and their families to meet in the restaurant after the march, have a meal and a few drinks and reminisce about their wartime experiences while they proudly wore their decorations and medals in front of adoring family members.

---

[8] ANZAC is an acronym for the Australian and New Zealand Army Corps which was formed in the First World War when the two nations' armed forces combined to fight under a single command.

Together with an embassy in Australia's federal capital of Canberra, Indonesia has a number of consular offices in the various state capitals of which the consulate in Sydney is the largest and most important. During the 1970s and 1980s the Indonesian Consulate General in Sydney used Warung Indonesia to cater for many trade missions and other official functions it was hosting, such as evenings for the Red Cross Society or the Australia Indonesia Association. For important occasions, such as Indonesia's Independence Day on 17 August, the Consul General, his entire staff and distinguished guests would come to the restaurant for a specially prepared feast when I would often organize Indonesian dancing and music to impress his guests.

In the mid to late 1980s the Indonesian Ambassador to Australia, His Excellency Major General August Marpaung, was a distant relative of mine and he used the restaurant for informal and official functions whenever he was visiting Sydney from the embassy in Canberra.[9] Also in the mid-1980s, senior staff from Indonesia's national airline, Garuda, attended one of the many Australia-Indonesia cultural functions at the restaurant. Afterwards, they approached me and said they were so impressed with the quality of the food that they wanted me to supply meals for their first-class passengers on Garuda flights from Sydney. This was a great honour, but before a commercial agreement could be reached the airline changed its mind and withdrew from negotiations.

I had many Australian and Indonesian staff working for me in the restaurant over the years and some of them went on to establish their own Indonesian restaurants, such as the Bali restaurant in Oxford Street, Darlinghurst, Ramayana restaurant in Sydney CBD, and Safari restaurant in Newtown. On many occasions my husband and I gave advice to ensure that their new ventures were a commercial success and sometimes we even paid for meals in their establishments to support them.

This was a very good time for us in our restaurant. As well as paying all our personal and business expenses, we still had enough money left over to repay all our debts and take two expensive overseas holidays to visit relatives and friends in Indonesia and Holland.

---

[9] Major General August Marpaung was the Indonesian Ambassador to Australia from 1984 to 1987. Born in 1926, he died in 1991 at the age of 65 and was buried in the Kalibata Heroes Cemetery in South Jakarta. General Marpaung was related to An via the marriage of his nephew, Pay Marpaung, to Tan Sian Ien, youngest daughter of Tan Siauw Djie (An's youngest brother).

The Decline in Our Business

After 1982, the business was undermined by three significant changes over which we had no control whatsoever. First, the New South Wales State Government introduced Random Breath Testing (RBT) in December 1982 to reduce alcohol-related road deaths.[10] Customers started drinking less when they ate at the restaurant or preferred to stay at home as they did not want to drink and drive. This especially depressed our night-time trade. Before the introduction of RBT, we had bought wines and spirits by the box-load, but afterwards we bought it by the individual bottle. From a high of $5,000 per week, the takings of the restaurant slipped to about $4,500 a week.

Secondly, in 1983 the Federal Government introduced tax changes which eliminated entertainment as a legitimate tax deduction for companies. This harmed our day-time trade as the majority of our luncheon customers were business people who had previously been claiming the cost of our meals as a legitimate tax deduction. Again our revenue slipped further, down to about $4,000 per week.

About this time, I was approached by two Balinese Chinese businessmen who were running a restaurant in Sydney and they offered me $100,000 to buy the restaurant, but I was of two minds. I recognized that the offer was an extraordinary amount — the equivalent of the price of two average homes in Sydney at the time — but I also needed the emotional satisfaction of owning and operating a successful restaurant. I reasoned that the offer of $100,000 was only their opening bid and therefore the restaurant was probably worth twice that amount, so I declined the offer. Unfortunately I did so in such an abrupt manner that the Chinese businessmen were convinced I was not interested in selling at all. There was some truth to their belief and to this day I really do not know whether I would have sold the restaurant for any amount.

The most serious shock occurred in late 1983, when Sydney Council announced a three-year restoration program for the Queen Victoria Building (QVB) opposite my restaurant to be completed by 1986, well in advance of the Bicentennial celebrations of European arrival in Australia (1988). York Street outside our restaurant and for the length of QVB was

---

[10] Random Breath Testing empowered Police to test the breath of any driver for suspected alcohol consumption without needing a legal justification in advance.

40th Wedding Anniversary Celebration at Warung Indonesia in December 1984 with Ingrid holding cake platter on right and grandson Daniel (3) in foreground

closed to all vehicular traffic for excavation of an underground car park and most pedestrians were kept away by barricades, hoardings, dust and noise. Over the three years of disturbance, the restaurant takings declined steadily from $4,000 to $2,000 per week. The reality was that the business never recovered from this massive blow. In fact, when the QVB reopened at the end of 1986, the restaurant was even more adversely affected than before. Pedestrians were now drawn directly into the QVB building from the nearby Town Hall railway station by new underground tunnels. York Street above ground became deserted. Business dropped off dramatically again and takings stayed as low as $1,500 per week from then on.

I was desperate to keep the restaurant operating as I needed to continue working. It may seem irrational now, but I had this abiding fear that if I stopped working, I would die! I convinced myself that if I worked harder, I could turn the situation around. Warung Indonesia was now losing money badly. I stopped keeping proper accounts because I did not want to know exactly how much money it was losing each month, but even without accurate figures I already knew that my outgoings were exceeding my income by more than $5,000 a month. One of the major costs was rent. From about $750 per week when I took over the premises in 1971, yearly rent increases had seen lease payments jump to almost $2,000 per week by the mid-1980s.

This is not a period of my life that I am proud of and I wish I had not behaved as poorly as I did, but I was obsessed with the fear of "losing face" in the community as my father had done sixty years earlier and I was determined never to repeat an episode like it. In extreme anxiety, I sought money from acquaintances, friends and family to support me. In late 1988, a friend of Ingrid's, Joyce Hoevenaars, invested $35,000 to keep the business afloat on the expectation of becoming a future silent partner. The costs kept on increasing, I never did offer her a partnership, and soon I found that again I could not even meet the monthly rental payments.

My husband was growing more upset by my increasingly obdurate attitude. We had frightful arguments and he even threatened to leave me, but nothing would divert me from my objective of saving the business and saving my dignity. One day at home he became so angry with me that he grabbed hold of my shoulders and started shaking me violently shouting, "Stop this nonsense woman. We are going broke! You stop this bloody restaurant or I'll divorce you, you stupid woman." I shrugged him off and resolved to take no notice of his frustration or his threat to leave me.

I discovered that the Westpac loan we had paid off earlier was in fact an overdraft facility which was still available. Without having to notify my husband, I reactivated the Westpac account and drew down the full amount of $20,000 to pay outstanding debts. I then obtained a loan from Citibank in late 1989 for $90,000 that was secured against the house in Chifley. Again, I forced my husband to sign the necessary documentation in spite of his objections. Most of that money merely paid off accumulated debts, such as rent, and soon I needed more money to not only keep the business going but pay off the Citibank loan as well. The interest rate was at an historic high of 22 per cent, and before long I could not even pay the monthly minimum amount on either of the outstanding loans.

I used every tactic I could think of to get more money, including emotional blackmail on friends and relatives. I told people the financial situation was so bad that I feared I would die and implied that if they did not give me money they would be responsible for my death. I even threatened suicide. One day at home I told my husband to get me money or I would hang myself in the garage. As a result, I received financial assistance from several fresh sources, but it was never enough. I needed a lot more money, tens of thousands more.

Up to now my children had been reluctant to help me financially even though they could both afford to do so. They had well-paid jobs and owned property. So I now put them under enormous pressure to help me. My son, John, absolutely refused. He repeatedly told me it was time to quit the business and retire gracefully, but I did not want to hear this. My daughter, Ingrid, however was a different proposition. She had always been more caring, more malleable, and I felt that if I applied the right pressure she would ultimately support me financially.

Personal Health

Twice in my life I have been under so much stress that I have experienced severe bleeding from my vagina for several months or years at a time. The first occasion this happened was in Jakarta in the early to mid-1960s, when I was convinced that Captain Said Pratalikusuma would throw us out of the house at Jalan Jogja 7 at any moment. The bleeding did not happen all the time. It came and went over a period of a few years and even fluctuated in volume, from spotting through to profusion. In 1964, as the Indonesian political climate approached disorder and violence the bleeding became more frequent.

By this time, I was in my fifties and had been post-menopausal for some years, so the bleeding could not be menstruation. I suspected cancer, but the doctors I consulted in Jakarta could find no evidence of cancer. They could not explain my condition, yet I continued to haemorrhage. During one of our regular trips to visit John in Sydney, I saw a doctor who told me she thought the problem was psychological,[11] but she was not certain and suggested that I follow the matter up in Indonesia or at the Dutch Institute of Cancer in Holland. Doctor Lie gave me a letter of referral.

Back in Jakarta the bleeding persisted and over the next year or so I had regular check-ups with Indonesian doctors who said they were also fairly sure I did not have cancer. But they also recommended that I should be checked out in Holland at the Cancer Institute if I wanted absolute certainty. It took Eddie over a year to arrange a free trip for me to Europe — his allocations were being used up on trips to Australia — and I got

---

[11] Dr Frances Lie, older sister of Chris Lie, who was a fellow University student of John Nielsen.

special leave from the Department of Education. While I was in Holland in October 1965, the news came through that there had been an attempted coup in Indonesia. I wanted to return immediately but all flights in and out of Jakarta were cancelled.

Family and friends were back in Indonesia and I did not know whether they were alive or dead. Suddenly my bleeding stopped, overnight. It took me close to a week to get back to Indonesia and the mysterious haemorrhaging did not return for decades.

The second occasion when I started regular bleeding was in the early 1990s, when I was fighting to keep my restaurant open. If I had thought about it then, I might have realized this was a pattern of behaviour repeating itself, but I was too self-absorbed to make the connection. Once again the bleeding waxed and waned and fluctuated in volume depending on my emotional state.

My Desperation to Keep the Restaurant Open

Over several months I kept ringing my daughter and demanding money, sometimes in the early morning before seven o'clock, sometimes late at night after nine, but often at work when she was emotionally most vulnerable. The pressure reached a climax in the first months of 1990, when she and her fiancé, Stuart Pearson, came to visit us at our home in Chifley. I waved some bloodied underwear of mine in Ingrid's face and said, "I am bleeding to death with worry about the restaurant. You need to help me or I will die and that will be your fault. I gave you money from the restaurant to buy your house but I want it repaid, now."[12] Yet, still she prevaricated.

Ingrid's wedding to Stuart was approaching, so I threatened my daughter with the ultimate catastrophe. I told her that unless she gave me the money immediately, I would commit suicide on the very day of her wedding! Within a week she gave me a cheque for $45,000, but Stuart said it was the very last "blood money" I would ever receive from her. The truth is that even this largesse was not enough. Within a few months I

---

[12] In 1981, Eddie had personally given Ingrid $45,000 out of his own individual bank account as a deposit on her home in Westleigh, Sydney. At the time it was a gift and had nothing to do with An or the restaurant, but now An was claiming the money came from her out of Warung Indonesia and that it was a loan which needed to be repaid immediately.

was facing the same desperate financial circumstances again. I knew that something had to be done to break this downward spiral, but I just did not know what.

Over the previous three years, through begging and borrowing, I had managed to inject almost $200,000 into the restaurant to keep the business afloat, but even I realized that no amount of money was going to save it now. In the end my landlord, Mr Vidor of Toga Properties Pty Ltd, solved this dilemma for me. The single largest outstanding amount I owed was for rent and this figure was growing by $2,000 each week. There was no way he was going to risk public condemnation by prosecuting a 78-year-old woman for rental arrears, but equally there was no way he was going to let the situation persist. In October 1990, after exploring every other possibility with me, he simply changed the locks on my restaurant which shut me out of my own business.[13] The restaurant ceased trading on that day, but he generously allowed us to remove our personal property from the restaurant and also waved half of the outstanding $90,000 debt. Coincidentally, my bleeding stopped completely.

After Warung Indonesia

We stayed in our house at Chifley for a short time, but as our major debtors like the banks were pressing us for payment, John invited us to live with him so that our house could be sold to pay off the most significant debts. The house was sold in 1991 for $300,000. After paying off our formal debtors under legal contract we had left a paltry $30,000. Everyone else — friends and family — simply lost their money.

We lived with John and his family in a room at their home in the Sydney suburb of Baulkham Hills for the next three years. It was not an agreeable time as there were differences between how the two families should live together. John found fault in just about everything we did. My husband would often clean the house or John's cars and I would cook a special meal for them to show our appreciation, but John would only criticize our actions. In the end it was becoming unbearable living under the same roof and we knew we had to find our own accommodation.

---

[13] Without An's knowledge, her son John and son-in-law Stuart had made arrangements for the landlord, Mr Vidor, to shut the restaurant without further warning.

During this time we travelled back to Indonesia twice on airfares paid for by my husband's relatives in Surabaya. They were pleasant trips because we were treated as honourable guests and could temporarily forget all about the troubles and embarrassments in Australia. On one of these visits our relatives invited us to stay permanently. They would give us our own house with servants and a driver and we would never have to worry about anything ever again. I was very much tempted at the prospect of becoming a respected elder citizen in the Indonesian community but my husband was more concerned about our increasing need for good health care.[14]

In 1994 our 50th Wedding Anniversary approached. My children in Sydney offered a modest party, while our relatives in Indonesia offered a more lavish celebration. Without hesitation, I insisted on accepting the latter proposal. I wanted a big party where hundreds of guests could deferentially pay me their respects. But this decision caused some conflict with my children. There was an economic recession in Australia and my children informed us that while they could afford a genuine but unpretentious celebration in Australia, they just could not afford to go overseas and contribute to a more lavish affair in Indonesia. It was either an intimate party in Australia, or a bigger event in Indonesia without any children present. Nevertheless, I still insisted on the Indonesian option.

At the end of 1994 my husband and I travelled to Indonesia and enjoyed our wedding anniversary with a lovely celebration in Surabaya, but true to their word not one of my children or close relatives from Australia attended. It was a strange and somewhat empty feeling. There we were as guests of honour at a party in Indonesia surrounded by many well-wishers, most of whom were strangers, while all the members of our immediate family were absent.

Since Warung Indonesia closed in 1990, we have had a total of nine overseas trips to Indonesia, Singapore and Bangkok to visit relatives and friends. Most of the trips were paid for by my husband's nephew Iwan Haryanto in Surabaya, or by our Sunrider business (more of that later), or by my daughter. In other words, out of nine trips overseas, my husband and I only paid for one of them.

---

[14] Eddie and An were respectively in their 70s and 80s, as were most of their friends and relatives in Indonesia. Several members of Eddie's family in Indonesia had already died because of poor health care in that country and Eddie insisted they should stay in Australia to receive the best health care possible as they grew older.

The home of An and Eddie Sudibjo at Girraween in Sydney that they moved into in 1994.

When we returned to Australia from our travels in 1994, our son-in-law, Stuart, helped us to secure a pleasant Housing Commission home in the western Sydney suburb of Girraween.[15] That is where we have lived ever since. We are so happy here I hope that we will stay in this place until we die. Of the monies remaining after our house was sold in 1991 to pay off the debts of Warung Indonesia, we currently have just under half the amount left. But I am not complaining.

We receive an Australian Government pension every fortnight, which is enough for us to live comfortably. Our children regularly augment the pension with generous financial contributions. I am comfortable with our current financial status and the knowledge that if we ever wanted to purchase something for ourselves we have a little "nest egg" set aside to afford that. This is a far cry from the hectic years a few decades ago when money flowed through my hands like water.

---

[15] Public housing that is affordable either to purchase (on time payment) or rent at heavily subsidized rates from the Government.

Children

In 1970 my son John met and married a Cypriot-Australian girl by the name of Tesula (Sue). I was happy about this marriage as I wanted John to settle down and Sue seemed quite a good woman. However, the two were not all that well suited. In winter, for example, John insisted on spending much time away from home snow skiing, a sport in which Sue did not want to participate as she was particularly susceptible to the cold. They started to drift apart and she began seeing another man. The marriage ended within two years when Sue left to live with this other person. Thankfully they did not have children and therefore the divorce was quite simple.

Nevertheless, the divorce was still emotionally hurtful and for the next five years or so John acted out his anger over the matter by having a string of casual relationships, smoking marijuana, and drinking heavily. Gradually he worked through this upset and in 1974 finally noticed a beautiful young Chinese-Indonesian girl who was working part time in Warung Indonesia while finishing her degree in Optometry at the University of NSW. Her name was Sally Suseno and they were married in 1978. They have been

John Nielsen and Tesula (Sue) Anastassiou wedding reception at Warung Indonesia coffee lounge in Piccadilly Arcade, Sydney 1970. L-R: An, Ingrid, Valeska Ong (wife of Ong Kiem Ping family friend who purchased Tebet properties from Eddie), John, Sue, Eddie.

Wedding of John Nielsen and Sally Suseno, 12 February 1978. L-R: Peter Hestelow, Gerda Nielsen, An Sudibjo, Roostien Liem, John and Sally Nielsen, Andrew Bray, Ingrid Hestelow, Eddie Sudibjo, and Jan Nielsen.

together ever since and have two fine children, Daniel (born 1982) and Jennifer (born 1987).

In 1971, Ingrid met Peter Hestelow when they were both working at the architectural firm of Kann Finch and Partners in Sydney. They started going out together. Peter was recently divorced and twenty years older than Ingrid, but we did not express our concern until the relationship became serious and they told us they wanted to get married. I knew Peter was sickly and my husband suspected alcoholism was the cause, but despite our objections Ingrid still wanted to marry him.

Peter had many redeeming and admirable features. He was a very charming and cultured person who obviously loved Ingrid deeply. However, I was more concerned about the age difference between them and his illness rather than his love for Ingrid. I feared that the marriage would end in his untimely death and cause much unhappiness for Ingrid.

I tried to talk Ingrid out of marriage and even got some of my friends and relatives to put pressure on her to end the relationship, but the more I tried, the more Ingrid insisted on going ahead. I guess that sometimes she can be as stubborn as me. In the end they were married in 1973, but my husband and I refused to attend the ceremony in protest. After the marriage, Peter's health continued to deteriorate and after several visits to

190

doctors my husband's fears were confirmed: Peter was an alcoholic and he was drinking himself to death. Ingrid kept insisting that her love would "cure" him of his habit, but his condition worsened to the point where he could not work any more and spent all day home along with his flagons of wine. Despite the best personal care and medical attention possible, Peter eventually died of an alcohol-related illness in late 1983 at the age of only 54.

Ingrid was heart-broken and for a long time blamed herself for Peter's death, but it was not her fault and we never indulged in the "I told you so" response. Ingrid needed our unconditional support and we gave it to her.

Many years later in 1989 she met a fine Australian whose name is Stuart Pearson. He had been divorced from his first wife for several years and his two children by that marriage lived with their mother in New Zealand. He was working as General Duties Master in a private college for boys, Knox Grammar School, on Sydney's North Shore and we liked him from the very first moment Ingrid showed us his photograph. Ingrid and Stuart had a whirlwind romance and they were married in April 1990.

I was then very much affected by the personal problems I was having with the restaurant and do not remember much about the wedding at all.

Pearson Wedding, April 1990. Standing L-R: John Nielsen, Jennifer Nielsen (2½ years), Sally Nielsen, Ingrid and Stuart Pearson, Daniel Nielsen (7 years), and Eddie Sudibjo. Seated: An Sudibjo.

What I do remember is that it was a drizzly day in the Blue Mountains to the west of Sydney and that the bride and groom were dressed in costumes that reflected their cultural heritage. Stuart wore an impressive Scottish kilt and Ingrid a beautiful Indonesian outfit. They looked radiant and the wedding was apparently a great success, but I was not in the mood to enjoy it. These two people have been happily married ever since, but because of physiological problems with Ingrid they have been unable to have children and I would have adored having more grandchildren. One thing I can say is that we have grown to love Stuart as much as Ingrid obviously does. He has been truly caring and we think of him more as a son than a son-in-law.

Health

In the late 1980s, our son John introduced us to a new health food company called Sunrider. It was a direct-marketing company that used the same method of multi-level selling as Amway or Avon. John has been devoted to a healthy life-style for most of his adult life and convinced us to try these products. We continued to use Sunrider products for years as we too believe that its products kept us healthy. We hardly ever got sick and the only times that we have needed medical attention was when we had suffered an injury of some sorts. I think we are healthier than anyone else at our own age and I put it down to this health food. We place a lot of faith in Sunrider, but its products are very expensive.

Under John's guidance, we established a business selling Sunrider to others in Indonesia and for several years things went so well that income from Sunrider paid for several return trips for both of us to Indonesia. Apart from the trips, the commissions we received also paid for all the Sunrider products we wanted at no cost to us. But in the late 1990s the Indonesian exchange rate plunged against the American dollar and this health food became unaffordable for our Indonesian customers. Sunrider dried up for us as a business, but we have continued to use it ourselves for many years since, only stopping briefly in late 2003 when our doctor said it would do no harm to discontinue as it was costing us a lot of money.

When I was visiting my doctor for a regular check up in the mid-1990s, some tests showed that I had several gall stones. My doctor recommended surgery to remove them but, consistent with every request for medical treatment up to this point in my life, I again refused. About a year later, I developed a high fever, became disoriented, and collapsed at home. I was rushed to hospital where my husband consented to the removal of my gall bladder, a procedure which thankfully saved my life. The gall bladder contained many stones, including one that was the size of an egg! Within days I was fine again and, with the exception of a minor stroke a few years later, have remained in the best of health until recently.

I actually do not know why I am so stubborn sometimes when it comes to my own health. I know that everyone has my best interests at heart, but if I can avoid medical treatment — especially hospitalization and surgery — I will do so, even if it jeopardizes my health. For example, a long time ago in 1988 I broke my leg through falling into a hollow in our front yard in Chifley at night. It was a silly mistake. Eddie had spent all day removing a tree, leaving a hole that he intended to fill in the next day.

When I returned from Warung Indonesia restaurant later that night, it was dark and I accidentally stumbled into the hole. For the next few days I was limping and suffering increasing pain from my right leg. In the end my daughter insisted on taking me to a medical specialist, where X-rays revealed that I had a badly cracked right thigh bone.

The doctor gave me a choice. I could either have an operation to place pins in my thigh, or I could rest my leg in bed for a minimum of ten weeks if I was prepared to keep it in the right position to heal properly. Naturally, I chose the latter, but to the consternation of my entire family I was out of bed and back to work within a few weeks! At the time my restaurant was more important to me than my health. The consequence of placing weight back on a fractured thigh bone too early was that my leg became curved and reset permanently at a bowed angle.

Stroke and Alzheimer Disease

One day in September 2001, during a dinner with visiting relatives from Surabaya, I had difficulty getting up from the table to go to the bathroom. I became disoriented and collapsed back into my chair unable to move. I was told that Eddie called John who came over straight away and once he saw my condition called an ambulance immediately. I was conveyed to Blacktown Hospital in a confused state. After the doctors had examined me, they diagnosed that I had suffered a stroke. My speech was slurred, my right hand was weak, I suffered memory losses and could not walk at all. I was admitted to hospital where my condition was stabilized. Because I was an 89-year-old, the therapists expected a long period of convalescence over several months. They were surprised by my speedy recovery and discharge from hospital just four weeks later. The only residual effect is some slight difficulty in mobility that requires me to use a walking frame and increasingly a wheelchair to get around. I attribute my current remarkable state of health in no small measure to the use of those Sunrider health foods.

However, I am increasingly forgetful about events and circumstances. For example, I continually press my husband to buy things that are not essential as I keep on forgetting how little money we actually have. In my mind, I think we are still enjoying a good income and can afford more than a basic lifestyle. I want a new car for my husband and to take another overseas trip before I die, maybe even to Europe. Why can I not do these things?

In July 2002, my children put on a big party to celebrate my 90th birthday. It was held in a church hall in the northern suburb of Pymble in Sydney with many friends and relatives attending. I know I had a very good time, but I confess I find it a little difficult to remember all the details. For a year or so now, I have become progressively more absent-minded. For example, sometimes I remember visiting people, but increasingly I forget. Likewise, sometimes I remember eating a meal, but increasingly there are times I insist that I have not and demand to be fed. Even if I can

An's 90th Birthday, Sydney, July 2002.

not remember my last conversation, I can still remember my youth with clarity.[16] Sometimes I recognise this is a sign of dementia, but increasingly I do not know what all the fuss is about.[17]

Dutch Citizenship

During the 350-year Dutch occupation of Indonesia, its people were never legally considered to be Dutch citizens. Instead millions of Indonesians were regarded as Dutch subjects (*Nederlands onderdaanen*).

In my early years I was perfectly content with being a Dutch subject and never once thought of becoming a bona fide Dutch citizen. After the new country of Indonesia became a reality and I saw the status of the Dutch go from the top of the social order to the bottom overnight, I had no desire to change my legal status and threaten my well-paid job in education.

However, there were a number of people in Indonesia who did manage to become Dutch citizens and the easiest way was through marriage, like my own sister for example. Roostien married Liem Sing Giap, the first suitor to whom she was introduced in 1926, and he was already *gelijkgesteld* (made equal) as a Dutch citizen. Liem Sing Giap had applied for and been granted Dutch citizenship earlier in the 1920s when he was in Makassar and responsible for the telephone system in the east of Indonesia.

His brother, Liem Sing Boen, who was one of the few qualified medical doctors in Indonesia, was also granted Dutch citizenship, but the same privilege did not extend to their sister who had no qualifications. You had to have a very important and crucial position with the Dutch administration, or to marry a person who did, before you were eligible to become a Dutch citizen. I did not comply with either criterion.

In 1962 when we were holidaying in Holland, we visited Mr Hoekendijk, my former teacher at the Teachers' College, in the town of Rijswijk. I had found him still living in Jakarta through the NIOG membership list when Eddie and I settled in Jakarta in 1947 and visited him regularly until he left

---

[16] Alzheimer's disease, or dementia, is manifested by the loss of recent memory first, followed by a gradual corruption and loss of memory going backwards in time.

[17] Following a fall in August 2005 that broke her hip, An had a 10-week convalescence in Blacktown and then Mount Druitt Hospitals. In November 2005 she became a permanent resident of Garden View Nursing Home in Merrylands, about 5 kilometres from her home in Girraween, where Eddie still lives.

Indonesia in 1957. We also visited my former Dutch headmaster, Meneer Lange. I had been his deputy at Jember primary school from 1930 to 1936 and he had remained in Indonesia until the government forced him to leave in 1958. For all this time I had maintained a friendship with him and his Dutch wife. Meneer Lange offered me a teaching position and house in Holland as well as the opportunity of becoming a Dutch citizen through his sponsorship, but my husband had already determined that he did not like the cold Dutch climate. I dismissed the offer as merely wishful thinking on behalf of an old colleague and friend. I never thought about Dutch citizenship seriously again until the mid-1980s, when Warung Indonesia was beginning to fail and I thought that a Dutch pension would help pay the mounting expenses.

Eddie and I went to Holland in the mid-1980s with the help of friends to see if I could receive a Dutch pension, taking along with us copies of relevant documents that had taken me years to put together. I thought I had a good chance of obtaining a Dutch pension until the Dutch authorities told me that my Australian citizenship obtained in 1976 made me ineligible for a pension from Holland.

My Relationship with Eddie

No marriage is perfect and I regret to say that there have been several times in my married life that I have suspected my husband of having affairs with other women. Over our long and happy marriage I have had one or two major confrontations with him over this suspicion and once I remember even throwing things at him in front of the children.

In 1954 a person arrived at our house in Menteng with a pistol in his hands exclaiming, "My daughter thinks she's pregnant and says that Eddie is the father!" We knew the family, and my husband had indeed taken this young woman — a fellow employee at Garuda Airways — to watch her brother race motor cars in central Java a month or so earlier. When she missed her monthly cycle, her mother became suspicious and that is when the parents demanded an explanation. Under intense pressure from the parents the daughter finally confessed that she was having an affair with a married man and nominated Eddie as the person involved. The father was furious and wanted to kill Eddie, but fortunately my husband was not at home at the time. The father left saying that if his daughter's pregnancy was confirmed my husband would have to divorce me and marry her.

Thankfully, a few days later this woman finally had her period and everyone was relieved. Embarrassed and apologetic, her father told us later that his daughter had falsely accused Eddie as she had been infatuated with older married men for some time and was having an affair with one particular individual whom she did not want to name.

She had falsely nominated my husband because she was in love with this other person and wanted to keep on seeing him. From the outset, my husband had strongly denied the allegation of sleeping with this woman and I should have believed him, but Eddie was only 33 and the other woman an attractive 28 year old, while I considered myself old at 42 years.

Later, when Eddie was working for TAI in the early 1960s I thought he was having an affair with his secretary, but I had no proof and gradually my suspicions receded.

In Sydney, during 1973, my sister Roostien in Indonesia sent one of her most loyal servants to help us in our businesses on a temporary basis for about a year. Her name was Kartini and she was a divorced 35-year-old indigenous Indonesian.

Kartini settled into the Australian way of life very quickly and after several months began saying how much she would like to stay in the country on a permanent basis. Meanwhile I started noticing her copying my mannerisms and dress, spending more time with Eddie alone and making him special meals. One day I overheard Kartini refer to Eddie as her husband in a conversation with customers and I confronted her. Kartini denied she was trying to replace me, but at 61, I was fearful that my husband would repeat what my father had done to his wife and marry someone younger.

In my mind, Kartini's motives were obvious. She wanted to remain in Australia and the easiest way to achieve that goal was to marry my husband. I confronted Kartini and sacked her on the spot. She ran away from us in distress. As her visa soon expired, she became a fugitive on the run from the Australian Immigration Department. Eventually she was arrested and deported back to Indonesia as an illegal immigrant. However, when my sister heard the whole story, Kartini was not dismissed as I had expected. She has continued to work for my sister and her family, including Roostien's grand-daughter till this day.

The fear of a husband replacing his wife with another younger woman has stayed with me ever since I was a little girl and witnessed my father do this to my mother, even though I knew it was with her consent. From the very beginning of our marriage I wanted to trust Eddie, but because he

An and Eddie cut the cake at their 60th Wedding Anniversary in front of their many friends and relatives.

was nine years younger, my father's actions still gave me a phobia that has only dissipated in my nineties. I can now truthfully say that I unequivocally and unquestioningly trust my husband. I only wish I could have felt this way over sixty years ago when we began our marriage.

Before I leave the subject matter of fears and foibles, there is another matter concerning my husband that raised its head only once in our marriage. That matter is gambling. His first and last major experience with heavy gambling happened in 1971 when he was staying in Jakarta for two months while selling a motor vehicle. Between 1968 and 1971, my husband had sold cars into Indonesia from Australia on three separate occasions. The first two vehicles were sold without Eddie actually leaving Australia, but changes to the Indonesian customs regulations in 1970 meant that Eddie had to take this third car personally into the country.

At the time the Indonesian Government had opened its first casino in Jakarta and Eddie went there to spend some time as he was bored waiting days for the car to pass through customs. He was staying with the station manager of UTA, Go Djoen Sian, whom my husband had employed years earlier. Eddie confessed to me later that he had never seen anything like this casino before and was fascinated with its allure, glitz and ostentatious glamour.

Moreover, the casino offered the attraction of quick money and my husband succumbed to that temptation. Over a period of only a few days he lost all the profit he was going to make on the sale of the car, over A$2,000. In today's terms that is the equivalent of a quarter of a year's salary! He returned to Australia saddened and chastened by the experience and we agreed that if he ever wanted to go to a casino and gamble again, we would go together so that my presence would temper any future compulsive behaviour. Since this one dark episode in the early 1970s, he has been in a casino to gamble less than a dozen times. The amounts invested have been petty and he has always been accompanied by a family member.

I raise this matter only because it shows how two people can overcome an episode of stupidity if they work at it together. I am actually very proud of Eddie in this matter. He said that he would stop gambling alone in a casino and with the assistance of a simple mechanism to support that commitment, he has stuck to his pledge for more than 30 years. We both occasionally buy some lottery tickets from the local newsagent, but this is only a trifling amount and gives us some pleasure without threatening our livelihood.

11

Final Statement

There are a number of people, including members of my own family, who believe that I am motivated primarily by money. They say that I need it, want more of it and that it is the centre of my world. Nothing could be further from the truth. For me, financial success has only been a tool to achieve a more important goal, namely one's reputation in the community. Money has not been the centre of my universe, it has been reputation. Allow me to give two very strong examples of this.

I started Harapan Kita originally to educate my children, but by 1964 this was no longer the case as both John and Ingrid were being educated in Australia. Even maintaining the school to continue our tenure at Jalan Jogja was not the real reason why I continued this loss-making concern. The true reason was to satisfy something far more important to me, that is my reputation in the community. A growing number of influential people in Jakarta had entrusted the education of their children to me and I had gained a name for being an outstanding educator. This was important recognition — especially from such an influential group of individuals — and in the end I was unable to refuse new enrolments, even though each new student took us further into debt.

The second example is my restaurant in Sydney. You have already heard all about that sorry saga in too much detail for my liking, but in summary it would be fair to say that I knew the business was losing money badly but I just could not stop trading. There was something more important to me than financial considerations, and that was my reputation in the community as a businesswoman and someone that the Dutch, Chinese and Indonesian expatriate communities could look up to and respect.

Before I conclude the story of my life, I would like to raise with you the one regret I have and it goes right back to when I was a little girl. From my earliest years I have always aspired to become a Doctor of Medicine, particularly a paediatrician healing sick children. During my youth there were few medical practitioners in Indonesia and even fewer paediatricians, so that they were held in the highest regard by the community. When I was a teenager, we discovered that my mother had a heart condition, but the family could not obtain or afford any medical treatment for her. Just to be a doctor was considered so important that often the colonial government rewarded indigenous and Chinese doctors with the ultimate privilege of Dutch citizenship, as happened in the case of my brother-in-law's sibling, Liem Sing Boen, when I was in my twenties.

However, my gender was against me and when my father lost all his money over his failed sugar venture in 1924, all chances of sending me to Holland to be educated as a doctor evaporated. There had been a Medical School in Indonesia for training native doctors since 1900 (STOVIA — *School tot Opleiding van Inlandsche Artsen*), but it was not open to females. A full Medical College (*Geneeskundige Hogeschool*) was not established in Indonesia until 1927, but by then it was too late for me as I had already embarked on a teaching career. Ironically, I could not enter the new College even if I wanted to because it too accepted males only.

Apart from healing children, I wanted to be a paediatrician to gain the respect and admiration of the whole community. I came close to achieving this goal through another profession, teaching, but even though I rose swiftly through the bureaucracy to become the Principal of a Teachers' College, I nonetheless felt my achievements were less significant.

Of course education is vitally important for society but it lacks the drama and recognition of medicine. Education develops the mind but medicine saves lives! I enjoyed teaching and felt much rewarded for my efforts, but what I really wanted was to save children from dying and to have the recognition and respect of a grateful society for it.

PART B

The Voices of Others

12

The Voice of Gerda Nielsen

I was born Gerda Kroeze on 3 January 1918 and like my late husband, Jan Nielsen (born 19 February 1915), we were both raised in Holland. We met and married in early 1943 during World War II, bringing two babies into the world in quick succession — Johannes (1944, nicknamed Hanjo, later shortened to Joe) and Nicholas (Nick, 1946). Although we were underfed during the war and conditions were harsh for the general population, the occupation of our country at the hands of the Germans thankfully did not result in any cruel treatment against us personally. Nevertheless, after the war and with much of Europe devastated by the conflict, we decided that our future lay elsewhere. My husband responded to an advertisement in an Amsterdam newspaper calling for teachers in the Dutch East Indies, and the Colonial Government accepted us.[1]

My husband set out for Indonesia first, arriving to commence a three-year contract at the start of their educational year in July 1948.[2] It was during the revolutionary period but at that time my husband's contract was organized by the colonial government. As soon as he arrived, Jan tried to find accommodation for us but the colonial administration took several months to find a government house that was suitable. Finally, he was billeted at Jalan Jogja 7 in the Jakarta suburb of Menteng, where I joined him

---

[1] The contract was to be paid out at the end of the three-year term, less all the living expenses paid by the Education Department in the interim.
[2] The Indonesian Educational calendar was, and still is, based on the European system that commences in late July and finishes in late June, with a long school holiday of one month in between.

sometime later in about September 1949, after waiting a total of fourteen months in Holland. That is when I first met An and Eddie Sudibjo (whose surname was then Kang) with their two young children (John, aged five, and Ingrid, an infant under one year old). They were also tenants in the house at Menteng, along with two officers of the Indonesian Army.

I had my third and last child in the first year I was in Jakarta (Alexander, born May 1950 and called Lex for short) and after my son's birth I worked for a few months as a clerical assistant in a gold business owned by our neighbour, Herman Braakensiek. He was delighted that he had another Dutch national with whom to work and converse.

We had a number of small rooms at the back of the garage adjoining the main house in Menteng and in a short time made the accommodation as pleasant as possible. It was a large house with sufficient space for all three groups of tenants to get along well with each other. Our family never had much to do with the Army officers; they kept to themselves pretty much and quietly went about their business.

Jan taught mathematics at a Dutch-speaking high school nearby until his contract expired in June 1951. He then had a number of choices. He could renew his contract with the new Indonesian Government for a further three years, or return to Holland, or emigrate to either Australia or Canada. We both agreed that we did not want to stay on in Indonesia because the political climate was unstable and discrimination against the Dutch was increasing, but neither did we want to return to Europe that was only slowly rebuilding itself from the after effects of war. Thus Jan applied for jobs as an actuary in both Canada and Australia. The Sydney office of Royal & Sun Alliance — an insurance company Jan had worked for previously in Holland — was the first company to accept Jan's job application without even interviewing him and that quick response determined the country to which we immigrated. We departed Indonesia for Australia in June 1951, approximately one year and ten months after I had arrived.

During the twenty months I stayed in Indonesia, my family and the Sudibjo family became friends. It was our respective children that drew us together as they were of similar ages and naturally wanted to play with each other constantly.

Apart from the servants, there was always at least one parent at home to watch over the children during the day.[3] We adults started talking to

---

[3] The Indonesian custom was to split the work-day into early morning and late afternoon work sessions, with a rest period at home for several hours during the midday heat.

each other — in Dutch of course — whenever two or more of us were present supervising the children and our conversations rapidly evolved into a friendship between the two families.

I would never describe our relationship as particularly close. We never went out together and my husband was only an ordinary teacher, while An held a much superior position in the Education Department. Nevertheless, the two families certainly did form a close bond in the short time we lived together. Before we left Indonesia, we agreed to maintain the relationship through correspondence.

When we arrived in Australia we had no money, so we rented a small house in Newport on the northern beaches of Sydney for about six weeks until our outstanding funds owed by the Indonesian Government finally materialized.[4] This amount was enough for us to purchase a house outright in the Sydney suburb of Manly Vale. Jan went to work immediately for Royal & Sun Alliance Insurance Company and I secured a part-time clerical job with a local Dutch baker. There was full employment in Australia at the time with job shortages in several key areas such as manufacturing, so that there was no difficulty securing a job.

I did not know that the Braakensiek family had left Indonesia for Australia (via Holland) in 1957 until the Sudibjos told me in 1960. They informed me that Herman Braakensiek had lost his gold business and all their money in Indonesia through government confiscation. This was a great shock to me.

My husband was a regular letter writer. He corresponded regularly with friends and relatives in Europe and after we arrived in Australia he included the Sudibjos on the mailing list. Once or twice a year we wrote to each other and exchanged Christmas cards. Sometimes I would read Jan's letters and any replies he received, but mainly the correspondence was directly between Jan and Eddie. In July 1960 we received a letter from Eddie Sudibjo informing us that his family was coming to Sydney for a visit and asking if we could assist with accommodation. The letter

---

[4] The Indonesian Government had argued previously that it should not be held responsible for paying out contracts entered into by the previous Dutch administration, but after some years of disagreement the Indonesian Government finally yielded to pressure to honour previous contracts. By the time the Nielsens left Indonesia in 1951, all contracts were being honoured by the Indonesian Government. The two months wait to receive the money was due to normal administrative delays.

was mailed much earlier, but because of lengthy delays in the Indonesian postal service arrived only three days before their visit.

We hurriedly moved our five children around the house to make room for four more visitors — in addition to our own three boys, we were fostering two girls. During the visit, they surprised me by raising the issue of leaving one or more of their children with us. I had never heard of this suggestion before and was greatly alarmed. We already had five children to look after and here were An and Eddie asking us to take on two more. But my husband was more relaxed about the matter. He may well have discussed the issue with them previously, but forty years later I can not recall ever discussing this issue with my husband prior to their arrival. What I do remember is my total surprise and shock at the proposal and its audacity.

They wanted to leave their children with us as they thought that Australia offered a better opportunity for them compared with Indonesia. We already knew Chinese Indonesians were having difficulties back in Indonesia and the Sudibjo family, through prior correspondence and discussions during their visit, confirmed this. They said that both children were facing growing restrictions on educational opportunities at home, but as John was four years older his limited future was being confronted earlier.[5] Therefore his problems were more immediate than Ingrid's.

As mentioned before, my husband was more positive about this proposal than I. He took the lead as to how best we could achieve the goal of keeping one or both of the children in Australia and over the course of the next week or so convinced me that we should cooperate. In the end, I saw it as our Christian duty to help other people in need. From the start, our friends sought to leave both children with us, but after talks between us adults it was obvious that John was their prime concern. If they had to choose between one child staying in Australia or none, then John had to be it. Also, the Sudibjo parents told me they had discussed the matter with both of their children and that only John had wanted to stay in Australia.

We had many hours of conversation stretching over several days, which involved advice from the Braakensieks, who we found out from the Sudibjos had arrived in Sydney two years earlier, and through them

---

[5] High schools could now only teach in Bahasa Indonesia and university places were restricted to a small percentage of Chinese-Indonesian students.

from a solicitor, Mr Henk Rutgers. Finally it was determined to organize a temporary student visa while we sought a more permanent resolution in the form of adoption. We all went to the Immigration office in person and arranged John's student visa, while Rutgers prepared the paper work for adoption. After two frenetic weeks of activity the Sudibjo family returned to Indonesia, leaving their son behind. From the outset, John was upset and felt abandoned by his parents. He did not even have all his clothes or possessions with him. He was a boy in anger and much of this anger was directed at us.

Before their departure, we agreed on a fairly liberal financial arrangement between ourselves to pay for John's accommodation and education. Even though I believed we had a Christian duty to help the Sudibjos, I still insisted they should pay a fair contribution for his upkeep. The deal struck between us involved the Sudibjos paying for educational fees, board and food at our home, plus incidental items, such as clothing, entertainment and sport. They agreed to pay around £10 a week to cover all these expenses and I agreed to accept payment on an annual basis as Eddie was paid once a year only.

For the next two and a half years, the Sudibjos regularly returned at least twice a year to visit John. However, during 1963, there had been several disputes over money and John still had not settled down. We had already agreed to adopt Ingrid by the time the Sudibjo family came to visit us in mid-1964, but they were now adamant that she should become a full-time boarder at a private school of their choosing and that all financial arrangements should be handled by the Braakensiek family instead. The Brothers at John's School, St. Augustine's College in Brookvale recommended Monte Sant' Angelo Mercy College in North Sydney which was run by an associated teaching order, the Sisters of Mercy.

Over the whole time John lived with us, it was a difficult relationship. He grew distant from all of us including Nick, who was the one son closest to him in age and behaviour. He and Nick had previously shared everything, including a love of model airplanes, but the longer John stayed with us the more distant he became. By late 1963, John had turned eighteen and was therefore legally an adult in Australia. He was now old enough to leave us and he chose to do so at the first opportunity in December 1963. He moved out and found alternate accommodation in Cremorne and shortly after in Chifley, at the house his parents purchased in late 1964. Since John moved out more than thirty years ago, we have not seen much of him or his family at all. He rarely visits and the few

John Nielsen at about 16 years of age taken at Jan and Gerda Nielsen's house in Sydney in about 1961.

occasions we do see each other have been at family events organized by others.

The Sudibjo family relocated to Australia in 1967 and moved into the house in Chifley. The two families have remained friends for over 50 years. Our children first played together in Indonesia and subsequently lived together in Australia. Even though there have been problems between us concerning such matters as finances, in the end we overcame them.

John may not have had a good experience with us, but Ingrid became the daughter we never had. I do love the family and I wish them the very best of luck for the future. It was a privilege to adopt the Sudibjo children as our own and I feel proud today that both children still use the name Nielsen when asked for their family name.

Author's Note: Gerda Nielsen died peacefully of natural causes at the age of 86 on 21 April 2004 while in respite care at Manly Vale Nursing Home in Sydney.

13

The Voice of John Nielsen

Earliest Memories

I am the first child of An and Eddie Sudibjo, born in the East Javanese city of Jember in Indonesia on 9 October 1945. My first memories, possibly at the age of three or four, are of our house in Jakarta. I remember it as a large open-plan home with high ceilings, slate or marble floors and enormous rooms for a young boy of my age. A gallery or veranda ran along the back of the house and the back yard was fairly open and unkempt. A modest outhouse was built to one side of the rear of the house to accommodate servants. I recollect our family living only in the back half of the residence as there were other people occupying the front. Our section of the house was busy with a succession of nannies, servants and relatives staying with us.

There were two parks nearby — Bisschopsplein and Taman Madiun — to which my parents took me for walks or to ride my scooter, which because of the newly introduced western innovation of pump-up tyres, was a rarity in Jakarta and made me feel special.

I remember the Nielsen family moving into rooms at the back of the garage of the house when I was about five. They had two young boys and I became very good friends with Hanjo (Joe) and Nick, who were respectively a year older and younger than me. One incident stands out vividly around this time. Gerda Nielsen was carrying a pot of boiling water when Joe accidentally ran into her, causing the water to spill over him. She threw cold water over Joe and my Mum assisted by applying chewed banana to the scalds on his arm. I do not know which remedy worked but Joe recovered without scarring.

One day my parents took me to Jakarta Zoo and there was a monkey my parents encouraged me to feed. But instead of taking the food, the monkey grabbed my hand and bit my finger. A kindly Dutch gentleman administered some iodine or mercurochrome while I screamed in shock and pain. My parents were quite concerned and took me to the local hospital, where I had a tetanus injection.

While I was at primary school, my parents gave me a blue boy's bicycle to get me to and from the nearby school, but I started to be picked on by a much bigger local street kid on my way home. This teenager would wait for me on my way home and try to beat me with a tree branch as I rode past. I could not take another route home to avoid the bully and the harassment continued for days with me getting progressively more upset. After one particularly close escape I arrived home in tears to find my father present. He put me on the back of his Vespa scooter, which was the only transport we had at the time, and returned to where the adolescent was, but as we approached the youth took off before my father could say anything. The next day the teenager was waiting for me again and angrier than before, so I decided to take matters into my own hands. I managed to get an unloaded air pistol from a friend of mine and the next time this person approached me I pulled the air pistol from my bag and pointed it at him. The bully ran away and I never saw him again.

I asked my father why this youth had singled me out for attention and Dad quietly explained the issue of racial discrimination to me for the first time. I was only about seven or eight and it was a new concept for me. My father explained that I was of a particular racial group, called Chinese, and that we had been subject to abuse ever since Chinese people started coming to live in Indonesia centuries earlier. I hated racial discrimination from the moment the concept was introduced to me and I have never stopped hating it ever since. I have firmly rejected the notion that one group of people can discriminate against another group of people simply because they look different.

Family Activities

My father introduced me to the popular Indonesian pastime of kite-flying when I was a young boy. After learning how to fly ordinary kites, he taught me how to fly fighting kites made with a glass-lined string to cut the lines of opponent's kites. Dad shared with me his own secret method for making the glass string that involved applying glass powder to the string with the resin from a particular tree, whose name I can no longer remember.

Dad first attached short loops of twine around each of the mangosteen and tamarind trees that stood about five metres apart in our backyard and then tightly ran the first part of the kite string backwards and forth several times between these two loops, like a very tight hammock. We taped our fingers and hands so the glass would not cut our flesh and slowly went along the lines applying the resin first and then the glass powder, which had to be squeezed onto the lines with our fingers and hands. Each of us took turns at holding a sheet of newspaper underneath the line at the point of application to capture the excess glass powder for otherwise we would quickly run out of glass.

The end result was about a 200-metre length of kite string, of which the first 15–20 metres was covered with finely granulated powdered glass. This first part was attached to the kite and the remainder wrapped around a home-made spindle. We then went off to the nearby parks during the kite-flying season and enjoyed many hours of fun with my father teaching me to fly a fighting kite. It takes many years of practice to become a master at this activity and, even though I never stuck at it long enough, I still enjoyed this sport for years.

Education

The first School I can recall attending was a Dutch-language primary school (CAS) nearby in Jalan Tegal, Menteng. I remember starting at the usual age of about 6, but in a class one year higher than normal because of what my mother later told me was my intelligence and her preparatory teaching at home. It was here that I met Lie Mu Lhan and Oei Tjong Hauw (Howard Winata) and we became lifelong friends. We would play together and regularly visit the home of Howard's grandparents in Jalan Lembang for they had a ten-metre swimming pool. A backyard pool was very unusual in Indonesia at the time.

My six years at primary school were fairly uneventful and I never had any difficulties with learning. I do not recall ever getting into trouble at school and generally my memories are positive. The principal's name was Meneer Camminga and he had a strikingly beautiful model of a modern fighter plane on display at school. I did not know what manufacture it was then, but looking back I think it was either a Hurricane or Spitfire and it was huge. The plane stood on its own timber pedestal and had a wingspan that seemed to me then to be over two metres wide. My fascination with the model plane was fostered by my father's employment in the airline industry. As a small boy, he would sometimes take me to the airport and point out all the planes and their various parts. Also, one of the people servicing his motor scooter gave me a scrapbook of early war planes from World War I and World War II which I treasured. With this heightened sense of awareness, I noticed parts of the model plane at school gradually disappearing over the years as other students removed items such as the propellers, a strut, or an aileron.

The first high school I went to at the age of about 12 was a Dutch-speaking HBS school, but I was there only for a few months (July 1957 to December 1957) before it was forced to close by government order. This high school was on Jalan Diponegoro opposite a main hospital. It was co-educational, as was the primary school I had attended earlier, and the students were mainly Dutch with only a few Chinese and indigenous Indonesians. I have a vague recollection of my mother trying to get me to take private violin lessons in the afternoons on my way home from this school, but I detested it so much she gave up.

My education up to this point had been taught exclusively in Dutch, but because the Government Decree stopped that practice by closing all the Dutch-speaking schools, including my HBS, my parents were forced to send me to an Indonesian-speaking school. Ironically, I ended up in the very same primary school I had left six months earlier in Jalan Tegal, except that now the Government had reclassified it as a high school. I stayed there only for a few weeks or months, because my mother was not satisfied with the standard of education. Teacher absenteeism was high and lessons were often cancelled or delivered by staff that did not care.

In March 1958 my mother decided to teach me at home and within a few weeks I was joined by two girls. We would mainly study on our own as Mum was working at the Teachers' College, but from time to time a very attractive Indonesian teacher called Tjiek (sister) Faisah would come and teach the three of us.[1] This was actually the inauspicious

---

[1] Even though some teachers were indigenous Indonesians, the Chinese title for "sister" was often used as a mark of respect for single female teachers. Once married, the title "Ibu" was used. Male teachers were always addressed as "Bapak" or "Pak", even if they were Chinese.

start of Mum's private school, Harapan Kita. As more students enrolled, Miss Faisah progressively attended more frequently until she became our first full-time teacher from the second half of 1958. I was educated at Harapan Kita for over a year until my parents sent me to Canisius College in July 1959.

During the year at Harapan Kita I think the numbers of students grew to about eleven or twelve. I finished my final exam for Junior High School in two years instead of the usual three and from July 1959 was sent to Canisius College to complete my final three years of high school. There were several reasons why my parents moved me back into mainstream education. The schooling at Harapan Kita was initially unstructured and undisciplined. We did not wear uniforms and really only worked on subjects that we wanted to study and when we felt like it. Students at Canisius College, on the other hand, wore uniforms and studied subjects when they were scheduled, whether we liked them or not.

I thought Harapan Kita was full of misfits and delinquents, whereas Canisius College was full of high achievers who were very motivated. I had also started to develop a very healthy interest in girls and Canisius was a boy's school.

Lastly, I was going through mid-adolescent angst. I was upset with my parents pushing me to achieve in sport (swimming) and scholarship. More than once I contemplated leaving home and even wrote away to the American Embassy seeking sponsorship for overseas study. I think my attitude also influenced my parents to send me to Canisius College for the extra discipline and direction. Returning to mainstream schooling at Canisius was a real challenge for me. I had to take eighteen subjects in total and the day was regimented strictly into teaching periods determined by the ringing of the school bell. I struggled, and then rebelled. Academically my results deteriorated badly.

My first mid-year school report in December 1959 was not good and my parents arranged for remedial tutoring in several subjects. For example, I remember a very kindly Indonesian gentleman trying to help me with Chemistry. But my final school report for my first year (June 1960) was a disaster. I failed most of my subjects and Mum took it personally. As the Principal of a Teachers' College, with her own private school, she believed my poor results reflected directly on her professional competence. The next thing I remember is that the entire family flew unexpectedly to Australia a week or so later.

Religion

I do not remember being baptized, but the story of how we ended up being Roman Catholics is fascinating. My mother told me that when Ingrid was a baby she got very sick and Mum made a promise to God that if Ingrid recovered she would convert both her children to Christianity. I do remember going to a Roman Catholic church in Jalan Malang on a weekly basis in my sub-teen years, but my parents never actually attended Mass themselves, apart from our first communion and confirmation services. Earlier on they walked my sister and me to church, but later after we had our own bicycles they would let us go by ourselves.

I was never a good church-goer and was constantly getting into trouble from the priests for sitting in the back of the church and creating mischief. I really could not stand church and sometimes we never actually attended, spending the time cycling all around the streets by ourselves and returning home an hour or so later, all innocent and full of smiles from supposedly confessing our sins at Mass.

Family Transportation

My Dad had a Vespa motor scooter in the early 1950s and I have some exciting memories of the whole family going on short trips outside the city to Bogor (an hour away) or to Puncak in the mountains (about 1½–2 hours away). It seems crazily dangerous now, but somehow all four of us sped through the busy streets crowded onto this tiny 125-cc scooter. Dad would sit forward on the rider's seat with Mum riding side-saddle behind him.[2] Ingrid would be perched on Mum's lap precariously over the road held by Mum with one hand and holding on to Dad for dear life with the other to avoid falling off the back. I stood on the floor boards between Dad and the handle bars trying to keep away from Dad's feet working the foot pedals and the handle bars digging into my ribs. I particularly remember one trip we took when I was very tired. For the whole journey I desperately fought to stay awake as I was petrified I would drift off to sleep and fall off! In 1954 Dad purchased a motor-cycle, but this was still

---

[2] In Indonesia, even though many women were aware of Western females wearing slacks (through movies and magazines), it was nevertheless considered too masculine. Modesty prevented women wearing skirts from straddling motor-cycle seats, forcing them to ride side-saddle instead.

not satisfactory to transport the family, so later that year he used family connections to purchase a second-hand car, a cream-coloured Skoda.

Typically, every important matter in my parents' lives has involved the use of contacts among family and friends. For example, this private motor vehicle was purchased from a relative of my father in Bandung (Tee Tiong Gak, nephew of my Oma Siem[3]); their permanent residency visas in Australia and their Australian pensions were obtained at the insistence of and coaching by customers at their restaurant; and lastly, their Government housing in 1990 was achieved through personal representations of their son-in-law.

The Skoda was mechanically so unreliable that when Dad secured a new job at a timber company in 1955, called Sioe Liem Kongsie, he still went to work on the motor-cycle. Within days of starting at Sioe Liem Kongsie, he had a fairly serious motor-cycle collision with a truck. It happened not far from home because Mum heard it and rushed out to attend. The truck and he were manoeuvring around a corner together when the truck cut across in front of him. Rather than hitting the tray of the vehicle, he aimed for the tyres and bounced off them onto the roadway. Within days the company supplied him with a green Fiat 1100.

From 1958 onwards, when Dad started working for the airline company TAI, he was lucky enough to purchase a succession of cars from the manager of the company. They were all Peugeots, of course, because the company was French, and all less than five years old. The cars were a vast improvement on the Fiat and Skoda he had driven earlier and we enjoyed being driven around in them. Nevertheless, he still retained the Skoda — the Fiat was returned when Dad left Sioe Liem Kongsie — and parked it permanently in the driveway where it rusted away.

Living with the Army at Jalan Jogja 7

Army officers lived at Jalan Jogja at the front of the house. For the latter part of the time my family also lived in the house, there was a war of attrition between one particular army officer and my parents. In the beginning the relationship between the army tenants and my family was fine, but sometime around 1956 Captain Said Pratalikusuma and his wife replaced one of the previous officers and the relationship rapidly deteriorated. He would snarl

[3] Tee Swat Siem, my father's aunt in Jember.

and yell at us children to get out of his way or stay out of the front yard which, although previously shared by all the tenants, had suddenly become his exclusive domain. He would also raise his voice at my parents, but I cannot recall what was said between them. In any event, his aggressive behaviour seemed to be directed at us children, or so it appeared at the time.

On my birthday (possibly my eleventh in 1956), my parents had invited a number of children to our place for a party. Captain Pratalikusuma's wife had just given birth to a new baby, who was not well, and the noise from the party upset the child and parents. He approached my father, exchanged words, and then suddenly Captain Pratalikusuma beat my father severely about the head. Only when my grandmother addressed the Captain in Madurese did he cease beating my father. One of my guests, a classmate from primary school, also witnessed the assault and was shaken badly by the incident. My Dad could not even go to hospital or report the matter because it would only invite further repercussions. There were many, many incidents over the years involving Captain (later Major) Said Pratalikusuma. For example, after I had left for Australia he took over more and more parts of the house, including my old rooms at the rear of the premises. On another occasion when I returned on holiday from Australia, my father's Peugeot had been blocked in by Captain Pratalikusuma's car. Captain Pratalikusuma refused to move his car, saying that the driveway was now exclusively his and he was not going to share it with anyone else.

Looking back, I suspect the Skoda was retained and parked permanently in a strategic position in the driveway to thwart Captain Said Pratalikusuma from taking over the driveway and, more importantly, the space behind which the school was using for assemblies, meetings and recreation. This would explain why the more valuable Peugeots were parked on the street with the increased risk of theft or damage, while the cheap Skoda was parked in the more secure driveway. My parents told me that one of the reasons for creating Harapan Kita was to prevent Pratalikusuma from kicking them out altogether.

Before the attempted coup of 1965, my whole family knew that Major Pratalikusuma was loyal to the communist cause. When I registered with him my visits from Sydney, he would spout communist slogans at me.[4] He

---

[4] Under Sukarno the army kept a close watch on its citizens by forcing them to register household guests with the *lurah* (local government authority, the equivalent of village head).

even stopped being a practising Muslim for it was philosophically impossible believing in Communism and religion at the same time. Sometime during 1966, I was visiting my parents in Jakarta. It was less than a year after the attempted coup and I passed a casual enquiry about Major Pratalikusuma to which my mother remarked, "Ah, Pratalikusuma. What a turncoat! When the coup was lost, he became a Muslim again overnight."

Visiting Relatives and Family Holidays

From our youngest years, my parents sent us children to stay with relatives by ourselves. When I was very young I vaguely remember staying with Tante Tien (Mum's sister, Roostien) in Bandung for weeks or even months. By the time I was about seven, Dad had moved from the cargo section of Garuda airlines to the passenger division, thus allowing him to obtain free or discounted airline tickets.

During this year, Dad put us on a two-hour flight to visit Tante Tien. It may have been the first time we went by air because Tante Tien's reaction to our visit was one of anger. Dad rang Tante Tien for her to collect us only when the plane was approaching Bandung. She was furious at the short notice and kept on speculating about what might have happened if no-one had been at home to receive the call and a seven-, and four-year-old had been left alone at a strange airport. This type of behaviour was not uncommon for my parents. They would often embark upon activities involving others, but only inform these other people about it at the last minute or not at all. This way, I suspect my parents felt other people could not say no. Later when I was about nine, I went to Jember and stayed with Tante Nanne[5] and her husband Leo. I ate so much durian that I got drunk on its fermenting fruit.

One day in early 1957 our family, including Lie Mu Lhan and a driver went for a big driving holiday to Surabaya, almost 1,000 kilometres away. Unfortunately, we had gone only half way when the exhaust fell off and we had to stop in Magelang overnight to have it welded back on. While there, Ingrid developed chicken-pox and was left behind with grandparents in Kediri, but the rest of us had already been infected and a few days later when we arrived in Surabaya, Mu Lhan and I had it too.

---

[5] Adopted daughter of my father's relative, Tee Swat Siem.

During my childhood and adolescence the family took many frequent trips. I can remember lots of daily or overnight trips a short distance away to Puncak, Bandung, and Lembang; several longer journeys to Semarang, Surabaya and Kediri by car, train and air; one annual holiday at Prapat on Lake Toba (July 1955) and another to Surabaya travelling first class by ship (July 1956).

I really enjoyed our annual family holiday to Lake Toba in Sumatra. However, it did not start all that well. I got an ear infection but my condition improved quickly enough for me to remember sitting in a taxi passing plantation after plantation of a crop I had never seen before. It was rubber. Later I watched fascinated as hundreds of workers tapped the bark and collected its sticky white sap in small buckets tied to the trees. The crystalline sand of Lake Toba was remarkable and looked like fine sugar. We rented a room in a *losmen* (lodge) beside the lake. I learned to paddle a canoe while Dad learned to water-ski.

The boat trip to Surabaya was wonderful. The ship was a Dutch passenger liner called *Tjiwangi* and was luxurious. We were the only children travelling first class and the crew loved to pamper us. I had been learning French for the previous six months and when I found out that some of the

Passenger liner Tjiwangi on which the An, Eddie and family travelled from Jakarta to Surabaya in 1956. (Image courtesy of <www.nedships. nl/liners/tliners/tjiwangi>)

crew spoke French I tried to speak it with them. Disembarkation at Surabaya was another experience altogether. The *Tjiwangi* was a duty-free ship and exempt from prohibitive import duties applying at the time, but the customs officials were causing a queue of passengers as they painstakingly inspected every piece of luggage looking for contraband. There was a huge crush of people as passengers anxiously tried to get themselves and their goods off the ship past these obstructionist officials. At one point Ingrid (then seven) got squashed and screamed in panic. Mum and Dad had to suspend her in the air above their heads while we and our baggage were bundled through a small doorway past the customs barrier to the outside world.

Australia

The journey to Australia was the first holiday my family had taken overseas, but the first I knew about it was when they suddenly announced, "Let's all go for a holiday to Australia", just a week or so prior to our departure. It all happened so quickly that I do not think I even had a chance to inform my friends and I suspected nothing of the events that were about to befall me. We packed only enough belongings for a short trip and nothing was said to us children on the long air flight to Australia about the true nature of the journey.

We arrived in Sydney early in the morning, were picked up by the Nielsens and driven back to their home in Manly Vale. The next day was spent sight-seeing, but on the third day my mother said to me, "Nick's going to school. Why don't you go along with him and check it out?" I was only 14 at the time and did not know what was going on, so I complied without question. From that point on every day of my supposed two-week holiday was spent at school.

Towards the end of this fortnight my parents sat me down and explained what they had in mind for me. They said I had a choice. I could continue my education in Australia or back in Indonesia. My parents cleverly structured the conversation in such a way that the choice of staying was far more attractive than returning. For example, they reminded me that if I returned I would be going back to all the problems I wanted to escape from in the first place and I would still have to repeat the year I failed as well. Whereas staying in Australia offered me a fresh start, no repeat year, and fulfilled my long held ambition of studying overseas. They even offered me a way out by saying I could return to Indonesia if I still wanted after trying out Australia for six months.

I agreed to stay and, with that decision made, my parents and sister returned to Indonesia the next day. Meanwhile, just a few months short of my fifteenth birthday in July 1960, I was left in Australia to start my new life and begin the process of being legally adopted by Jan and Gerda Nielsen.[6] During the time I was in Australia separated from my parents and sister in Indonesia, I felt I was missing out on their love and attention. My family still visited me as often as they could, but at best that was only a few weeks at a time, once or twice a year. Meanwhile, they had each other's company 365 days a year and on top of their trips to visit me in Australia enjoyed two trips to Europe without me.

Dad tried to make up for this sense of loss by buying me expensive presents, such as a camera and transistor radio, but that actually made me feel worse. The Nielsen family could not afford these expensive gifts and it singled me out as someone more privileged living among them. In other words, I felt not only physically separated from my Indonesian family but also emotionally separated from my Australian family.

I completed my Leaving Certificate at the end of 1962 at Saint Augustine's High School in Brookvale and matriculated to University, but with insufficient marks to be awarded a Scholarship.[7] Saint Augustine's was a new high school and Nick Nielsen and I were part of its "pioneer" students, meaning that the twenty or so students in our year were the first to complete high school there. I performed remarkably well at the trial exams the school conducted internally to prepare students for the common Leaving Certificate, but when the results of the actual Leaving Certificate were announced everyone from our school accomplished mediocre results, even the dux. It showed that our School's academic quality was below average.

My mother convinced me that I should repeat my final year in order to obtain a scholarship because they said they could not afford to pay university fees themselves. I spent February of the 1963 school year attending Manly Boys High School as it had a better academic record, but soon realized that I really did not want to repeat the year. I was determined that I would attend university instead and do so without my parent's financial support.

---

[6] The official process would take twelve months to complete.

[7] At the time the Australian Government awarded Commonwealth Scholarships to University entrants who had attained sufficiently high marks in the high school Leaving Certificate. The Scholarship paid for university tuition fees and was designed to encourage students from low- and middle-income families access to tertiary education.

Staying with the Nielsen Family

The two and a half years I stayed under the Nielsens' care were not very pleasant for me. I had to adjust to a household that was more strictly organized than I had been used to previously. For example, each child had domestic tasks to perform that in Indonesia would have been performed by servants and, if you were deficient in some way, you would answer to Gerda who ruled the household as a demanding matriarch. I got on well with all the boys, the two foster girls who stayed for a while, and even my adoptive father Jan, but my relationship with Gerda was acerbic from the start.

Gerda was a harsh but fair disciplinarian who managed the household through verbal and corporal punishment. Even though this practice was initially a shock for me — coming from an unstructured, permissive family environment — I admit it was the usual way children were then raised in Australia. She probably did have a heart of gold but it did not show itself in a way that I appreciated.

There were a few minor occasions when Gerda let slip that she resented my presence, but I ignored them as they were usually said in the heat of the moment. However, there was one incident I could not ignore as it became the cause of a major conflict between us. It was towards the end of my second year of living with the Nielsens (August–September 1962) and my Leaving Certificate examination was fast approaching. I asked Gerda to return a small amount of money for some item I had bought for her[8] and suddenly she turned on me angrily and yelled in Dutch, "How dare you ask me for money. Your whole family is nothing but *sponsen* (sponges) and *opleggen* (impose) on our charity. I spend so much money on you, but hardly get a penny back from your parents. You're an ungrateful sponge, that's all you are."[9] I was stunned. Up to this point I had been blissfully unaware of the financial arrangement between my parents and the Nielsens, but clearly Gerda was now telling me it was unfair. I objected to her criticism of my family and told her I wanted to leave. I hurriedly

---

[8] John took on a number of part-time jobs, such as working in a service station, to earn a little pocket money to support his hobby of building and flying model aeroplanes in competitions. Occasionally, Gerda asked him to buy an item such as a newspaper or pay a bridge toll, sometimes forgetting to repay the money.

[9] The majority of conversations in the Nielsen household between John and his adoptive parents were conducted in Dutch.

penned off an urgent letter to my family in Indonesia informing them of the conversation and my desire to return to Indonesia, but I heard nothing back from them. Despite writing six letters over the next three months, I continued to hear nothing from them and my feelings of anger turned to concern for the well-being of my parents, especially when I was now beginning to read stories in the press about rising civil disorder on the streets of Jakarta.

In the end, I wrote directly to my father's boss at UTA, Monsieur Richez in Indonesia with the following appeal, "Please help me. I have written to my parents repeatedly over the past three months, but I have not received any response. Jakarta is in turmoil with riots and if something's happened to them I am better off knowing. I am prepared for the worst, but if they are alive please help as I need to contact my parents urgently."

One afternoon soon after, I returned home from school to find my parents had abruptly arrived on a hastily arranged visit. I was surprised by their sudden appearance as I was expecting their response to be in the form of a phone call, or telegram, or even a letter. Mum greeted me by saying, "Why are you being so silly in writing to Richez to contact us?" to which I answered, "Because you have not responded to any of the six letters I have written to you over the past three months!" Mum ignored the implied criticism in this comment and continued, "Well, we're here now. What do you want?" I said, "You did not have to come in person. All I want is an airplane ticket back to Jakarta. Get me out of here."

Over the next several days my parents talked me into staying in Australia with the Nielsens for the remaining few months of the academic year. They most likely also settled any financial problems with Gerda, because her attitude towards me did improve afterwards. My parents dangled the carrot of an Asian holiday in front of me at the end of the year on the proviso that I would stay with the Nielsens and get a good enough pass to enter university. It was not the outcome I wanted but it was a solution I could accept.

I completed my Leaving Certificate a few months later and, true to their word, my parents gave me an overseas flight to Asia, during which I met a Chinese student, William Chan, on the plane who was studying at a university in Sydney. We struck up a friendship that continued after our return to Australia and when I decided again that I could not stand living with the Nielsens any longer, I moved into William's flat in Cremorne, ceased going to Manly Boys High School and started at University in March 1963.

I politely thanked the Nielsens for taking care of me over the previous three years, but the parting was not a sad occasion for me. I saw Gerda a handful of times only in the forty years since, but I did attend her funeral.

University

I commenced studying Engineering full time at the University of New South Wales in Kensington in the eastern suburbs of Sydney. I took on tutoring and part-time work to pay for incidentals, but the major expenses of education and rent came from my parents via their friend Herman Braakensiek, whom I would see on a monthly basis for payment. With my parent's approval, I bought a little Vespa scooter like the one my father had purchased years previously in Jakarta and spluttered my way around Sydney on that for a long time. I guess my parent's cry of poverty was just a ruse for me to obtain a University Education at the Government's expense, because within a year they had paid cash for a new house in Sydney.

My first year at University was one long party for me. I did not do much study at all and consequently I failed many subjects. I sat for some post exams and passed most of my units, so thankfully did not have to repeat the whole year. However, I did commence my second year of studies with the extra burden of having to carry over one or two first year subjects as well. I settled down a little better during my second year at university with fewer failed subjects and in July 1964 Ingrid came to study in Australia as a boarder at Monte Sant' Angelo Mercy College, North Sydney.[10] During this year I also developed a strong desire to become a commercial airline pilot.

I had enrolled in Engineering mainly because I did not know what I wanted to do and my parents had suggested that Engineering was a prestigious and worthwhile career. Now, I was in love with the idea of becoming a commercial pilot. I wrote away to Qantas and successfully passed all the physical and psychological tests to gain a scholarship in this company's trainee pilot program. To confirm my commitment I needed

---

[10] During a trip Ingrid took to Europe with her parents in 1963, Ingrid then fourteen and approaching her final year of high school in Indonesia, had concluded that Europe was too cold a location to further her education and decided instead to join her brother John in Australia.

to buy my initial flying kit for the sum of £200, but when I asked my parents for the money — through Herman Braakensiek — they refused. I let the matter drop, but it is to my eternal regret that I did not present a strong enough argument to my parents directly.

To be reasonable, at the time they did not know how strongly I felt about becoming a commercial airline pilot and I have been disappointed all my life that I did not do enough to seize this opportunity then. Over the years since, I have flown the occasional small commercial aircraft at an air school, but the desire to fly is still as strong today as it was forty years ago. I am now seriously contemplating learning to pilot gliders in the near future.

During 1964 when my parents were visiting Australia, I talked them into buying a house in Sydney. My parents said they had enough money readily available and we looked at a number of locations around Sydney. They seriously considered one particular house in Balgowlah on Sydney's North Shore, but it was over twenty kilometres from the University of New South Wales where I was studying. Proximity to the University was a major issue for me, so I prevailed upon them to purchase a house in Chifley, which was only a few kilometres away.

In retrospect it was bad investment advice on my behalf because the Balgowlah property subsequently appreciated in value at twice the rate of the property in Chifley. My parents were in a hurry to buy the property as they were only here on another temporary visit, so it came as a minor irritation to Mum when she was unable to move into the new house straight away. Despite paying cash, it would still take another six weeks to exchange contracts and settle property title.

I moved into the house as soon as possible after settlement with some of my flatmates from Cremorne and chose to enter my third year at university as a part-time student because I wanted to join the work force and earn some financial independence. Also, my heart was no longer in completing an Engineering Degree, if it ever was, and pursuing life experiences and personal happiness was now more important to me than pursuing a tertiary education. In the end it took me a total of nine years to obtain my degree in Engineering, which normally takes only four years to complete.

For the next year or so, I continued the routine of work, part-time University and developing long-term relationships with females, while Ingrid also attended the University of New South Wales to pursue a degree in Architecture. We had regular parties at Chifley but life appeared settled and content.

My Parents Move to Australia

In mid-1965 I again started picking up disturbing news from friends and media sources concerning Indonesia. As usual my parents were not commenting but I knew the political situation was deteriorating again. At least I felt comforted in the knowledge that my father's position in the airline industry would allow them to depart the country quickly if anything dramatic happened. On October 1 that year the Australian news reported an attempted coup in Indonesia and my concern rose significantly.

For days and weeks the news out of Indonesia was sketchy and I heard nothing from my parents. Then, as if nothing had happened, my parents calmly arrived in Australia about two months after the coup according to their normal schedule of twice-yearly visits, but kept silent about their experiences during the coup attempt. I found out much later that Mum was on a Communist "death list" during this period, but to this day I remain ignorant of the details of the coup and its bloody aftermath.

Then in mid-1967 while here on another visit, my parents received a phone call from Indonesia telling them that their possessions had been removed from their home of twenty years in Menteng and that the future of Mum's school, Harapan Kita, was in doubt. Dad hastily returned to Indonesia alone and shortly after phoned back saying that all had been lost. Major Said Pratalikusuma had taken over the entire household and the school furniture of Harapan Kita had been removed to a nearby school. What was left of our possessions had been saved by servants, who removed these and themselves to my parent's other house in Tebet, where my father's parents lived. My Dad sadly informed Mum to remain in Australia as there was nothing in Indonesia for her to return to.

Mum now stayed permanently in Australia, living with us in Chifley, while Dad continued to work in Indonesia, flying back and forth over the next year. Mum objected to my free-wheeling lifestyle, told me to straighten up and curtail the regular parties and staying out all night. Coincidentally, my live-in girlfriend returned to Hong Kong after finishing her university degree and broke off the relationship with me. I think this secretly pleased my mother, who thought I needed to refocus on my academic career. Meanwhile in Indonesia, the special relationship Dad had enjoyed under UTA's Territory Manager came to an end when Monsieur Richez was replaced by another French national, who took away Dad's privileges and stopped paying him in American dollars. Dad obviously realised there was no future for him in Indonesia for he settled his affairs and came to join us on a permanent basis in Australia in mid-1968.

Travelling Overseas

The January holidays of 1966 were spent with my sister on a six-week European holiday by ourselves. Our parents provided us with an open ticket requiring us to arrange all the flights and gave us a combined advance of US$2,000 to pay for all our accommodation, food and transfer expenses. We stayed with friends and relatives wherever we could to save money, but still we ran out of money fairly quickly because, as a hot-blooded 20-year-old, I insisted on hiring an expensive red Fiat 128 sports convertible in Italy to show off.

Nevertheless, it was one of the best holidays ever. We returned to Sydney via Jakarta, where we caught up with our parents for about a week and told them all about our fabulous holiday. We knew about the coup attempt six months earlier, but surprisingly noticed very little physical evidence of it in Jakarta itself. Of course there was a strong military presence in the city,

Son John and daughter Ingrid feel pretty pleased with themselves at hiring the latest Fiat 128 sports car in Italy on their European tour of January 1966.

but that was not unusual in itself as the military had always had a strong presence there. When we asked our parents about the coup and whether it had affected them personally, we received the non-committal response. Mum waved her hand about dismissively saying, "It doesn't matter. Now, what do you want for dinner?"

In January–February 1967, our parents shouted Ingrid and me yet another short overseas holiday. This time it was to Hong Kong and Thailand and we returned to Australia via Jakarta to visit our parents, whom we had not seen for a few months.

At the time both my father and I smoked heavily. After staying up all night chatting and smoking together, my father pronounced he would give up smoking. I jokingly said to Dad, "Couldn't you have stopped smoking before you finished off all my duty-free cigarettes?!"

My Parents' Businesses

Neither of my parents were working in Sydney during 1967 and Mum grew concerned that their savings were rapidly dwindling. She started looking in the papers and came up with the idea of buying a coffee lounge in the city as a business. I did not take a lot of notice of these developments as I was moving jobs from Pye Industries[11] to pharmaceutical manufacturer Johnson & Johnson at the time, but I do remember my parents purchasing the Toby Coffee Lounge in the Piccadilly Arcade of central Sydney in early 1968. The Toby Coffee Lounge was a shop-front café within the arcade with two rows of tables seating about forty customers along the right-hand wall and a counter most of the way down the opposite wall to a modestly sized food preparation area beyond that. It was a typical milk bar and café of the time that served Western-style light meals, cakes and sandwiches accompanied by tea, coffee, milk shakes and soft drinks. From the counter, the public could buy cigarettes, sweets, hot food such as pies, pasties and sausage rolls, beverages and sandwiches.

In addition to the traditional fare of bacon and eggs, steak and chips and toasted sandwiches, my parents gradually added Indonesian meals such as *opor ayam* (light curry chicken), *rendang* (beef curry) and *ayam goreng* (fried chicken), which could be pre-cooked at home and easily served at

---

[11] In 1966, the family of Howard Winata (Oei Tjong Hauw) had previously secured John the position of Quality Controller at Pye Industries, television division in Marrickville.

the coffee lounge. They also moved away from a reliance on fast food counter-service to sit down table-service and employed a cook and waiter to assist. One of the smartest moves my mother made was to advertise in the Dutch-Australian weekly newspaper. Expatriates from Indonesia — Dutch, Chinese and indigenous Indonesians — started frequenting the coffee lounge, but her success was not limited to just expatriates. The Australian public too responded well to the "indonesianization" of the coffee lounge. A growing number of Australians willing to try out exotic cuisines were turning up for lunch or an early dinner before a show or the movies, and they liked the result. I suggested the name Warung Indonesia and a friend of Ingrid's drew a logo on the front glass window.

At the end of 1971, I helped to remove and store some property out of the café when all the tenants of Piccadilly Arcade had to vacate for a total redevelopment. A few months later in early 1972 my mother started a restaurant in York Street, Sydney, taking with her the Warung Indonesia name. There were only two or three Indonesian restaurants operating in Sydney at the time and the positive customer response I had observed at the Coffee Lounge to Indonesian cuisine convinced me that the new restaurant was a good business move. Regrettably the restaurant started losing money from day one.

I have thought about this since and concluded that my parents went into the business without any plan as to how they would convert the Granny's restaurant from an American style bar and grill into an Indonesian restaurant. There was very little change to the décor, hardly any alteration to the menu and too many former staff — set in their past ways — continuing in employment. Some key personnel, such as the cook (Wendy) and kitchen hand (Elsie), were still working in the restaurant three years later, passively resisting change and continuing to produce the same American-style meals, like pancakes and steaks.

In hindsight my parents should have made the transition to an Indonesian-style restaurant much earlier, as had been done previously at the Toby Coffee Lounge, but the restaurant was a bigger, more onerous prospect and they chose to change it slowly so as not to lose the existing customers. When they finally did make a concerted effort to change in 1975, takings picked up rapidly and the restaurant became profitable for the first time.

However, the main reason why the restaurant languished for its first three years was that my parents were actually operating two separate businesses and were waging a subtle war between them. In 1972 Dad started a fish shop at about the same time as Mum started the restaurant and for almost three years the two would not agree on which food outlet they should concentrate their efforts.

In late 1974, while temporarily unemployed, I performed a review of the restaurant's cash flow with a view to operating the bar concession myself as a separate business, but discovered the restaurant was losing $1,000–2,000 a week, of which the major cost items were rent and labour. I was not interested in the fish shop and therefore did not conduct a similar review of its operations. I advised Mum that the restaurant was not commercially viable, but she dismissed my concerns and my parents stubbornly refused to resolve their continuing conflict. However, when the building which housed my father's fish shop burned down in 1975, he underwent a remarkable volte face in his attitude towards the restaurant. From being implacably opposed to Warung Indonesia, he now told me he would unreservedly support it. He finally accepted that Mum would not give the restaurant up under any circumstances and therefore decided to focus all his efforts on turning the restaurant into a commercial success.

From that point on, Warung Indonesia started to make a profit. Dad played the role of the welcoming host so well — by remembering customers' names and attending to their needs personally — that a growing number returned and started bringing along friends and family. My parents started building up their own regular clientele and the last employees of the previous restaurant were replaced.

My parents organized regular special evenings twice a month, such as disco nights to attract young people, but the very first event actually came from a suggestion I made. It was the days immediately after the devastation of Darwin, the capital of Australia's Northern Territory, by cyclone Tracy on Christmas Eve, 1974. People were organizing charity events to raise donations for the stricken population. From the radio I heard that another restaurant was hosting one of these charity events and thought it would be a good opportunity for Warung Indonesia to lift its profile by doing likewise. The evening was planned as a Dutch-Indonesian style banquet (*rijsttafel*) with entertainment included for a set amount per ticket. Within days the whole family quickly organized the entertainment and food and I obtained free radio publicity for the evening. We arranged for a master of ceremonies, dancers and an Indonesian folk band. Mum guaranteed that a percentage of the evening's receipts would go to the Darwin Relief Fund.

On New Year's Eve of 31 December 1974, the place was packed with more than 120 paying customers. Every available seat had been booked in advance with still more insisting on paying at the door. The bar and food takings amounted to about $5,000 gross and after paying $1,000 to the Relief Fund and $2,000 in costs the restaurant netted the previously unthought of profit of $2,000 for one night's trading! Following that success people started calling for more special nights, so my parents organized these events on a regular basis. Each evening followed the same format of a rijsttafel and entertainment provided for a set price, but the themes would often change. Sometimes they were based on promotional events, other times fashion parades, youth nights or cultural evenings.

One of the benefits of these special evenings was that customers who had enjoyed themselves on the special night would often return at other times to partake of lunch or dinner and bring family or friends with them. Conversely, the more customers who came for lunch or dinner meant that more people became interested in attending the restaurant's special evenings. It was a constant circle of mutual reinforcement and the customers responded to it exceedingly well.

Change of Fortunes

These were truly good times for the restaurant and lasted from the mid-1970s to the early 1980s. However, there were obvious changes approaching which my parents did not see, or simply chose to ignore. In the first few years of the 1980s the State Government brought in Random Breath Testing to reduce drink-driving on the roads. Then there was a change to Company Tax, removing entertainment expenses as a legitimate corporate deduction. These regulatory changes were both announced in advance, but my parents did not take any notice of them until they affected their business.

Although these changes led to a cumulative reduction in income of 15–20 per cent, their effect was not ruinous and my parents could have easily recovered if it had not been for the third and most significant event to affect the restaurant, the refurbishment of the Queen Victoria Building (QVB) opposite their restaurant. The QVB covered an entire city block and had been the main vegetable and fruit markets for the city until they were moved elsewhere in the 1940s. After that the building had fallen into disrepair and by the 1960s many people were suggesting that the entire block should be demolished. Just when this seemed to be its likely fate, Sydney began to rediscover its heritage and a groundswell of public opinion swung firmly behind the authorities saving the building and restoring it to its former glory.

In the early 1980s the City of Sydney Council announced a major redevelopment of the QVB that was intended to make it one of the main shopping locations in the city. The project would take three years to complete and be opened in plenty of time to celebrate the bi-centenary of European settlement in Australia in 1988. In 1982 construction began and the street outside the restaurant became a building site. The negative effects of the massive redevelopment opposite had not yet had the full impact when a buy-out offer came out of the blue to save the business.

There was a group of businessmen who operated an all-you-can-eat Chinese restaurant nearby which had to close down. They offered my mother a sizeable amount of money to buy Warung Indonesia and I advised her strongly to accept. She refused. This was a cause of serious friction between my parents as Dad wanted to accept the offer as well. Whenever there were conflicts between my parents, my mother would inevitably win as she can be very stubborn. On this occasion mother resolutely rejected the offer and even threatened suicide if she was pushed further on the matter.

The restaurant struggled amid the hoardings, noise and other impediments from a full-blown construction site outside the front door and restaurant trade plummeted. Meanwhile with rent and labour still having to be paid, Mum now dreamed of better days ahead and kept on saying, "We'll wait until the QVB opens. We'll see this (temporary downturn) out and then the restaurant will pick up and everything will be all right again." Everyone knew that the completed building would house many new restaurants and a whole new food centre as the plans were publicly available and even the hoardings displayed artist's renditions of the proposed food court. When I pointed this out to Mum, she refused to even discuss it.

The restaurant underwent pretty lean times during the three-year renovation, but, as I suspected, suffered even greater hardship when the QVB finally opened in the mid-1980s. Through direct underground connections to all the nearby buildings and railway station, all previous above-ground pedestrian traffic was cleverly redirected into the QVB and the dozens of food outlets awaiting them. The street outside the restaurant was now virtually deserted and the little remaining revenue soon evaporated. It is about this time that I noticed Mum, despite her optimistic rhetoric, anxiously raising money from a number of sources to keep the business afloat. When times got tough my mother would raise the perennial issue of a Dutch pension and in the mid-1980s my parents departed to Holland to pursue this cause again and to seek investments in the restaurant from distant relatives.

One night in the late 1980s my mother introduced a stranger to me in the restaurant as a distant family member recently arrived from Holland.[12] When my mother was out of earshot, this middle-aged Chinese woman started asking me about the difference between compound and simple interest on business investment in Australia. I thought the conversation a little strange, particularly from a person I had never met before, but nevertheless obliged her with an answer. Then she surprised me by asking specific questions about why I had not injected money into Warung Indonesia.

I realised that my mother had either borrowed money from this lady or was attempting to, and understood it was obvious this lady was naturally concerned that my parents would seek investments from distant relatives in Holland while immediate family members in Sydney would not do likewise. I told her in no uncertain terms that in my opinion the business was unviable and she left to speak with Mum. A few minutes later my mother came over and angrily told me I had no right to interfere with her business affairs. I never found out what actually transpired between these two people and I never saw this lady again.[13]

Once or twice a year I would receive phone calls from relatives in Indonesia whom I barely knew accusing me of being an ungrateful son and demanding that I assist my mother financially. Even my wife's mother told me that I now had a terrible reputation from her friends back in Indonesia as a rich son who refused to help his own mother. I tried to ignore this emotional pressure but it was a difficult task having repeatedly to defend my actions to strangers and it was very hurtful to me that my own mother was the original source of this personal attack.

Over this time I heard that an acquaintance and part-time dancer at the restaurant, Joyce Hoevenaars, had invested a sizeable portion of her life savings in Warung Indonesia, much to the embarrassment of her friend and my sister Ingrid, who had apparently advised her not to. I knew that a regular patron of the restaurant and wealthy drunk, Basil, had also been approached but thankfully he did not contribute. It seemed that Mum was now out of control and attempting to obtain money from everyone

---

[12] Eddie Sudibjo has since confided that this person was Bertha, wife of Go Ing Tjoh, who is a cousin of Go Ing Hoe, co-owner of the timber company Sioe Liem Kongsie.

[13] According to Eddie, An had already borrowed $5,000 from Go Ing Tjoh during their visit to Holland in the mid-1980s. Following Go Ing Tjoh's death, Bertha travelled to Sydney as An was seeking further investment. Eddie further explained that Bertha decided not to invest and demanded repayment of the previous loan, which Eddie paid prior to Bertha's return to Holland.

and everywhere. Without my knowledge, a mortgage was organized from Citibank in 1989 or 1990 which was secured against their property in Chifley, but still debts were accumulating faster than they could be repaid. Dad wanted to walk away from the business and was now threatening to divorce mum if she would not retire.

The end came when Ingrid's fiancé Stuart Pearson and I contacted the landlord, Mr Vidor of Toga Properties, to discover that my mother's rent was about $90,000 in arrears! We informed him that she was unable to pay that amount as she was virtually bankrupt but, if he closed the restaurant by changing the locks on the premises and allowed her to retrieve personal possessions, we would guarantee he would receive half the amount owing him from the sale of their house in Chifley. As Stuart and I pointed out to Vidor, a quietly negotiated half settlement was better than receiving nothing at all from legal proceedings, especially when we would ensure as much adverse publicity as possible if he went ahead and took an 80-year-old woman to court.

I guess Mr Vidor saw the logic in this compelling argument as a day or two later my parents arrived at the restaurant to find their keys no longer opened the premises. When they spoke to Vidor directly, he informed them that he had decided to bring the business to a close. To the great relief of the rest of the family who had observed and suffered years of emotion, subterfuge, threats and broken promises, my parents thankfully gave up the struggle to keep trading without so much as a whimper. My explanation of my mother's behaviour over this wretched five-year period is that she was obsessed. She was like a gambler with an addiction: she could not stop and refused to see the reality of the situation around her while everyone else did. Nevertheless, I have never fully understood what the underlying motivating factor was producing this obsessional behaviour.

We collected personal possessions from the restaurant but Mum refused to visit the restaurant again or help in the removal of items. Day after day she stayed in Chifley, grieving over the loss of her restaurant. Meanwhile I negotiated with the banks and other secured creditors and collectively they agreed to hold off legal action, as long as we arranged to sell the Chifley property quickly and pay them out with the proceeds.

The Aftermath

My parents lived at Chifley until the property was sold a few months later for $300,000, of which $270,000 went to pay off creditors (Citibank

$150,000, Landlord $45,000, Westpac $30,000, Credit Cards $30,000 and sundry other creditors $15,000). Investors, family and friends who had collectively lent or given them more than $100,000 lost everything, as did a large number of unsecured creditors who had supplied goods and services to the restaurant. In all, the business collapsed leaving over $400,000 owing, of which $270,000 (a creditable 67.5 per cent) was repaid, but it cost my parents everything. Knowing they would lose all their savings and assets and face starting life again at their age with nothing, I managed to retain a meagre $30,000 for my parents out of the sale of the house. It was not a huge sum, but I hoped it would be enough to salvage some self-esteem out of the whole sorry debacle.

After the Chifley property was sold, my parents came to live with me and my family in a room at our home in Baulkham Hills for the next three years. It was a very stressful time and we did not get along at all well. At this time I was running a consulting business from home. Despite my instructions on professional phone protocol, they would constantly answer the phone in a casual manner and it cost me customers. Our lifestyles were very different. While I was going through a vegetarian phase, the pungent smell of meat and seafood dishes they cooked filled the home every day. Dad loved feeding birds and soon the backyard was littered with excreta and food scraps. Even our clothes drying on the outside washing lines were regularly soiled by the birds that flocked to our backyard in their dozens.

However, there were good times too. Dad tried to help around the house whenever he could and took on the task of transporting my children and doing the cooking for the extended family. Their physical presence was comforting to me and the rest of my family and it was good to see us become closer after so many years of animosity over the restaurant. Even though there was a degree of friction caused by two families living under the same roof, on balance it was good to have them live with us. Having said that, it was obvious to all concerned this arrangement was never going to succeed as a permanent solution to their accommodation problem.

Whilst they were living with us, I suggested to Dad that he earn a little extra money through buying and selling motor vehicles, an activity he had performed successfully years earlier, and he threw himself into this hobby with a vengeance. He went off to the auctions and purchased cars cheaply, detailed them well and sold them a few weeks later privately for a small profit. He sold three or four cars this way and made enough money to buy a Mitsubishi Magna station wagon for himself outright.

I introduced my parents to Sunrider health food as another money-making opportunity. I had become fairly successful as a Sunrider distributor before they came to stay and it was not all that difficult to share with them the health and commercial benefits of becoming involved in the business. Initially my parents started as consumers, but when they reported significant improvements to their health they began selling the product to others as well. Coincidentally, the Sunrider company was about to expand into the Indonesian marketplace and I saw this as a golden opportunity for them to get in on the ground floor through their contacts, their ability to speak the language fluently, and their own good health to promote the product.

They flew to Indonesia for the company's launch into that country and were celebrated as one of the company's most notable ambassadors. For years they managed a successful business distributing products out of Australia, but the Asian Financial Crisis of 1997–98 put an end to that when collapse of the exchange rate made Sunrider products too expensive for Indonesians to buy. However, my parents continued to consume the products personally and tell me that Sunrider still contributes to their remarkable health to this day.

Stuart organized all the paper work for a Housing Commission home for them and pursued their application vigorously on their behalf. In 1994 my parents moved into a small well-presented house in Girraween, where they lived together happily until my mother's deteriorating health required her to be moved into a nursing home in 2005.

My mother is now in her nineties and as well as dementia has recently been diagnosed with abdominal cancer.

Swimming

On a particularly hot Indonesian day when I was eleven or twelve, I was invited to swim socially with family friends Howard Winata, Mu Lhan and her father, whom I called Oom (Uncle) Fritz, at the Manggarai Olympic swimming pool in Jakarta, one of only two Olympic-sized pools in Jakarta at the time. We were splashing around and I happened to find myself in the lanes reserved for club swimmers, who were training at the time. Something in my pathetic attempts to keep afloat caught the attention of two middle-aged men, whom I later found out were the Dutch swimming coach (Oom Dick) and an Indonesian swimming coach (Aman Siregar). One of them invited me to join the club.

I did not think much about the offer initially but over the course of the next few weeks I returned several times to the pool and slowly started to get involved in the club. Mu Lhan, the girl I was interested in, was already a club member and her family often showed 16-mm foreign movies — then a rarity — in the evenings. It really was not a difficult choice for me and I decided to join Kuang Hua Swimming Club, where they began teaching me some skills.

At the beginning lessons were twice weekly in the afternoons but as I became more committed and showed better skills, the number of afternoon training sessions increased until I was swimming five afternoons each week. Then it stepped up again with the addition of morning sessions until finally I was training ten sessions a week, five each in the morning and afternoon, plus attending time trials and competitions regularly on the weekends. As my commitment increased, so did that of my parents. They started coming to watch me during the afternoon sessions, then driving me to the early morning ones. Gradually they became members of the club themselves and took turns to cook meals for the swimmers as well as transport swimmers to meetings and sessions.

I joined the Club in 1956, but the level of intense involvement — ten sessions of training a week and competitions — started in 1957 and continued for three years until I left for Australia in mid-1960. During that period I rose to become Captain of the Swimming Squad and held every club championship and almost every club record possible for freestyle, medley and relay events in the middle to long distances.[14] I found that the longer the distance, the bigger the winning margin. I would struggle to win the 200-metre races but would win by two laps of the pool for 1,500-metre races.

During competitions many swims broke the existing national records at the time, but the government would not acknowledge my achievements because ethnic Chinese swimming clubs were not recognized as legitimate organizations. While other swimmers would occasionally swim for different clubs to gain official recognition for their achievements, I steadfastly refused to do so. It was discrimination and I did not like it. I can particularly remember one swimming carnival at which I came first in an event and set a new Indonesian national record in the process. I stood on the podium

---

[14] These events included the 200m, 400m, and 1,500m freestyle; 100m and 200m butterfly; 4 × 50m and 4 × 100m individual medley; and the 4 × 100m as well as the 4 × 200m relay.

as the winner and received a medal for my performance, but the official record published next day in the paper only reflected the names and times of swimmers from government-approved clubs who had finished behind me.

Incidents like this have left a permanent scar on me. I detest discrimination of any kind but reserve a special loathing for state-sponsored discrimination. It is racism and it is wrong! Another abhorrence is corruption. In Indonesia I found the two closely intertwined. Since leaving Indonesia, I have never really wanted to return and I think I have only done so once or twice over the past forty years, mainly out of family obligation, not personal choice. Even the last time I visited Indonesia in the early 1980s, to introduce my own family to relatives, I witnessed several examples of discrimination and corruption. We were at Jakarta airport about to board a plane with Chinese relatives when suddenly they were taken away by customs officials, only allowed to re-join the flight at the last moment after they had paid these officers a bribe, otherwise they would have missed the plane. I have a negative opinion of Indonesia but it is a result of years of bitter personal experience.

After relocating to Australia, I still wanted to continue competitive swimming, even though I knew that the standard of swimming was considerably higher. In October 1960, I went to the North Sydney Olympic Pool and tried out for a twelve-month coaching sponsorship from the Jansen swimwear company. I was successful and the coaching was provided by Sam Herford at his pool in The Spit. It caused a stir in the media that an adolescent from Indonesia had obtained an Australian sport scholarship and the "Manly Daily" wrote an article titled, "Boy, new swim hope", on the subject.

I learnt a lot from Sam Herford and I knew he was one of the best swimming coaches in the world,[15] but by the end of 1960 my passion for intense competitive swimming had waned. I was in a new country, eating new foods, living a different lifestyle and, at the age of 15, finding that girls were far more interesting than the black line at the bottom of the pool. I kept up the regime for almost a year, but with my heart no longer in competitive swimming, my performance deteriorated.

---

[15] Sam Herford was Australian swimming coach from 1958 to 1966. He personally trained a number of champion swimmers, including the great Murray Rose, who won gold medals at the 1956 and 1960 Olympic Games.

At the end of the twelve-month sponsorship I was facing the daunting prospect of moving from junior to senior level swimming and competing against world class swimmers when I was not even holding my own at junior level. I was realistic enough to know that I would never make a swimming star and I quietly stopped swimming on a competitive basis. Nevertheless, I still very much enjoy water sports and activities on a social basis.

My Marriages and Family

I met Tesula Anastassiou, a Greek Cypriot whose anglicized name was Sue Anastasi, at a friend's party in 1970. I was 25 and she was 21. We liked each other, started going out, but when we wanted to get married her parents who lived in the Sydney suburb of Ashfield tried to stop us and threatened to kill me. My parents were in favour of the marriage, so with their help we hid from Sue's parents, got married at the Registry Office in a civil ceremony and held the reception in the Toby Coffee Lounge, all within a few months of meeting. For several weeks leading up to the wedding, Sue's parents heard nothing from their daughter. When we finally made contact and informed them of our marriage, they were so grateful their daughter was alive and well that they forgave us instantly for the marriage and over the next few months grew closer.

We were both quite young and immature and entered the marriage with no real understanding of what it actually meant to be wed. In retrospect we should have spent longer getting to know each other. I continued my pursuits and personal activities as if I was still single and told Sue I was not ready to have children. Sue and I moved from our rental accommodation in Maroubra into her parent's home in Ashfield and they transferred title of the property to us when they relocated to Melbourne about six months after our marriage.

Sue worked as a secretary in an insurance office at the time and we held a few office parties for staff at our home. One of the guests included a male work colleague about my age who was going through an upsetting divorce of his own. We took pity on him and he stayed at our place occasionally, sometimes whilst I was away snow skiing. Sue was obviously unhappy and the two started seeing more of each other. In May 1972, almost two years to the day of our wedding, Sue left me and two years after that we were divorced. In the meantime I heard that Sue had moved in with this other person. We sold the Ashfield property and I bought a unit in Bondi with my part of the proceeds of the divorce.

For several years afterwards I was deeply unhappy, took to alcohol and marijuana heavily and had a succession of casual relationships with women whom I treated badly. I can particularly remember my sister's wedding to her first husband Peter in 1973. Sue and I were only recently separated, but she still agreed to be Ingrid's bridesmaid. I turned up with a girlfriend, got drunk and spent most of the night trying to pick a fight with Sue, who ended up in tears, spoiling the wedding celebrations. To this day, I am sure Ingrid has not forgiven me for my unpleasant behaviour.

In late 1974 my mother asked me to drive one of the girls who worked at the restaurant home. Her name was Sally Suseno and she was a nice young woman working part time at the Warung Indonesia while studying Optometry at the University of New South Wales, my alma mater. I did not know it at the time but I think my mother was probably pushing us together.

We started going out together, became close and in late 1975 Sally moved into my Bondi flat to live with me. We were married in February 1978 with the approval of both sets of parents and later had two children, whom we both love very much.

Mum's Suspicions of My Father's Supposed Infidelity

During my life I have observed the occasional incident when my mother has suspected Dad of infidelity. For example, I was visiting my family in Indonesia in the early 1960s when Mum was accusing Dad of spending too much time with his secretary or personal assistant, called Netta, at UTA. Mum was upset that he was working back late at the office with Netta and taking this woman to company functions instead. Even though I was only in Indonesia for a few weeks, I got the clear impression this conflict had been going on for some time. I am not aware how, or if it was resolved, because I returned to Sydney whilst the disagreement was still in progress.

During the early 1970s, Mum accused Dad of having an affair with one of their employees, Kartini. This elevated the conflict between them to a new personal level. Kartini came to my home one day crying on my shoulders and denying that she had slept with my father or done anything else that would warrant my mother's growing outbursts of jealousy and anger. The matter was finally resolved when Kartini was deported to Indonesia for overstaying her visa.

It would seem that my mother's suspicion about father was even shared by her sister, Roostien. On the occasion of my marriage to my second wife,

Tante Tien who had come to Australia to specifically attend the wedding was overheard saying she hoped I did not turn out to be like my father, who had the "roving eye". I wonder to what extent my grandfather's behaviour in taking a second wife or mistress affected both his daughters.

Assessment of My Parents' Character

I have never really analyzed my mother's character before but, on thinking about it, I can see education has always been the paramount motivation. This issue not only dominated her own life but also influenced her decisions as to how we children were raised. In this regard my mother is no different than generations of others who grew up during the nineteenth and twentieth centuries.

Education was seen as the single most effective tool for people to raise themselves out of poverty and mediocrity. By and large this belief proved highly successful as the majority of Western populations educated themselves out of the lower class into the middle class and a better life-style over the period of a century or so.

My mother is not motivated by money but by society's acceptance and recognition of her achievements. Achievements, according to my mother, are not financial; rather they are the institutions, legacies and effects on others that your actions have accomplished during your life. This is why her school, Harapan Kita, meant so much to Mum. She changed the lives of many misguided, aimless and delinquent children who eventually went on to become valued, important and even esteemed members of society. It did not matter to her that Harapan Kita was a commercial failure: making profits was not as important as improving people!

My father's main motivator in life is to be liked by other people. He takes great pleasure in socialising with people and assisting them whenever he can. He has always had great inter-personal skills and this is why he was such a good salesman and host in the restaurant. In summary, I would say that Mum is primarily motivated by social recognition, whereas Dad is motivated by social acceptance.

My father had a very close working relationship with Monsieur Richez at UTA that withstood any intrusion, but Dad was not able to establish the same close bond under subsequent management that replaced Richez. Seizing the opportunity, Dad's assistant naturally promoted himself. However, my father did not regard this as unusual and dismissed the machinations as normal office politics which he could handle with ease. Indeed he did, but

Mum blamed this person's behaviour with somehow causing my father's departure from UTA. In truth my father's privileged position or special status had simply come to an end under new management at UTA and his subsequent resignation had nothing to do with undermining from his assistant. It was just a change in executive style.

Sometimes, when adversity strikes our family, my mother is quick to sheet home responsibility to some other individual whose actions, according to my mother, are malicious rather than accidental. The truth is that all people and families go through cycles of success and failure and everyone is as much responsible for their highs as they are for their lows. To claim ownership of achievements only, but to blame every mistake, every mishap, every wrong on someone else is a sign of insecurity. Yet that has been another character trait of my mother I have observed all of my life.

My mother is strong-willed and strong-minded and has great intestinal fortitude to tough out the bad experiences that beset us all. As much as possible, my mother has done a fantastic job in protecting her family. She is capable of manipulating others and often does, though I do not think she does it consciously or malevolently. I think she is such a perfectionist that she needs to impose order around her. Some of her relationships are based on a perceived value that my mother would place on the other party. If she did a favour for someone else, my mother would expect a favour in return and sometimes my mother would actually initiate a good turn purposefully to receive one back. This has led to my parents often associating themselves with people of more influence, power and prestige than themselves, such as captains of industry, politicians, community leaders, and senior military personnel. If my mother did a small favour for one of these other people, such as tutoring a son, then it was hoped they would receive a larger benefit in return.

Conclusion

If you asked me what role would best epitomize my mother, I would have to draw an analogy by going back a few hundred years to the court of a rich and powerful Sultan and say she would have been perfect in the male position of Grand Vizier. Mum would play the part of adviser and confidant superbly well and be the focus of all the courtroom intrigue with absolute conviction and success. My mother would thrive as the power behind the throne.

I suspect that if someone asked my mother whether she regarded her life as successful, she would answer in the negative. She would be rather critical on herself and judge it as falling short of her very high expectations. I personally think that she has had a fantastic, wonderful life of which she should be very proud. I am certainly very proud of her.

14

The Voice of
Ingrid Pearson

I was born on 10 January 1949 in Jakarta, Indonesia and the first of many names I have had in my life was Kang Tjay Ing. Kang is my family name and Tjay Ing means "gift of joy". Of course, I do not know anything about my conception or birth but I can pass on my mother's recollections about these matters because she spoke to me about it many times.

After the birth of my older brother John in 1945, when my mother was 33 years of age, she found it difficult to conceive again. Eventually she went to see a doctor, a gynaecologist I think, in Jakarta who prescribed a course of fertility pills. According to my mother, these pills must have worked because she fell pregnant almost immediately. However, Mum was 36 years of age at the time, which was late for childbirth in those days and knew this was probably the last child she could have, so she hoped it would be a boy. Her reason for preferring another son was that the two boys would be very good company for each other. They would grow up playing with each other, wearing the same clothes and following the same sports. My mother was so convinced that she was going to have a boy that she had only purchased blue-coloured baby clothes in advance of the birth.

On a wet and stormy night, I was born in a Jakarta hospital and my parents were surprised that I was a girl. According to Mum, my father rushed out and hastily bought me a dress to wear home, as they had only brought baby wear for boys to the hospital. Even though they expected a boy, my parents have always told me how grateful they have been for having a girl in the family. There has never been discrimination in my family based on gender. If anything, I learned from an early age that women are not only equal to men. They are in fact stronger! This was not a point of view that was popular anywhere in the world at the time and particularly not in a Third World country like Indonesia. Nevertheless, my mother's strong character and personality taught me from the beginning that women can achieve anything they want.

Childhood

I lived at Jalan Jogja 7 in the suburb of Menteng in Jakarta from when I was a baby until I was fifteen. With the advantage of hindsight and my profession of Architecture, I now know that the house was a spacious five-bedroom Dutch-colonial home set on a large suburban block of land in a central and prestigious suburb of Jakarta. At the time I can only remember it as a big rambling house. The sitting room furniture had been designed by Mum and made for her quarters in Jember. The furniture had travelled with her to Salatiga and finally Jakarta. I recall the generously proportioned black lacquered arms that cradled the seats and the rich, burnt orange upholstery in cotton. The set comprised a divan with integral side tables and two armchairs in a style that I later learned was Art Deco.

Glimpses of memories, augmented by tales told by parents and relatives have created a patchwork of recollections from my early childhood. Memories such as spending the day in a rattan playpen on the front veranda of the house; being bathed in a tub in the rear yard, the water a pretty purple colour,[1] being put on the potty at night and given a drink of weak, sweet milk tea.

I was told that when I was about 15 months old, my parents left me in the care of my paternal grandmother while they travelled to East Java on family business. When they returned several days later, I was very ill with a kidney infection, apparently as a result of being left in the playpen in wet diapers. Mum had a dream that Mary, the mother of Jesus Christ, approached her and said, "Give your child to me, and I will look after her." Mum awoke with a start and related her dream to Dad, saying that she would place my health in Mary's hands. If I got better Mum vowed that both John and I would be baptised into the Roman Catholic faith. In later years, when I was troubled she would often relate this story and ask me to pray to Mary for comfort.

---

[1] Potassium Permanganate was added to the water to act as a disinfectant.

246

My strongest early memory, probably at the age of three or four, is being taken by my parents to a nearby public park in Jakarta, called Taman Madiun, where I threw a tantrum. I cannot recall the reason for my anger, though that in itself is not unusual for I was generally angry most of my childhood, but I do remember shouting, screaming, running around and generally behaving badly in public.

In my childhood, I was actually more interested in the animal life at home than in the architecture. We had chickens, birds, rabbits, cats, and dogs, and they seemed to have taken up most of my time when I was a child. Sometime between the ages of four and five (1953–54), my father was breeding chickens in our back yard and he frequently incubated and hatched more chickens at a fellow breeder's house nearby. I often went along to watch the hatchlings emerge from their eggs and I became so attracted to these cute little hatchlings, that I begged my father to be given a few to raise myself. Unknown to me these birds were very valuable, but my father reluctantly agreed and I was given two or three little chicks to raise personally. The young birds became my pets until the day that I took them into my bath with me to let them have a swim. Having no concept of what drowning was, I was surprised when the chicks lay on the bottom of the bath and would not move.

I was lucky to have a number of influences on my life in my childhood years, but my mother was first and foremost. She laid the foundation stone of my future life and convinced me that I could achieve anything I wanted if I set my mind to it. After my mother, the most influential character on my development was Tante Tien, my mother's sister. When I was growing up, Tante Tien lived with her husband and family in the city of Bandung in West Java and every occasion of being with her always began with an exciting trip.

I have been told that when I was a baby suffering from heat stroke, my parents left me with her for a few months in the cooler climate of Bandung. When my parents returned to claim me, I had been away from them so long that I called my parents Tante and Oom! In retrospect, life in Jakarta was hectic and I was constantly vying for my parents' attention amongst their obligations from work, career and socializing, whereas my aunt's house in Bandung, although full of activity, felt calmer. Tante Tien had three children, two girls and one boy, and my cousins were much older than I was. While I was still a pre-schooler, Evy was at high school and Ida at university. Both looked after me and spoiled me whenever I visited.

Tante Tien ran a dressmaking business from home and she had many European fashion magazines, which I loved to leaf through. At her home, I was introduced to beautiful fabrics such as silk, brocade, and lace. To me, it was a wonderful world of luxury. My aunt also trained beauticians for an Austrian cosmetics firm, Vitaderm, and she later took over the business when the owner returned to Europe.

My childhood was not idyllic. I was a difficult, angry young person. Looking back on that part of my life, I can now say that I felt unloved and neglected and showed it through temper tantrums on an almost daily basis. A typical morning was spent with servants or relatives instead of Mum and Dad. Although Mum and Dad would sometimes wake up my brother and me in the mornings, it was always the servants who dressed us, fed us and sent us off to school because our parents had already left for work.

In the early afternoon, when school had finished we saw Dad briefly as he usually returned home for a meal, but we were all instructed to keep quiet as he took the opportunity to have the customary nap before returning to work again. Occasionally, Dad would read to us before his afternoon nap in return for us tickling the soles of his feet. These were very special times for me. However, it seemed there were many, many afternoons and evenings when we did not see Mum or Dad at all. They always seemed to be studying, working or socializing. Thankfully, John and I had the supervisory company of adult relatives during these years, from Mum's cousin whom I called by the Chinese title *Wak Ie* (first aunt), or in later years from my paternal grandparents who lived with us.[2]

Of course Mum and Dad did spend time with John and me, holidaying together and often spending weekends at Cibulan, a mountain retreat where we swam and played in their company. In fact, despite my comments above, I would say that our parents spent a lot of time with us, but unfortunately it was not often exclusive. In mixed adult company, the rule for children of being seen but not heard applied and, even when they were alone with us, they spent most of their time talking to each other. At the time, John and I were fighting constantly, often making Mum cry. We sometimes received corporal punishment for our fighting or other misdeeds delivered

---

[2] Mum's cousin, Tjie Hwie, and one daughter, Marie, stayed with the Sudibjo's from 1949 to the early 1950s because her husband and one of her children had been murdered by fellow villagers in the kampung of Prambon (near Ngronggot) in early 1949. The family were victims of a violent robbery (*rampok*) and were left destitute.

by the rattan end of a handy feather duster or the thick sole of a shoe. In retrospect, I think we might have been trying to attract the attention of our parents. If we did not fight, sometimes our parents would take us to a well known and popular ice cream parlour Tjan Njan as a reward.

When John and I were not fighting, we were finding some mischievous activities to occupy our time, such as blocking up the drains in the bathroom to create a swimming pool; sprinkling talcum powder on the polished floors to slide on, having mock battles with blowpipes made out of thin bamboo tubing and using mung beans as projectiles; or smoking tobacco behind the water drum in the bathroom.

Moral Debts

For much of my life I have noticed that my parents, and especially my mother, have placed a value on everything and everybody. Not only were physical items given a value but intangible items such as family and friends were also judged by a perceived value. Mum and Dad sought out and deliberately developed relationships with people of wealth or influence such as high-ranking military or captains of industry. For a period they even tried to get close to the President of Indonesia by attending meditation sessions with Sukarno's personal dukun.

During my childhood, I began to notice differences between Aunt Roostien and my mother. I felt that Roostien was genuine in her relationships with other people, while my mother appeared manipulative. Roostien seemed to do things for other people out of genuine friendship and there appeared to be no ulterior motives for her actions. Nor did her favours appear to be motivated by any expectation of reciprocity. Her acts of charity and assistance appeared to be spontaneous, generous and without any strings attached. However, Mother was different. The impression that has remained with me ever since my earliest days is that my mother was more deliberate and calculating about her relationships. She would do a good deed for someone on the basis of what that person could do in return. It made no difference whether the people were friends, relatives, acquaintances, or work colleagues — they all appeared to be valued according to what they could do for my mother and the family.

Sometimes people needed reminding of the basis for the relationship with expressions such as "I did this for you; therefore you must return the favour". In these cases I felt that these people never understood how Mum regarded the relationship in the first place. Some examples come readily to mind:

- Mum's brother, Tan Swan Bing, still "owes" my mother because she believes that way back in the 1920s she financially assisted his way through University;
- Her nieces Evy and Ida (Roostien's daughters) still "owe" my mother because she believes she looked after and educated them when they were children staying with her during part of the Japanese occupation in World War II;
- A relative in Surabaya "owes" my parents many favours because my father believes he prevented a "gold digger" from marrying and then stripping the assets off this millionaire relative.

In fairness, Mum also taught me that a good turn in one's favour should always be remembered and reciprocated whenever possible. My adoption by the Nielsen family is a case in point. My mother instilled in me that you owed people if they did good deeds for you. To this day she believes that Jan and Gerda Nielsen performed a special favour for the Sudibjo family by adopting and then looking after both John and me, and for this good deed they should always be remembered. In Indonesia there is a well-known and well-used phrase *berutang budi* (to be under great moral obligation) and it permeates all the communities and cultures of Indonesia.

For some people in the West, it may seem foreign to perform good deeds on the basis of obliging the recipient to perform a good deed in return. However, on the island of Java and especially in the Chinese community it was not unusual, because the Chinese had to rely more heavily than most on informal deals and deeds amongst themselves for survival. Maybe this is the Asian way with favours begetting favours, but perhaps other cultures have similar attitudes as well. I would like to think that most people would help others in the same way that I remember Roostien did. I felt that she was so special that she was worth copying.

A House Full of People

From my earliest recollection, we had a succession of relatives staying with us in Jakarta. Apart from Wak Ie and my paternal grandparents, we also housed a number of cousins[3] and, on one occasion, my mother's

---

[3] Cousins Lioe and Bing (daughter and son of Tjioe Swie Hian) and Kwie (Dad's niece — daughter of Kang Hoo Tjong) stayed with the family at various times during the 1950s and 1960s.

youngest brother, Tan Siauw Djie and his daughter. It made for a diverse and busy household, but there was a great deal of tension in the house. I was constantly reminded to keep quiet and not upset my parents, guests or army officers in residence. There were also verbal fights between Mum and my father's mother over differences about almost everything. It appeared that the two families were struggling to cohabit under the same roof. My mother told me later that her mother-in-law had not been happy that she married Eddie, being much older than he was, although no one ever formally objected to the marriage taking place.

My grandmother's main concern was that Mum was a career woman and not a dutiful wife. Even though the Indonesian Government campaigned tirelessly for gender equality, the traditional belief that women were second class to men never really abated. She took over the running of the household and servants in the absence of my mother, which was a constant source of friction between the two women. She would insist that only she could cook special dishes for my father, denying my mother the pleasure of preparing his favourite foods.

The other issue of conflict between my mother and her mother-in-law was over money. According to Mum, my paternal grandmother kept asking my parents for housekeeping money, which she would then pass on to her more needy relatives. In the early to mid-1950s, Mum felt put upon to support members of her mother-in-law's family when her own family's financial position was not yet secure, even though traditionally the eldest son supported not just his immediate family but the extended family as well.

At times it was like walking on egg-shells around the house but, to be fair, at other times the house was filled with laughter and boisterous activity. However, I did not know when to be noisy and when to be quiet and it seemed that my behaviour was being arbitrarily determined by my parents. However, in Bandung with Tante Tien it did not matter how noisy you were. The house was always full of love, joy and noise and there did not seem to be any tension in the atmosphere at all, except when Oom Sing Giap was at home. To me, Roostien's husband appeared surly and complained about every minor thing, such as the food being too salty or the house being unclean, and this made me uncomfortable in his presence. Later in my life, I learnt that I was Oom Sing Giap's favourite niece! I loved going to Bandung to see Tante Tien.

When I was about twelve I spent my entire summer holidays with Aunt Roostien in Bandung, where I attended her beautician's course and graduated with a diploma. This was a wonderful month for me and decided that I would model myself on her from that time on. It was not a dramatic change and it did not happen overnight. I observed how she behaved and slowly begun to copy her as much as possible. This change from being an angry young child into a calmer adolescent coincided with puberty and occurred over a period of two years or so. It could well have been that my so-called "modelling" on Tante Tien was part of my normal maturation process into womanhood.

Sayings

Sometimes you hear a particular phrase repeated so often that it becomes part of your own vocabulary, part of your own thought processes. I learnt a few statements from my relatives that have remained with me the rest of my life. I often felt physically unattractive when I was growing up and my mother reflected a similar experience. She told me that her Grandmother Njoo constantly referred to her as an "ugly duckling". Whenever she heard this, my mother would remember her father's reassuring words — "It is better to be beautiful on the inside than beautiful on the outside" — and she conveyed these wise words to me. I am sure these words were meant to reassure me, but instead they seemed to convey that I was less than beautiful too. It explains why in my adult years I was surprised to hear from others that I was beautiful and attractive.

The next lesson I learnt from repeated sayings was again from my mother. When I grew older and reached puberty, my mother would often take me aside and repeat the following words of wisdom, "You'll have to use your brains to keep your man." At least I felt that my mother and I had something in common, our plain physical features! I have since found out that at the time my mother was experiencing her own crisis of confidence as she suspected my father of having an extra-marital affair.

Lastly, two sayings about money have influenced me all my life. One statement was by my mother and the other by Tante Tien. My aunt would often say, "Money doesn't lie", by which she meant that you should always be prepared to spend more for superior quality. My mother would say just as frequently, "Money doesn't matter", meaning money is not as important as other issues, such as health and happiness. These two statements helped me to conclude that possessions are not as important as your well-being, but if you have them make sure that they are quality products.

From an early age, I was made aware of the value of possessions, to look after them and to take responsibility for them. I was not very good at it at first and damaged or lost many items before I learnt this important lesson. I was also taught to take responsibility for my actions and choices. For example, my mother allowed me to choose the one pair of shoes I wore each year, but warned me that if they did not fit well (because of the fancy shape I might have insisted upon) I would have to live with those shoes until next year. Mum made my undergarments and dresses, a couple of plain everyday ones and one good dress for going out to church or visiting people.

Once, my aunt was so outraged at my lack of apparel that she made me several extra dresses and bought me another pair of shoes. My mother said this act was "wasteful" and would cause me to treat possessions with contempt. I now realise that my mother's actions were gifts of love and she was still sewing dresses for me 30 years later when I was a corporate associate director and could easily afford expensive designer clothes.

Cultural Influences

From a very young age my parents exposed me to a wide range of cultural activities and influences, such as ballet when I was 4, singing when I was 5, music recitals from about 8 and opera when I was 14 in Rome, Italy while in Europe with my parents. Most of the culture was Western, but it was not exclusively Western. For example, when I was about nine I started learning Balinese dancing at a dance academy in Jakarta originally run by Ludwig Werner and later by Valeska Ong.[4]

My mother made John and I learn to play a musical instrument from about the age of 5 or 6. John played the violin and I learned to play the piano. I attended a piano recital by the famous Artur Rubenstein in Jakarta when I was about 13 or 14. I loved singing and burst out in song at every opportunity I could. People said I had a lovely voice and my mother told everyone that I must have inherited the musical gene from her father. It was said that my Grandfather loved music and singing too and not only played in the gamelan orchestra he helped establish in the village of Ngronggot decades earlier, but also took every chance he had to join the villagers in song.

---

[4] Coincidentally, Valeska Ong's husband Ong Kiem Ping (also known as Ping Kadarusman) later purchased father's property in the Jakarta suburb of Tebet when Dad left for Australia permanently in 1968.

During one visit from John — possibly 1962 — my parents decided it would be a good idea if John knew how to dance, so they enrolled him into the dance academy they had attended in the 1950s. As he needed a partner to practise the dance steps, I was enrolled too. We learnt the Fox Trot, Waltz, Quick Step and Samba, but our personal favourites were the Jive and Cha Cha, at which we excelled.

My parents took me to the main museum in Jakarta several times. It was known as the Musium Gajah (Elephant Museum) after the little bronze elephant statue outside the entrance which had been donated by King Chulalongkorn of Thailand. There we saw artefacts, textiles, and other items of significant Indonesian heritage. There was batik, silverware, costumes, weapons, paintings, pottery, murals and statues going back six hundred years to the greatest of the pre-Islamic states in Indonesia, Majapahit. These visits sparked a continuing fascination I have with archaeology and ancient cultures to this day.

Adolescence

There was no sudden transformation from childhood into adolescence. Even though I physically matured early at about the age of 11, puberty was not a dramatic event for me. One minute I was running around without a top on and bathing communally with the rest of the family and the next I am being told to put on a blouse or singlet and shower alone. My mother took me aside and explained all the facts of life to me and without any further fuss I gradually found myself turning into a woman from a fairly early age. However, even though my body matured early, my mind took a few more years to catch up, as my attitudes to life remained naïve for years into my adolescence.

Because of accelerated learning, I was placed in classes where the other students were one, two or even three years older than me. These older students were starting to demonstrate and politically agitate for and against such things as democracy, Third-World poverty, the Cold War, and nuclear proliferation. I was oblivious to it all and played with my pets or surreptitiously listened to the latest overseas Western popular music on Radio Australia, which was banned under the Sukarno regime. I never developed a strong sense of politics in my youth as these matters were strictly forbidden at home. My parents were so determined to remain politically neutral that they never allowed politics to be discussed. Consequently, I never took an interest in the real world until much, much later in my life.

Education

After my mother's initial tutoring in my early years, just like my brother, I was first educated at a Dutch primary school, and then at a local Indonesian primary school until I was eleven. When I started high school it was at my mother's school, which was then only in its third year. There were only about fifteen students then but when I left four years later in 1964 the student numbers had risen to over eighty.

In the 1950s and 1960s the Indonesian education system was expanding rapidly to make up for the lack of investment by the Dutch but, no matter how many new schools were being opened each month, there was always a chronic shortage of teachers and schools. Further, the physical infrastructure provided was very basic, just walls, desks and chairs and a blackboard. Harapan Kita was no different and lacked physical resources. For example, we did not have any science laboratories of our own but were lucky to be able to use the laboratories at the Air Force Academy in Kebayoran.

However, what we lacked in physical infrastructure was more than compensated by the quality of the teaching staff. Our teachers were amongst the very best graduates of the Indonesian teaching system and hand-picked by my mother, who paid them up to three times a normal teacher's salary to work at Harapan Kita. The quality of the teaching staff produced outstanding academic results that were the envy of many other schools and colleges. Every year, every student passed their university entrance exam (a common exam across the country) and some with the highest marks possible. Consequently, there was a flood of enrolments as more parents wanted the Harapan Kita "magic" for their children as well. The school was informal. For example, we wore uniforms (white shirt or blouse, light grey trousers or skirt) only to the two official assemblies a week, at the start of the week when the Indonesian flag was raised and at the end of the school week when the flag was lowered. Otherwise, dress was casual, as was the way we addressed our teachers, such as Pak or Tjiek.

Classes were conducted in the veranda, garage, bedroom, dining room and lounge room and we were encouraged to question and explore within the confines of the subject. However, no matter how inquisitive we were, there was always one matter that remained permanently off-limits to discussion — politics. Time after time, our teachers instantly shut down any discussion about our Constitution and any perceived shortcomings with the Sukarno Government. Some of my fellow students were not pleased with this censorship and on occasions became very agitated, but to me, this was a waste of energy. As I have mentioned before, I had already been conditioned by my parents to steer clear of politics.

It is only decades later that I now realize just how perilous a tightrope my mother was walking with Harapan Kita. Captain (later Major) Pratalikusuma wanted to remove us from the house at Jalan Jogja 7 and take over the property completely for his own purposes, but the school became the major barrier preventing him from achieving that ambition. As long as ambassadors, military, bureaucrats and other influential people sent their children to Harapan Kita, Pratalikusuma could never legitimately shut it down. However, it would be another story entirely if Pratalikusuma could prove that the school was spreading seditious material. Thankfully, my mother denied Prataliksuma any chance of victory by ensuring that politics was never discussed at her school.

Instruction on Civic Studies

What we did learn about Indonesian history is probably laughable by today's standards. I did not know it then, but Indonesian civic studies were taught as "heroic and revolutionary". In simple terms the message was:

- Indonesians struggled for centuries to overthrow the "evil" Europeans and in 1949 finally achieved this goal without any help from others; and
- By 1960 Indonesia as the fifth most populous country in the world and the largest Muslim country was well on its way to becoming a world power; and
- Not being aligned with the East or the West, Indonesia would become the leader of the world's non-aligned movement with the potential of influencing up to half the world's population.

Unfortunately, the reality was very different. Indonesia certainly had a large population but the majority were poor, sometimes desperately so. Our national living standard was that of a Third-World country and to say that we were becoming a world power and a rich nation was laughable.

During one of our lectures on Civics at Harapan Kita, other students began criticising the nation's manifesto and the Pancasila, which represents the five fundamental principles of the Republic of Indonesia. As the criticism grew louder our teacher grew more frightened and in the end begged the class to stop. He told us, "There could be spies listening", but what made us really take notice was when he said that if reported to the authorities we would be arrested and he would be shot!

Coming to Australia

From the time that my brother had gone to Australia to further his education in 1960, my family had also discussed my educational future with me. It was agreed that I would either continue my education in Holland or join my brother in Sydney. Going overseas was not the issue. The only matter was which country. As I neared the completion of my high school studies in Indonesia, my parents discussed the matter with me again and I told them I wanted to join my brother in Australia. I had already been to Holland twice in the previous five years and on both occasions I felt very cold, so I wanted a warm climate and to be closer to my family.

It had been established that the easiest way for me to study and stay in Australia was by adoption with the Nielsen family, but when I arrived in Australia I was surprised to find out that I was not going to stay with them. Although they were to adopt me, I was to board for the next year and a half at Monte Sant' Angelo Mercy College in North Sydney. Something had caused my parents to change their minds regarding my accommodation but I was not party to it and therefore I just went along with their decision without question.

I knew in advance that I would not be going to university in Australia directly from an Indonesian high school and for some years we had planned the move by accelerating my high school education in Indonesia from the usual six years down to four to account for spending time at a bridging course in a secondary school in Australia. Therefore, when I arrived in Australia I was only 15 years old and discovered that I would not be allowed into an Australian University until I was 17. Hence the bridging course I thought would take only six months, turned out to be eighteen months.

I was used to a co-educational environment and it was alien to me to enter a school that consisted only of girls. At Monte Sant' Angelo Mercy College there were girls boarding from Hong Kong, Papua New Guinea, Singapore and Thailand, but I tended to stay amongst the Australian boarders and other Asian girls who did not speak Chinese. There were only about thirty-six boarders out of a total student population of approximately three hundred from Form 1 to Form 5. My time at school was the last year of a five-year high school system in NSW. After I finished, high school was expanded to its current six years.

I stayed in boarding for the rest of Form 4 (1964) and half-way through Form 5 (1965) until the rivalry between the Hong Kong boarders — who only spoke Chinese amongst themselves — and every other boarder from Australia and the rest of Asia broke out into open conflict on a daily basis. I was more interested in studying for my matriculation into University than the petty rivalry between these two groups, so I obtained permission to move out and stayed at the Nielsen home for the last few months or so leading up to and through the final exams. The house at Chifley, which had been purchased a year earlier, was too far away from school at North Sydney to justify moving there. From the Nielsen home in Manly Vale, it was a simple half-hour bus ride.

I passed my Leaving Certificate at the end of 1965 with sufficient marks for me to matriculate to a number of universities on a Commonwealth Scholarship. The reason why I chose to pursue Architecture is that an aptitude test in Indonesia when I was ten years old had shown that I was suited to this discipline. My mother had wanted me to fulfil her lost dream by becoming a medical doctor, but I deliberately chose to follow my own career rather than one laid out for me by my mother. To my surprise, she accepted my decision without comment. Sometimes Mum would be wistful at not having a doctor in the family but she seemed satisfied that at least I had chosen to pursue another highly regarded profession.

From the end of 1965 I lived at Chifley and it was like shared accommodation with John and his university mates. After years of being separated from John, it was a joy to now be living with him again. I adored him and tried to do everything I could for him, including cooking and cleaning up for John and his mates. In the next year or so, my parents would arrive from Indonesia on regular visits once or twice a year. Prior to their arrival, everyone in the house would madly clean and tidy the place, putting it in order for my parents' approval. Whenever she was visiting in Sydney, even though I could stay out as often and as late as I felt like, my mother would inevitably wait up for me and ask me questions about the evening.

During my time at university my political awareness was still underdeveloped. At the time the university was a hotbed of radicalism. There were frequent demonstrations against Australia's involvement in the Vietnam War and sometimes they became violent, but while the tear gas and protests swirled around the campus, I ignored it all completely.

Socially I was growing up quickly and entered into my first sexual relationship with the person I thought I was going to marry. Richard Lewandowski was my first true love. He was of a Polish migrant family and my parents never objected to the relationship. However, after two years I discovered he was seeing another girl and with sadness, I broke off the relationship at around the time of my twenty-first birthday.

Throughout the next few years, as my parents settled into life in Australia, the relationships between all the family members never really developed. John and I had been separated from our parents for about six years. I was a twenty-one year old and John four years older, but when my parents moved to Australia to live permanently it seemed as if our relationship took up from where they had left off. They were disapproving of one of John's girlfriends which caused some friction between them. Mum and Dad were still making decisions about our lives, or at least my life. For example, I was encouraged to accept overtures from a fellow architecture student because I would be marrying into money, which I ignored.

Peter Hestelow

In the architecture course at the time, students were obliged to spend their fourth year at university in an architectural firm learning the practice of architecture. At the age of 22, my fourth year was spent at Kann Finch and Partners and there I met Peter Hestelow, who was 20 years my senior. He was a senior Architect and a charming man who was full of confidence and held women in the palm of his hands.

I admired him from the start. He was recently divorced and lived alone. When I found out that he was often away from work through illness, I began to care for him and this quickly turned into a form of love. I thought he appeared vulnerable and that I could make him whole again. As our relationship grew more serious, my parents expressed their opposition to it. They never actually told me that they suspected Peter of being an alcoholic, they only told me that he was sick, but I took their rejection of Peter as a personal rejection of me and became determined to prove them wrong. I ignored his heavy bouts of drinking when in company and when I visited him at his flat, did not see the many flagons of wine piled up outside the door as a serious matter. Against my parents' express wishes, I married Peter in 1973, without my parents being present but with the full support of my adoptive parents.

The first two years of the marriage were very exciting and adventurous. I felt like a woman being tutored in the ways of the world but everything came to a sudden stop when Peter ended up in hospital near death from cirrhosis of the liver. The doctors told me that Peter was a dependent alcoholic and would soon die if he did not stop drinking. He was in hospital for almost two months and was lucky to survive. My parents rallied around me and that is when I realized that they did love me but they just did not like my decision to marry Peter.

Peter swore that he would give up alcohol and appeared to do so for the next few months, but when I started finding bottles and flagons of wine hidden around the house I realized that he had again succumbed to temptation. For the next seven years, Peter was in and out of hospital on a number of occasions. Once, we were on a coach trip to Perth to attend a family wedding when he had a fit from alcohol withdrawal. He had to be removed to a nearby hospital just outside Adelaide, where for the next few days I did not know whether my husband would live through this latest episode or not. He did, but it was always uncertain whether he would survive each successive incident.

Peter held a number of jobs at decreasing levels of responsibility while his illness grew progressively worse, including working for my mother at Warung Indonesia. His last full-time position was as a poorly paid counter clerk at Ku-ring-gai Municipal Council, during which time we purchased a house in the Sydney suburb of Westleigh. Finally, he became unemployable and remained at home in a constant alcoholic haze.

I left him briefly during this time as he kept breaking his promises to stay clear of alcohol, but returned when Peter's doctor informed me that my husband did not have long to live. Near the end he was hospitalized where he died in November 1983. My parents were incredibly supportive during and after the funeral. I took a very long break to grieve with relatives in Indonesia, where I cried my eyes out for weeks on end until I was spent. I returned to Sydney and threw myself into work, where I would often put in 12-hour days.

I also started helping my mother more and more in the restaurant, with dancing performances or waitressing for money. Once, I took all of my annual holidays in one lot to manage my parents' restaurant for a month while they visited Europe on holidays. I think this was in the mid-1980s. I would sleep over at my parents on a regular basis and on several occasions they came to stay Saturday night at my place in Westleigh and we would all go for a country drive the next day. Between work, friends and family I found I had no time for myself nor the possibility of romance and that is exactly what I wanted. As far as I was concerned, at the age of 33 I was now a busy single woman and that is the way I thought it would remain for the rest of my life.

For the next six years or so, I took many trips·interstate and overseas. A few domestic trips were taken by car or train, but I enjoyed it most when I travelled overseas by aeroplane. It reminded me of the days of my youth when Dad would arrange flights for the family. Some overseas trips during this period were for work but several were personal and in 1988 I returned to Europe with friends for a six-week holiday.

Stuart Pearson

Soon after my return from Europe in 1988, I met Stuart Pearson on a blind date organized by Bill and Marelle Dive, who were mutual friends. The Dive family were Knox Grammar School parents and knew Stuart as the General Duties Master at the School. Bill Dive was a surveyor whom I would occasionally use in my architectural profession. My first impression of Stuart was not favourable. He smoked tobacco and consumed alcohol — both habits which I dislike — and I thought him overweight, loud and uncouth. I never thought any more about him until, by accident, we met again at the Dive household several months later. I had a completely different opinion of him the second time around and from that moment on we were inseparable.

That same weekend we had dinner at the Summit restaurant in the Centrepoint tower in Sydney, where we had our first picture taken. When I showed my parents this picture the next day they liked his open face and manner and approved immediately. They also appreciated that Stuart had the added advantages of youth for he was three years younger than me, healthy and in a steady, well-paid job. .I continued the relationship and we married after a whirlwind courtship in April 1990.

Restaurant

About the time of my marriage to Stuart that I came to realize that my parents' restaurant was in terminal decline. Years earlier, I had tried to prop up the restaurant by providing cheap labour for them and organizing friends, neighbours and business acquaintances to dine at the restaurant whenever possible. However, as time went on and Warung Indonesia continued to decline I began to question my mother, who by then was in her late seventies, whether she should still be operating a restaurant. Yet every time I approached the subject, my mother would insist that if she stopped working she would die soon after.

While I was struggling to maintain a consistent position on what I thought should happen with the restaurant, my brother had no such qualms. He was adamantly opposed to the family's continued involvement in Warung Indonesia and from about the early 1980s he had wanted my mother to get out of the business by selling the restaurant. Looking back, I initially wanted my mother to make the decision to leave the business rather than force a decision upon her, but as the years wore on I came to realize that this approach was unworkable because my mother was steadfastly refusing to leave a declining restaurant. Even her most ardent supporters, myself included, could see that this was futile.

In 1990 Stuart and John, at their own insistence, conducted an investigation on the state of the restaurant's finances with the full co-operation of my father. We were horrified at the level of indebtedness. When I was informed that the amount of money owing was so enormous that my mother could never possibly repay it, I finally decided that the situation was hopeless and accepted that drastic measures were needed to bring the matter to a rapid close. Yet there was still another ugly episode I had to go through before this matter was finally resolved.

At about the time I came to realize the situation was beyond hope my mother demanded I return to her a sum of $45,000, which she claimed was lent to me earlier as a deposit on the house at Westleigh. In 1990, Westleigh was valued at about $120,000, so the money represented over one third of the value of my house. I did not want to give her the money, preferring to keep it for my parents as a nest egg after the restaurant closed, but she put me under great emotional pressure saying that I was killing her, that I owed her the money, and she had brought me into the world so I must do as she commanded.[5] Comments like these triggered deep emotional responses in me and I was made to feel very guilty and obligated to my mother. Ever since I was a young girl, my mother had used the tactic of emotional blackmail whenever she wanted me to do something to which I was opposed.

---

[5] Ingrid's father had given his daughter the money in 1981 as a deposit for the house in Westleigh, indicating that it was a gift in lieu of her inheritance as the house in Chifley would be left to John.

Sensing my deep opposition to her request, she went further with her threats than she had ever done before. With just days to go to my wedding to Stuart in April 1990 she said, "I won't be present at your wedding because I will kill myself. I'll hang myself in my garage in Chifley on the day of your marriage if you do not give me the money." This was more than I could resist. Up to that point in my life I had never been certain that my mother really loved me and now I was terrified that her conditional love would be withdrawn altogether. As I saw the matter, I had no choice and over Stuart's strong objections I arranged for an immediate loan to return the amount to my parents.

Australia was going through a recession at the time and interest rates were at a historical high level of over 15 per cent. Our loan was at 15.5 per cent and was disastrous for us financially because we had to pay a third of our combined earnings each month just in interest repayments alone. I soon found out that our $45,000 did not make the slightest difference to my mother's indebtedness. After spending all the money to pay off less than half her rental arrears, her debt still remained insurmountable. It was all a total waste of effort and the restaurant was forced to close in any event in late 1990, but at least I felt that the repayment of money had cut the control my mother had over me and made me a much stronger person.

Fifteen years later the relationship with my mother is very different and far healthier, but up to that point I was a middle-aged woman who had allowed herself to be manipulated all of her life. I now believe that my mother's love for me is unconditional and we have a much more equitable relationship where we are more like equals than mother and daughter.

My parents hit rock bottom after the closure of the restaurant and the subsequent sale of their house in Chifley to repay a few of the more substantial amounts owing. For the next three years they lived with my brother John and his family at Baulkham Hills but it was not a good time for anyone. There were constant disagreements, sometimes over the pettiest of matters, and it was obvious that the two families were not suited to living together. Eventually Stuart helped them into their own two-bedroom villa in Girraween where they lived very happily for a number of years until Mum was moved to a nursing home in 2005. Mum is not as healthy or as strong-willed as she was previously and she is getting progressively more frail.

A Final Word

I love my parents very, very much and I want to make their lives as pleasant as possible in the few remaining years we are privileged to have them amongst us. Having been almost as intimately involved in this biography as my husband Stuart, I can say that my mother has lived an extraordinary life. I am amazed at her tenacity and determination. In the face of overwhelming odds against her, she has managed to survive and thrive.

Group photo of family taken in March 2004. L-R: Daniel Nielsen (21), Sally Nielsen (50), Eddie (83), John (58), An in wheelchair (91), Ingrid Pearson (55), Stuart Pearson in background (52) and Jennifer Nielsen (17).

I know that life has not been easy for her and she would view it as bittersweet, but my husband and I share a very different viewpoint. Both of us believe that she should be proud of what she has achieved, not disappointed. Any person who has endured what she has and gone on to live into her nineties deserves to be treated as a champion.

Appendix

Appendix A: Tan Family Tree

Tan Kim Hok — Tan Tik Ie — Tan Ting Bie MALE LINE

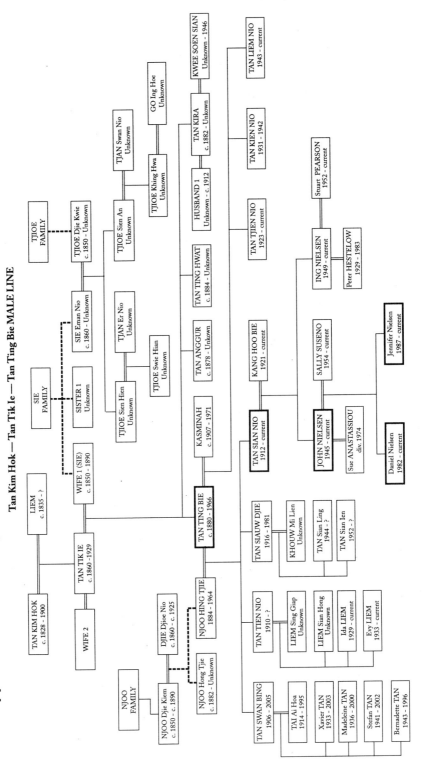

Appendix B: Maps

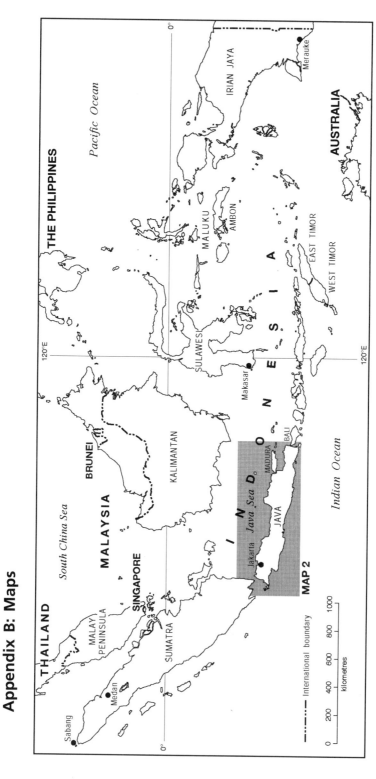

MAP 1. Indonesia

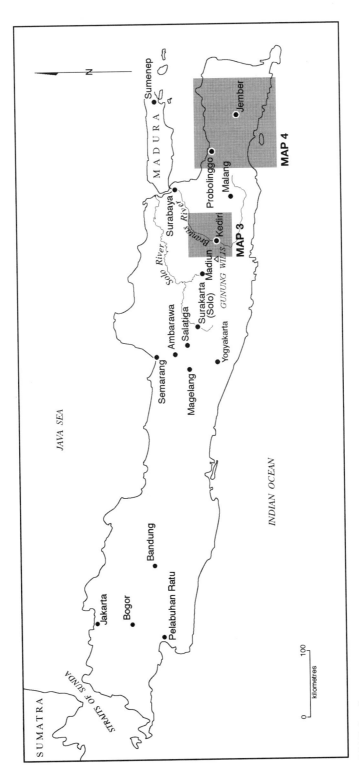

MAP 2. Java

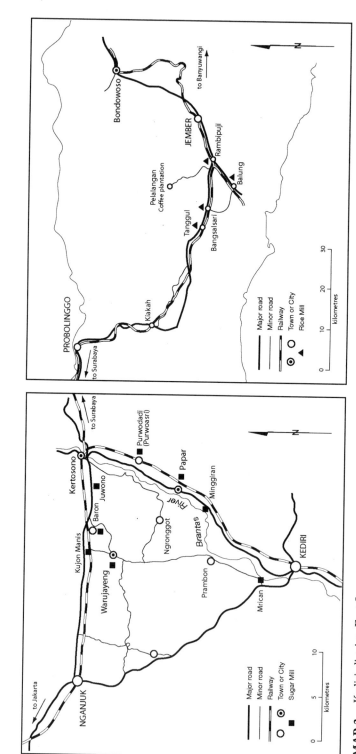

MAP 3. Kediri district, East Java

MAP 4. Jember district, East Java

GLOSSARY

Abbreviations, Symbols and Acronyms

Name	Full Name	Meaning, or Equivalent in English
£	Australian Pounds	Former currency of Australia until 1966 when the decimal system was introduced
ABRI	Angkatan Bersenjata Republik Indonesia	Armed Forces of the Republic of Indonesia
AURI	Angkatan Udara Republik Indonesia	Air Force of the Republic of Indonesia
BB	Binnenlandsche Bestuur	Dutch Civil Administration of the NEI
CAS	Carpentier Alting Stichting	Carpentier Alting Foundation
ELS	Europeesche Lagere School	Government-run Primary School attaining European (Dutch) standards of education
f	Dutch guilder	Monetary currency of Holland and her colonies, including Indonesia up to 1949
GIA	Garuda Indonesia Airlines	The national airline of Indonesia
GANEFO	Games of the New Emerging Forces	Major international athletic competition introduced as an alternative to the Olympic Games
HBS	Hogereburgerschool	Government-run High School
HCS	Hollandsche-Chineesche School	Government-run Primary School for Chinese students
HIS	Hollandsche-Inlandsche School	Government-run Primary School for indigenous Indonesians with Dutch as the medium of instruction
HOB	Huisvesting Organisatie van Batavia	Housing Organization of Batavia
IMF	International Monetary Fund	International Regulator of currency

Name	Full Name	Meaning, or Equivalent in English
KITLV	Koninklijk Instituut voor Taal-, Land- en Volkenkunde	Royal (Netherlands) Institute of Linguistics and Anthropology
KLM	Koninklijke Luchtvaart Maatschappij	Royal Dutch Airline
KNIL	Koninklijk Nederlandsche Indisch Leger	Royal Netherlands Indies Army
KPM	Koninklijke Paketvaart Maatschappij	Royal (Dutch) Shipping Company
MULO	Meer Uitgebreid Lager Onderwijs	More Extended Lower Education (school) – Junior High School
NEI	Netherlands East Indies	Indonesia under Dutch Colonial rule
NICA	Netherlands Indies Civil Administration	Equivalent of the BB while it operated from Brisbane during and shortly after the Japanese Occupation of Indonesia in WW II
NIOG	Nederlands Indisch Onderwijzers Genootschap	Netherlands Indies Teachers' Society (Association)
PETA	Pembela Tanah Air	Defenders of the Fatherland
PKI	Partai Komunis Indonesia	Communist Party of Indonesia
PNI	Partai Nasional Indonesia	Indonesian Nationalist Party
PRC	People's Republic of China	(Communist) Government of China
PTT	Post, Telegraaf & Telefoon	National Telephone and Postal System in the NEI
QVB	Queen Victoria Building	Major shopping building in the centre of Sydney
SGA	Sekolah Guru Atas	Teachers' College (after 1948)
SMA	Sekolah Menengah Atas	Senior High School (after 1948)
SMP	Sekolah Menengah Pertama	Junior High School (after 1948)
STOVIA	School Tot Opleiding Van Inlandsche Artsen	School for Training Native Doctors
TAI	Transport Aériens Intercontinenteaux	France's national airline for Charter flights (merged with France's domestic airline to become UTA in early 1960s)
TNI	Tentara Nasional Indonesia	Indonesian National Army
UTA	Union de Transports Aériens	National Airline of France for normal commercial flights (renamed Air France in the 1980s)

Foreign Words

Name	Origin	English Translation or Meaning
adil	Indonesian	just, righteous, fair
adviseur	Dutch	adviser, or counsel
afgelopen	Dutch	finished
air	Indonesian	water
akte	Dutch	academic qualification equivalent to a degree
algemeen	Dutch	general, or universal
alma mater	Latin	Literally, "fostering mother", but means school or college you graduated from
alun-alun	Indonesian	open square or field
amah	Indonesian	personal nurse or nanny
ambtenaar	Dutch	public servant
andong	Indonesian	horse-drawn wagon carrying several people
arang	Indonesian	charcoal
asli	Indonesian	original, as in indigenous
atas	Indonesian	on / upon
ayam	Indonesian	chicken
batik	Indonesian	traditional style of painting or cloth using wax and dyes
bahasa	Indonesian	language
bapak	Indonesian	father, respected elder (usually shortened to pak)
becak	Indonesian	pedicab, usually three-wheeled
bersiap	Indonesian	stand ready
berutang budi	Indonesian	moral debt: to be under great obligations
bestuur	Dutch	government
bikkelen	Dutch	jacks
Bisschopsplein	Dutch	Bishop's Park (now Taman Suropati)
boekendelegatie	Dutch	book allowance
bung	Javanese	brother (shortened from abang)
bupati	Indonesian	Government officer in charge of regency
cikar	Indonesian	ox-drawn wagon for goods
Cina	Indonesian	Chinese (derogative term)
concordante	Dutch	in accordance with (Dutch education in Holland)
controleur	Dutch	junior Dutch government official
coup	French	shortened form of coup d'état
coup d"état	French	sudden overthrow of the political order
dagang	Indonesian	commerce
dalang	Indonesian	puppeteer and story-teller
danau	Indonesian	lake
Darul Islam	Arabic	literally, abode of Islam; rebel movement

273

Name	Origin	English Translation or Meaning
Demokrasi Terpimpin	Indonesian	Guided Democracy, under President Sukarno
desa	Indonesian	town
ding (es)	Dutch	thing (s)
dokar	Indonesian	horse-drawn cart for a few people
dukun	Indonesian	native healer, spiritual adviser and sometimes sorcerer
durian	Indonesian	tropical fruit (*Durio zibethinus*)
en masse	French	as one, all together
fabriek (en)	Dutch	factory or mill (s)
gajah	Indonesian	elephant
gamelan	Indonesian	traditional percussion orchestra
gelijkgesteld	Dutch	made the same as, made equal
genduk	Javanese	girl (also nduk for girl maid)
goreng	Indonesian	fried
groot	Dutch	great
guilder	Dutch	unit of currency in Holland and its colonies (now replaced with the euro)
gunung	Indonesian	mountain
guru	Indonesian	teacher
haj	Arabic	pilgrimage to Mecca in Saudi Arabia
haji	Arabic	one who has done the pilgrimage
handel	Dutch	commerce
handelaar	Dutch	merchant (with groot, means wholesaler)
harapan	Indonesian	hope
huisvesting	Dutch	lodging, accommodation
ibu	Indonesian	mother, also used as title of respect
ingenieur	Dutch	engineer, entitled to use the initials Ir before surname
istana	Indonesian	palace
jalan	Indonesian	road/street (abbreviation Jl.)
jihad	Arabic	holy war
kali	Indonesian	river
kampung	Indonesian	village
kapelmeester	Dutch	urban bandmaster
kapitein	Dutch	captain
kelontong	Indonesian	small goods, or general goods
Kempeitai	Japanese	Japanese secret police
keris	Indonesian	traditional dagger with wavy-edged blade
keroncong	Indonesian	traditional folk music
kiai	Javanese	religious teacher
kita	Indonesian	us/our
klenteng	Indonesian	Buddhist temple

Name	Origin	English Translation or Meaning
Konfrontasi	Indonesian	Confrontation campaign against Malaysia
kongsie	Indonesian	company (usually Chinese)
koning	Dutch	king
koninklijk	Dutch	royal
kota	Indonesian	city
kraton	Javanese	palace
kretek	Indonesian	Indonesian clove cigarette
kuli	Indonesian	peasant worker or unskilled labourer. Derived from the Chinese "coolie"
kulon	Javanese	west
kweekschool	Dutch	Teachers' college
laan	Dutch	lane
Lebaran	Arabic	Muslim new year
Loro Kidul	Javanese	Goddess of the south
losmen	Indonesian	lodge or inn
luitenant	Dutch	lieutenant
lurah	Indonesia	Local Government authority
Mahabharata	Indian	famous Hindu epic story of love and war between gods and man (similar to ancient Greek mythology and tales)
majoor	Dutch	Major, senior Chinese officer
makan	Indonesian	to eat
makanan	Indonesian	food
malaise	Dutch/ French	in the context of this book the great depression of the 1930s
mas	Indonesian	literally gold, but also an honorific male title
matahari	Indonesian	sun
medan	Indonesian	square
Melayu	Indonesian	Malay
meneer	Dutch	mister
menengah	Indonesian	middle, secondary (school)
Merah Putih	Indonesian	Red and White (Flag of Indonesia)
merdeka	Indonesian	independence
musium	Indonesian	Museum
nasi	Indonesian	rice (cooked)
ndoro	Javanese	honorific title for gentleman of noble birth
nyai	Indonesian	concubine (traditional) mistress (modern)
oma	Dutch	Grandmother
onderdaan	Dutch	Subject
oom	Dutch	Uncle
opa	Dutch	Grandfather
opleggen	Dutch	Impose
orde	Dutch	Order

Name	Origin	English Translation or Meaning
organisatie	Dutch	organization
Pancasila	Indonesian	Five fundamental principles of the Republic
pasar	Indonesian	market
pax neerlandica	Latin	peace under Dutch colonial rule
pembela	Indonesian	protector, defender
pemuda	Indonesian	a youth, youth groups
peranakan	Indonesian	Chinese born in Indonesia whose cultural orientation is towards Indonesia rather than China
peraturan	Indonesian	regulation
pertama	Indonesian	primary school
plein	Dutch	park
pribumi	Indonesian	indigenous Indonesians ("of the land")
proefstation	Dutch	experimental research station
raden	Javanese	lord, a term of respect for one of the Javanese noble class
raksasa	Indonesian	giant
Ramadan	Indonesian	Islamic fasting month
Ramayana	Indian	Hindu epic story of love between King Rama and Queen Sita, her abduction and subsequent rescue
rampok	Indonesian	to rob or plunder
rantang	Indonesian	lunchboxes of food in round containers
ratu	Indonesian	king or queen
ratu adil	Indonesian	the just king of Javanese messianic expectations
raya	Indonesian	great
regentswoning	Dutch	regent's house
rijst	Dutch	rice
romusha	Japanese	forced labour
rupiah	Indonesian	currency unit of the Republic of Indonesia
rust	Dutch	tranquillity, calm
sake	Japanese	rice wine
sarong	Indonesian	piece of cloth the ends of which have been sewn together, wrapped around the waist and legs like a skirt.
sashimi	Japanese	raw seafood
sawah	Indonesian	rice fields, using flood irrigation to grow crop
Schouwburg	Dutch	Playhouse or Theatre
sekolah	Indonesian	school
selamat	Indonesian	good, blessed
serekat	Indonesian	united (older spelling, now serikat)
siang	Indonesian	daytime
siap	Indonesian	ready

Name	Origin	English Translation or Meaning
sikat	Indonesian	wipe out, or erase
sirih	Indonesian	betel vine whose leaves and nuts are used to mix with tobacco for chewing usually by women
sponsen	Dutch	to sponge
Staatsspoorwegen	Dutch	State (government) Railway
suiker	Dutch	sugar
sushi	Japanese	rice snack
taman	Indonesian	garden
tanah	Indonesian	land, country
tante	Dutch	aunt
tengku	Indonesian	prince
Tionghua	Indonesian	Chinese
toko	Indonesian	shop or store
totok	Indonesian	pure, full-blooded (in a racial sense); usually referring to ethnic Chinese or Dutch born outside Indonesia whose cultural orientation is towards their places of birth rather than Indonesia
tjiek	Chinese	sister
touwtje springen	Dutch	skipping rope
tuan	Indonesian	sir
van	Dutch	of
waras	Javanese	healed, or healthy
warung	Indonesian	little shop, booth or stall (compare with rumah makan which is a restaurant)
wayang	Indonesian	Javanese puppet story-telling
wedana	Indonesian	Indonesian head of a district (colonial times)
wiskunde	Dutch	mathematics

Bibliography

Booth, Anne, 1995, "Real Domestic Income of Indonesia, 1880–1989: A Comment and an Estimate", *Explorations in Economic History*, Vol. 32.

Blussé, Leonard, 2002, *Retour Amoy: Anny Tan, Een vrouwenleven in Indonesië, Nederland en China*. Balans, Amsterdam.

Brown, Colin, 2003, *A Short History of Indonesia: The Unlikely Nation?*, Allen & Unwin, Sydney.

Chang, Queeny. 1981. *Memories of a Nonya*, Eastern Universities Press, Singapore.

Coppel, Charles, 1983, *The Indonesian Chinese in Crisis*, ASAA.

Chandra, Siddharth, 2002, "Race, Inequality, and anti-Chinese Violence in the Netherlands Indies", *Explorations in Economic History*, Vol. 39.

Cribb, R. (ed.), 1991, *The Indonesian Killings 1965–1966: Studies from Java and Bali*, Melbourne Centre of Southeast Asian Studies, Monash University.

Cribb, R., 2000, *Historical Atlas of Indonesia*, Curzon, Richmond, Surry.

Creutzberg, P., *et al.*, 1979, *Between People and Statistics, Essays on Modern Indonesian History*, Telkamp, The Hague.

Dick, Howard, 2002, *Surabaya, City of Work: A Twentieth Century Socioeconomic History*, Ohio University Press, Athens (Ohio); Singapore University Press, Singapore.

Eng, Pierre, van der, 1992, "The Real Domestic Product of Indonesia, 1880–1989", *Explorations in Economic History*, Vol. 29.

Govaars, Ming, 2005, *Dutch Colonial Education: The Chinese Experience in Indonesia, 1900–1942*, Chinese Heritage Centre, Singapore.

Grant, Bruce, 1964, *Indonesia*, Penguin Books, Sydney.

Haven, Violet, 1944, *Gentlemen of Japan*, Ziff-Davis Publishing Company, New York.

Koo, Hui-lan [Madame Wellington Koo], 1943. *An autobiography as told to Mary Van Rensselaer Thayer*, Dial Press, New York. [Later version published as Koo, Madame Wellington (with Isabella Taves) 1975. *No feast lasts forever*, Quadrangle/New York Times Book Co, New York.]

Korver, A. P. E., 1982, "Sarekat Islam 1912–1916", Historisch Seminarium van de Universiteit van Amsterdam (Ph.D. diss., University of Amsterdam).

Levert, P., 1934, "Inheemsche arbeid in de Java suikerindustrie (Native Labour in the Sugar Industry of Java)", Doctoral Dissertation, Wageningen.

Library of Congress, *Country Studies*, 1994.

Mackie, J. A. C (ed.), 1976, *The Chinese in Indonesia. Five Essays*, University of Hawaii Press, Honolulu.

Matthews, Tony, 1993, *Shadows Dancing: Japanese Espionage against the West, 1939–1945*, St. Martin's Press, London.

Palmier, L. H., 1965, *Indonesia,* Thames and Hudson, London.

Pausacker, Helen, 2005, "Peranakan Chinese and Wayang in Java", in Tim Lindsey and Helen Pausacker (eds.), *Chinese Indonesians: Remembering, Distorting, Forgetting,* Institute of Southeast Asian Studies and Monash Asia Institute, Singapore and Clayton.

Penny, D. H., 1967, "Survey of Recent Developments", *Bulletin of Indonesian Economic Studies*, Vol. 3, Iss. 6.

Regeeringsalmanaak voor Nederlandsch-Indië.

Ricklefs, M. C., 2001, *A History of Modern Indonesia since c. 1200* (3rd Edition), Palgrave Press, London.

Roos, John, 2006, *Pretext for Mass Murder: The September 30th Movement and Suharto's Coup d'Etat in Indonesia*, University of Wisconsin Press, Madison.

Rush, James R., 1990, *Opium to Java: Revenue Farming and Chinese Enterprise in colonial Indonesia, 1860–1910*, Cornell University Press, Ithaca and London.

Tan, Hong Boen, 1935, *Orang-Orang Tionghoa Jang Terkemoeka di Java* [Prominent Chinese in Java], The Biographical Publishing Centre, Solo.

Van Niel, R., 1960, *The Emergence of the Modern Indonesian Elite*, van Hoeve, The Hague.

Winter, J. A., 1999, *Dosa Dosa Politik Orde Baru* [*Political Sins of the New Order*], Jambatan Anggauta, IKAPI, Jakarta.

Online References

Brommer, B., "Semarang Beeld van een Stad", Asia Maior, Purmerend, 1995, p.19 translated by Marianne van Rees Vellinga, found at <www.semarang.nl.org/oeitiongham> (accessed 12 November 2004)

<www.chez.com/utawebfan/html/new/UAT_TAI> (accessed 12 November 2004)

Miller, Michael B., "The Business of the Hajj Seaborne Commerce and the Movement of Peoples", paper presented at Seascapes, Littoral Cultures, and Trans-Oceanic Exchanges conference, Library of Congress, Washington D.C., February 12 through 15, 2003, found at <www.historycooperative.org/proceedings/seascapes/miller> (accessed 1 November 2004)

<http://www.kitlv.nl/index.html> (accessed 21 December 2004)

<www.gimonca.com/sejarah> (accessed 8 January 2005)

Hampton, Paul., "Communism and Stalinism in Indonesia", article Worker's Liberty # 61, February 2000, found at <http://archive.workersliberty.org/wlmags/wl61/indonesi.htm> (accessed 5 November 2004)

<www.immi.gov.au/facts/06evolution> (accessed 26 May 2005)

<www.indonesianembassy.org.uk/photo_history> (accessed 18 July 2005)

<www.nedships.nl/liners/tliners/tjiwangi> (accessed 2 February 2006)

Windmill Herald, 8/3/1958, found at <www.godutch.com> (accessed 8 November 2004)

<www.workers.labor.net.au> (accessed 12 November 2005)

<http://www.geocities.com/dutcheastindies/balikpapan.html> (accessed 12 November 2005)

<www.internationalgames.net/ganefo> (accessed 14 March 2004)

<http://www.nusindo.co.id/menu.cgi?2> (accessed 22 August 2007)

Suggested Additional Reading

Anderson, B. R. O'G., 1972, *Java in a Time of Revolution, Occupation, and Resistance 1944–1946*, Cornell University Press, Ithaca.

Blackburn, S., 2004, *Women and the State in Modern Indonesia*, Cambridge University Press, Cambridge.

Dahm, B., 1971, *History of Indonesia in the 20th Century*, Pall Mall Press, London.

Dick, H., Houben, V., Lindblad, J. Th and Thee Kian Wie, 2002, *The Emergence of a National Economy: An Economic History of Indonesia, 1800–2000*, University of Hawaii Press/ KITLV Press/Allen & Unwin, Hawaii/Leiden/Sydney.

Frederick, W. H., 1989, *Visions and Heat: The Making of the Indonesian Revolution*, Ohio University Press, Athens (Ohio).

Furnivall, J. S., 1939, *Netherlands Indies: A Study of a Plural Economy*, Cambridge University Press, London.

Gordon, A., 1979, "The Collapse of Java's Colonial Sugar and the Breakdown of Indonesia's Independent Economy", in Francien van Anrooij *et al.*, *Between People and Statistics: Essays on Modern Indonesian History*, Martinus Nijhoff, The Hague.

Kahin, G. McT, 1961, *Nationalism and Revolution in Indonesia*, Cornell University Press, Ithaca.

Koentjaraningrat, 1967, *Villages in Indonesia*, Cornell University Press, Ithaca.

Pelzer, K. J., 1963, "The Agricultural Foundation", in R.T. McVey, *Indonesia*, Yale University, New Haven.

Salmon, C. and Lombard, D., 1980, *Les Chinois de Jakarta/ The Chinese of Jakarta* (bilingual), University Microfilms International, Ann Arbor.

Index